CONSTRUCTING THE INEFFABLE: CONTEMPORARY SACRED ARCHITECTURE

KARLA CAVARRA BRITTON, EDITOR

YALE SCHOOL OF ARCHITECTURE

YALE UNIVERSITY PRESS

Copyright 2010, Yale School of Architecture

All rights are reserved. No part may be reproduced
without permission.

Published by
Yale School of Architecture
180 York Street
New Haven, Connecticut 06520
www.architecture.yale.edu

Distributed by
Yale University Press
P.O. Box 209040
New Haven, CT 06520-9040
www.yalebooks.com

Library of Congress Cataloging-in-Publication Data

Constructing the ineffable : contemporary sacred
architecture / Karla Cavarra Britton, editor.
    p. cm.
 Includes index.
 ISBN 978-0-300-17037-5 (cloth : alk. paper)
1. Religious architecture. 2. Architecture, Modern—
21st century. 3.
Architecture and society—History—20th century.
I. Britton, Karla.
 NA4600.C62 2011
 726—dc22
                            2010037918

Edited by Karla Cavarra Britton
Publications Director: Nina Rappaport
Editorial Assistant: Heather Kilmer
Designed by Think Studio, NYC

title page: Moshe Safdie, Yad Vashem
Museum, Jerusalem, 2005, reception building
with skylight and trellis

Printed in China

6 **PREFACE** ROBERT A.M. STERN

8 **INTRODUCTION** KARLA CAVARRA BRITTON

12 **PROLOGUE:** THE CASE FOR
SACRED ARCHITECTURE
KARLA CAVARRA BRITTON

PART I.
ARCHITECTURE AND THE SACRED

24 INTRODUCTION

26 THE EARTH, THE TEMPLE, AND TODAY
VINCENT SCULLY

48 UNTIMELY MEDITATIONS ON THE NEED FOR
SACRED ARCHITECTURE
KARSTEN HARRIES

60 ARCHITECTURE, MEMORY, AND THE SACRED
MIROSLAV VOLF

66 REVEALING CONCEALMENT
MARK C. TAYLOR

72 CONSTRUCTING THE IMMATERIAL IN SPACES
LARGE AND SMALL
EMILIE M. TOWNES

PART II.
**PRECEDENTS: SACRED SPACES
CONSTRUCTED AND IMAGINED**

  80 INTRODUCTION

  82 RUDOLF SCHWARZ AND MIES
       VAN DER ROHE: THE FORM OF THE SPIRIT
       THOMAS H. BEEBY

  96 THE SECULAR SPIRITUALITY
       OF TADAO ANDO
       KENNETH FRAMPTON

112 TEMPLES OF LIGHT
       DIANA ECK

120 VISIONARIES OR LUNATICS? ARCHITECTS
       OF SACRED SPACE, EVEN IN OUTER SPACE
       JAIME LARA

PART III.
**PERSPECTIVES: CONTEMPORARY EXPRESSIONS
OF THE INEFFABLE**

132 INTRODUCTION

134 THE TRIBE VERSUS THE CITY-STATE:
       A CONUNDRUM FOR THE JEWISH PROJECT
       STANLEY TIGERMAN

148 JUBILEE CHURCH
       (DIO PADRE MISERICORDIOSO), ROME
       RICHARD MEIER

158 ARCHITECTURE AS A VEHICLE FOR RELIGIOUS
       EXPERIENCE: THE LOS ANGELES CATHEDRAL
       RAFAEL MONEO

170 FAITH AND FORM: CONTEMPORARY SPACE
       FOR WORSHIP AND PILGRIMAGE
       FARIBORZ SAHBA

182 THEISTIC—POLYTHEISTIC—NON-THEISTIC
       STEVEN HOLL (WITH DAVID VAN DER LEER)

192 THE ARCHITECTURE OF MEMORY:
       SEEKING THE SACRED
       MOSHE SAFDIE

206 IS THERE A RELIGIOUS SPACE IN
       THE TWENTY-FIRST CENTURY?
       PETER EISENMAN

216 THE CONTEMPORARY MOSQUE
       ZAHA HADID

222 **EPILOGUE:** ON THE RELEVANCE OF SACRED
       ARCHITECTURE TODAY
       PAUL GOLDBERGER

232 CONTRIBUTORS

236 ACKNOWLEDGMENTS

237 INDEX

244 IMAGE CREDITS

While religion is a central motivating force behind many political and social movements in the world today, the religious building type is seldom discussed in a critical manner within the classrooms or design studios of most American schools of architecture. However, the design of sacred buildings (including not only mosques, synagogues, churches, and temples but also monuments and memorials) remains an important aspect of practice, and many of today's most important architects have designed notable new sacred spaces and religious buildings that receive wide public attention.

Historically, the religious building type has often been a locus for advancement and invention in architectural design. This fact remains true today: many recent religious works creatively address architecture's contemporary concerns with innovative technology and material expression, engaging these factors in relation to the heightened challenges of liturgical tradition, cultural identity, social memory, and spiritual and symbolic form.

Recognizing that it was important to examine the topic of religious architecture through a contemporary lens, the Yale School of Architecture, in collaboration with the Yale Divinity School and the Yale Institute of Sacred Music (ISM), convened in the fall of 2007 the symposium, "Constructing the Ineffable: Contemporary Sacred Architecture" to begin the discussion that lies behind this book. Because such a broad cultural exchange necessarily needs to be addressed from a variety of perspectives, this event was from the start shaped as a collaborative inter-disciplinary and inter-faith dialogue. The project was also representative of a long tradition at Yale of treating architecture—in the words of Vincent Scully—as a "social art" and "a conversation across time," concerned with building as an interplay between form and meaning and history.

Demonstrating an expansiveness beyond traditional disciplinary boundaries that is uniquely possible in the multi-faceted environment of a research university, this book, an enlargement of the original themes aired at the symposium, represents a rare exchange between architects, philosophers, historians, and theologians to engage one another in considering the sacred building type. Remaining true to the original intentions of the project, the book seeks to address a wide audience, both in architecture and religious studies, and indeed all who share an intellectual curiosity about the role religious space has to play in contemporary life. The essays offer multiple points of entry into this conversation, whether through the reflective and self-critical reflections of architects themselves, or of those working from the perspective of more philosophical, theological, or historical disciplines.

This book would not have been possible without the robust support of Martin Jean, Director of the Yale Institute of Sacred Music, and Harold Attridge, Dean of Yale Divinity School. Their leadership from the earliest stages helped to give concrete form to the collaborative and cross-disciplinary ambitions of this project. The book also owes a debt to the sustained efforts of Barbara Shailor, who in her role as Deputy Provost for the Arts was instrumental in facilitating this collaboration among the three professional schools. The Edward J. and Dorothy Clarke Kempf Fund provided financial support for the symposium, and Rob Nelson of the History of Art Department at Yale helped to secure this funding. I would also like to thank Yale School of Architecture Publications Director Nina Rappaport for facilitating the production of this book.

Finally, I would like to acknowledge the role of Karla Cavarra Britton of the Yale School of Architecture, together with the ISM's Jaime Lara, in convening the original symposium. Karla's successive work in editing this volume has resulted in a significant contribution to the discussion.

Robert A.M. Stern
Dean & J.M. Hoppin Professor of Architecture

INTRODUCTION

KARLA CAVARRA BRITTON

The role of religion, once assumed by many to be waning in the wake of progressive secularization, has in recent years reasserted itself in the shaping of social and political life. Corresponding to this phenomenon is a shift in many academic disciplines, which had in recent decades tended to give scant attention to religion as a significant social fact, toward an increasing recognition that religious conviction, or at least the search for recognizable patterns of meaning, persists as a potent force in our cultural and personal identities in surprisingly complex and powerful ways. Indeed, Jürgen Habermas, one of modernity's most perceptive interpreters, has recently observed that we have entered a "post-secular" age when the secularization hypothesis (which held that growing modernization necessarily results in increased secularism) has to be nuanced to take into account the continuing influence of religious convictions in social discourse, albeit at a more individualized level.[1] Amid this growing discussion around the role of religion in cultural identity, this documentary anthology seeks to open a dialogue between architects, historians, philosophers, theologians, and sociologists as one important entry into the much larger field of the re-appraisal and re-assessment of religious and sacred space in the world today.

[1] Jürgen Habermas, "The Resurgence of Religion: A Challenge to the Secular Self Under standing of Modernity," The Castle Lectures, Yale University, October, 2008.

[2] A number of recent publications document the extent of new religious building: Phyllis Richardson, *New Spiritual Architecture* (New York: Abbeville Press, 2004); Samuel D. Gruber, *American Synagogues: A Century of Architecture and Jewish Community* (New York: Rizzoli, 2003); Martin Frishman and Hasan-Uddin Khan, *The Mosque: History, Architectural Development and Regional Diversity* (London: Thames and Hudson, 2002); Edwin Heathcote and Laura Moffatt, *Contemporary Church Architecture* (London: Wiley-Academy, 2007); Michael J. Crosbie, *Houses of God: Religious Architecture for a New Millennium* (Mulgrave, Victoria: Images Publishing, 2006); and *Architecture for the Gods*, 2 vols. (Mulgrave, Victoria: Images Publishing, 1999, 2002); Randall S. Lindstrom, *Creativity and Contradiction: European Churches Since 1970* (Washington, D.C.: American Institute of Architects Press, 1988).

A key premise of this book is that the exploration of such questions can only progress if it reaches across those disciplinary boundaries that tend to separate intellectual life into the isolated spheres of academic discourse. As an inter-religious and interdisciplinary endeavor, this collection of essays seeks a more expansive idea of sacred space than the self-imposed limitations any one discipline allows. Indeed, as a means of addressing this challenge, the central intention in this volume is to place prominent architects who have recently built significant sacred and religious buildings in dialogue not only with their own work, but also with scholars from other fields who serve as interlocutors from a variety of intellectual disciplines and religious traditions. The essays thus raise both concrete and theoretical issues of the nature of the sacred in a deliberate encounter between concept and realization. Moreover, with this principle of theoretical eclecticism in mind, the essays in this volume collectively explore notions of transcendence that are not specific to any one religious tradition, but in fact interact and influence one another in multifarious ways.

This collection of essays comes at an opportune time, when a corpus of newly built work valuably coincides with the renewed intellectual awareness of those buildings' social importance. This book therefore recognizes that sacred places take many forms, and are not necessarily limited to those typological buildings we think of in strictly "religious" terms. While it would be difficult to ignore the recent resurgence in the construction by well-known architects of overtly religious spaces—mosques, temples, synagogues, chapels, and churches—contemporary sacred spaces also surely include less obvious expressions, such as landscapes, monuments, and museums which evoke great commitment, pathos, and sacrifice on the part of a community of individuals.[2] In this respect, religious buildings and sacred landscapes rarely function simply as isolated expressions of largely sectarian experiences. Rather, these sacred spaces often contribute in critical ways to shaping the larger cultural and urban fabric of contemporary life. The themes presented in the book should be read, then, as an important cross-section of a broader investigation with the unifying intention of opening up a renewed discourse, especially for students in the academy and in professional schools, on religious architecture and sacred spaces today.

The essays in this book are arranged according to the categories of theory, precedent, and practice. The distinction between these three organizing categories is obviously not rigid, and many of the authors represented here move with fluidity between them (just as the reader is invited to move freely among the essays). Nevertheless, the organizing editorial intention is that the first essays deal in a more explicitly conceptual way with the philosophical and theological contexts of religious architecture, and with its sociological, formal, and even ethical challenges. The sacred as it relates to architectural form is thus described in the first section in a wide variety of ways: as an abstracted form of nature; as the descent in an ethically consequential manner of the transcendent into the visible and material; as a memorialized collective memory. The section includes essays that significantly broaden the parameters for a critical reading of religious architecture by discussing it in terms of the importance of cultural identity, the vernacular and everyday life, and the inescapable reality of religion's ties to forces of violence and evil.

As for the essays in the second section, these may be read as investigations into historical precedents which offer consequential interpretations of the sacred in both modern and late modern architecture. The essays in this section address a series of precedents that remind us that in important instances ritual and visionary expression continue

Le Corbusier, Notre Dame du Haut,
Ronchamp, 1950–55, interior construction
photograph by Michel Sima

to inform experiences of cities and landscapes, both natural and otherworldly. These essays are something of a montage of concrete embodiments of the sacred, yet they together form the link between the more conceptual reflections of the first section and the actual reflections of practicing architects on their own work in the third section.

The eight essays in the final section, then, are all written by prominent contemporary architects who have faced the challenge of considering how to express the inexpressible in built form. The focus in this section is on recently constructed religious and other sacred spaces that are viewed through the self-described experience of the architect as the product of his or her own imagination and effort. Many other examples of recent sacred architecture could surely be added to this category, especially when one considers the number of leading architects who have been actively engaged in building such works. The examples offered here, then, are

representative rather than exhaustive, and their presentation is more dialogical than descriptive. Moreover, while some of these works may by now be well known and even familiar, the focus here is on providing a collection of reflections on the actual process of designing and constructing sacred spaces that is more introspective and reflective than analytical. The result is an exploration not only of many important investigations into contemporary religious building, but also of the creative process and the existential questions which often lie behind those investigations.

To a large extent, all the contributions may be read as responses to the two seminal questions posed by Vincent Scully in his opening essay: What is sacred to us today? And how may it be embodied in architectural form?

PROLOGUE:
THE CASE FOR SACRED ARCHITECTURE

KARLA CAVARRA BRITTON

I am the inventor of the phrase "ineffable space," which is a reality that I discovered as I went on. When a work reaches a maximum of intensity, when it has the best proportions and has been made with the best quality of execution, when it has reached perfection, a phenomenon takes place that we may call "ineffable space." When this happens these places start to radiate. They radiate in a physical way and determine what I call "ineffable space," that is to say, a space that does not depend on dimensions but on the quality of its perfection. It belongs to the domain of the ineffable, of that which cannot be said.

—Le Corbusier, from an interview recorded at La Tourette, 1961[1]

[1] Quoted in André Wogenscky, *Le Corbusier's Hands* [Les Mains de Le Corbusier], English trans. Martina Millà Bernad (Cambridge, Mass: MIT Press and London, 2006), p. 81. The full conversation was published in *L'Architecture d'Aujourd'hui* in issue No. 96, June–July, 1961, a special issue on religious architecture.

[2] Le Corbusier, "L'Espace indicible," in *L'Architecture d'Aujourd'hui*, January, 1946, *numero hors serie* Art, pp. 9–10. English trans. published in Le Corbusier, *New World of Space* (New York: Reynal & Hitchcock, 1948), pp. 7–9.

The title of this book, *Constructing the Ineffable*, is intentionally reminiscent of Le Corbusier's famous characterization of the experience of ineffable space. First published in 1946, and translated into English in 1948 as the opening of *New World of Space*, Le Corbusier's essay "L'Espace indicible" presents in a condensed philosophical tract an argument for the living being's foundational need to control space and the "aesthetic emotion" that is the potential outcome of such control.[2] The occupation of space, Le Corbusier argues, is a proof of existence, and a fundamental manifestation of the human search for "equilibrium and duration." Architecture, sculpture, and painting, he asserts, are those disciplines bound up with a fuller understanding of this fundamental need for spatial control. When perfected, the "action of the work" of the architect, sculptor, or painter produces a "phenomenon of concordance" as exact as mathematics, a manifestation of "plastic acoustics," so one may speak of sound either as a conveyor of joy (music) or of oppression (racket). Le Corbusier describes such a carefully controlled experience as being close to the Cubists' own spatial experiments around 1910, with their search for a mathematical *"fourth dimension"* capable of providing a unique human phenomenon extending beyond real time and space. As Le Corbusier describes the spiritual power of this aesthetic experience: "The fourth dimension is the moment of limitless escape evoked by an exceptionally just consonance of the plastic means employed … Then a boundless depth opens up, effaces walls, drives away contingent presences, *accomplishes the miracle of ineffable space*."

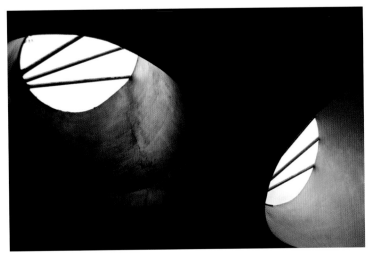

above: Le Corbusier, Monastery of Notre Dame de la Tourette, Eveux, 1952–60, interior view of light cannons in crypt

above, right: Monastery of Notre Dame de la Tourette, detail of west façade

[3] Curtis, for example, says of Le Corbusier that "when questioned about his beliefs in relation to Ronchamp, he replied: 'I have not experienced the miracle of faith, but I have often known the miracle of ineffable space …'" William J. Curtis, *Le Corbusier: Ideas and Forms* (London: Phaidon, 1986), p. 179.

[4] Le Corbusier, *Modulor 2: 1955: la parole est aux usagers: suite de "Le Modulor 1948"* (Boulogne: Editions de l'Architecture d'Aujourd'hui, 1955). Translation, *Modulor 2: 1955: Let the User Speak Next* (London: Faber and Faber, 1958), p. 27.

Le Corbusier would return repeatedly to the theme of "l'espace indicible" throughout the 1950s and into the '60s, republishing his earlier essay in both *Le Modulor* (1950) and *Modulor 2* (1955), as well as leaving notes for a book by the same title that he thought of writing as late as 1959. Although not religious himself in any orthodox sense, Le Corbusier was deeply attentive to the need to address the spiritual dimension in life as a fundamental human condition and on more than one occasion famously distilled his personal understanding of faith by quoting his own essay on ineffable space: "I am not conscious of the miracle of faith, but I often live that of ineffable space, the consummation of plastic emotion."[3]

Seemingly, the repetition and return to the concept of ineffable space was born out of the strength of Le Corbusier's own personal experience of mystical transcendence, brought on by staring at one of his own paintings: "One day—at a very precise moment—I saw inexpressible space come into being before my eyes: the wall, with its picture, lost its limits: became boundless."[4] It is perhaps not surprising, therefore, that Le Corbusier's concern with ineffable space paralleled his intensive explorations in the latter part of his career with metaphysical and religious themes: from the mystical project for Edouard Trouin at the legendary site of the retreat of Mary Magdalene, known as La Sainte-Baume near Aix-en-Provence (1948); to his iconic work for Notre Dame-du-Haut at Ronchamp (1950–1954) and

the Dominican monastery of Sainte-Marie de La Tourette near Eveux-sur-Abresle (1957–1960); to the cosmological Philips Pavilion for the Brussels World Exhibition of 1958 (in collaboration with Iannis Xenakis) and the Church of St. Pierre at Firminy-Vert, begun in 1960, left unfinished at the time of his death.

Recognizing that such modernist reflection as Le Corbusier's fascination with "ineffable space" stands in the background of, and might be said to have been rediscovered by, many recent architectural explorations of the sacred (including many of those documented in this volume), this introductory essay calls attention to the long historical trajectory of engagement and experimentation with sacred and religious space in modern architecture. By way of providing an intellectual framework for the essays that follow, this introduction thus seeks to suggest some key categories which may be understood to connect the fields of modern architecture with the study and history of religion. In this sense, Le Corbusier may be seen as just one of many prominent modern and late modern architects who were interested in sacred space and religious architecture. Through the religious building type, many modernists may be seen as exploring alternative forms of expression as a tentative response to the dominant rationalist and techno-scientific *Zeitgeist* typically understood to be the underlying common denominator in the evolution of twentieth-century architecture. Within this latter mindset, Le Corbusier's

engagement with the concept of ineffable space, and its manifestation in his religious architecture itself, has often confounded historians and critics who see this concern as an abrupt departure from the rationalist themes of his early and middle career. Yet, this surprise should only be indicative of the degree to which many narratives of the history of modern architecture have overlooked the significance of the religious building type and sacred space as sites of exploration and experimentation.

———————————

The Portuguese architect Álvaro Siza recently noted that it would almost be possible "to do the history of architecture, through the history of religious buildings."[5] Throughout human history, the religious building—from the Babylonian ziggurat, to the Greek temple, from the domes of Byzantine churches to the great mosques of Sinan, or from medieval Gothic cathedrals to the Hurva synagogue of Jerusalem—has served as a record of architecture's technical, symbolic, and material transformations. Yet, the religious building in the history of modern architecture has at best tended to be understood as a kind of marginal "counter-history." Categories frequently assumed to be the underpinnings of twentieth-century architecture (such as the new spirit, progress, and cultural modernity) are often understood as being at variance with the essence of the religious building as representative of more entrenched cultural underpinnings (ritual, memory, historical continuity, cultural identity, and tradition). In spite of the *retardataire* implications often attached to discussions of the religious building, one has to acknowledge (as many of the essays in this volume do) the many remarkably innovative religious buildings in the twentieth century which exhibited a considerable originality in terms of language,

structure, material, and the arrangement of space and form.

To name just two seminal architectural figures in this regard, we could take Frank Lloyd Wright and Auguste Perret. These two architects, whom Le Corbusier declared in 1959 to be "the two stars of the contemporary architectural firmament,"[6] realized religious buildings in the first decades of the twentieth century that had implications far beyond the need to seek an appropriate accommodation of religious worship in a new era. Rather, their ecclesiastical buildings provided essential foundations for a "new architecture" and its evolution in the twentieth century.

So, for example, Wright's Unity Temple of 1905, similar to the Larkin Building which preceded it, broke with almost every existing rule of American and European religious architecture while laying the groundwork for newer forms of construction and the handling of material. Using concrete in a totally new way, the Temple would be among the first monumental buildings in the world to be comprised entirely of poured-in-place, exposed concrete. Its cubist themes, geometrical manipulations, and even its interior furnishings were all part of a tightly constructed and unified organizing system suggestive of a new direction in architectural form. Like Unity Temple, Auguste Perret's church of Notre Dame du Raincy (1921) also elevated the otherwise much maligned

Portrait of Le Corbusier with a model related to his *Modulor* philosophy of proportion and design, photograph by Michel Sima

[5] "Álvaro Siza and Alexandros N. Tombazis in Conversation," *Arquitectura Ibérica*, special edition on Holy Trinity Church, Fátima, September 2007, p. 92.

[6] Le Corbusier, "Il laisse son œuvre," *Zodiac* 5, November 1960, p. 28.

material of reinforced concrete to a new aesthetic level by treating it in a completely new controlled architectural language. Built in the working-class town of Le Raincy to the northeast of Paris, Perret's church is structurally an extension of the asperities of the French Greco-Gothic tradition, and of new precedents in concrete construction technology established by the French architect Anatole de Baudot in his Saint-Jean-de-Montmartre of 1904. As Le Corbusier wrote about Notre Dame du Raincy, "The interior, which has the effect of a section, is splendid. This section is the conquest of reinforced concrete, administered by a Sage, by someone artful and daring." Here, as Le Corbusier celebrated, the use of the new material of reinforced concrete allowed for a spatial reconsideration of the traditional religious space in light of the industrial building type.[7]

To these decisive examples of new religious building design in America and France prior to the Second World War, one must also surely add those eminent architects and teachers whose work was representative of architecture in their respective countries during the first decades of the twentieth century: Hendrik Petrus Berlage's Wrightian First Church of Christ, Scientist in The Hague (1926); Karl Moser's concrete church of St. Anthony in Basel, Switzerland (1926); Sigurd Lewerentz and his Chapel of the Resurrection at Woodland Cemetery near Stockholm, Sweden (begun in 1914); and Otto Wagner's St. Leopold am Steinhof in Vienna, Austria (1902).[8] Indeed, Wagner's St. Leopold, perhaps the most spectacular work of Wagner's career, provided a new reading of materials and their relationship to structure. Above all, it presented a fresh interpretation of ornament in relation to the metalwork and the radial ribwork. Here the thin sheets of Sterzig marble and the gold and copperwork reveal the salient features of the building's structure. This building would have a notable impact on the work of Wagner's

prize student Jože Plečnik (whose Church of the Sacred Heart in Prague is described in the epilogue of this volume). Collectively, these representative works demonstrate key moments in the evolution of modern building where significant advances in the use of structure, material, and technology were combined in a serious attempt to address the unique challenges of imagining sacred space.

The constructional emphasis in the ecclesiastical work of Wright and Perret, in particular, suggests a core paradox that lies at the heart of a question that the essays in this volume attempt to address: Is it possible to speak coherently of constructing the ineffable? In assembling a variety of responses to this question, the book as a whole recognizes the paradox of trying to speak of (much less construct) that which, by definition, cannot be put into words. In this manner, it seeks to draw the reader's attention into a consideration of certain cases wherein the ineffable does seem to be given constructed form. Inevitable doubts are raised by some of the authors whether or not the ineffable can coherently be discussed; others, however, draw upon the idea that the ineffable can by definition only be expressed non-verbally. If the ineffable is incapable of being put into words, then for it to have any representation accessible to human consciousness and experience, the ineffable will only be manifested in those forms of expression which do not rely on spoken language, such as music and architecture. In this manner, the cases considered here raise for us the question of what risk an individual architect must take in entering into this uncertain terrain of the sacred.

Indeed, as one enters into the paradox of "constructing the ineffable," the word "ineffable" itself becomes increasingly problematic. Coming from the Latin root *effare*, "to speak out," the

[7] Le Corbusier, "Perret" in *L'Architecture d'Aujourd'hui* VII, October 1932, p. 9.

[8] For a fuller treatment of the evolution of modern church architecture, see such recent works as Wolfgang Jean Stock, *European Church Architecture, 1900–1950: Towards Modernity* (Munich: Prestel Verlag, 2006) and *European Church Architecture, 1950–2000* (Munich: Prestel Verlag, 2002); Edwin Heathcote and Iona Spens, *Church Builders* (London: Academy Editions, 1997); or the more historical Ferdinand Pfammatter, *Betonkirchen* (Einsiedeln: Benziger, 1948); Albert Christ-Janer and Mary Mix Foley, *Modern Church Architecture* (New York: McGraw-Hill, 1962); and John Knox Shear, ed., *Religious Buildings for Today* (New York: F. W. Dodge, 1957).

right: Frank Lloyd Wright, Unity Temple, Oak Park, Illinois, 1904–06, exterior

below: Auguste Perret, Notre Dame du Raincy, Le Raincy, 1921, showing the façade described by Le Corbusier as a "masque" of its luminous interior

negated adjectival form of that word, *ineffabilis*, suggests the impossibility of speech, that which cannot be spoken. The reasons for such an impossibility of speech, however, can be multiple. In some cases, ineffability has a mystical connotation and is the result of an ecstatic experience that no words can adequately represent. Yet, ineffability can also be used in a restrictive sense, such as the biblical injunction against speaking the "ineffable name of God," or the Islamic prohibition of representational images of the divine. The variety of words approximating the meaning of the ineffable suggests other connotations as well. "Unspeakable" might be used to describe horrors such as the Holocaust that leave one shocked beyond words; "unutterable" might evoke treasured words or sentiments too intimate to be articulated out loud; or "inexpressible" might point in the direction of a surplus of meaning that lies beyond any communication, verbal or otherwise. Thus, the ineffable may, for a variety of contrasting reasons, impose a rule of silence upon what might otherwise be awkward or inadequate expression. Thus, any one of these meanings, or even some combination of them, is potentially included in the challenge an architect faces when confronted with the task of designing a space that will "speak" of the sacred (however that might be understood), even though the sacred may ultimately be ineffable. And, in fact, each of these meanings is in some way engaged by the variety of projects discussed in this volume.

It is striking that the plethora of meanings of the ineffable points in a direction that a number of major architects of modernism explored through their own intellectual and spiritual alignment with religious intellectuals or clients who proved to be decisive influences on their work. Again, to name two telling examples, one might think first of Mies van der Rohe's association with the religious architect and theorist Rudolf Schwarz and the Catholic intellectual Romano Guardini. Schwarz

Abbey of Le Thoronet, Provence, c. 1170, cloister

was also a friend of Guardini, who praised Schwarz's austere asceticism and absence of imagery in the unadorned interior of his Corpus Christi Church in Aachen, Germany, completed in 1930. A second influential relationship in this regard was Le Corbusier's close association with the Dominican Marie-Alain Couturier (known as Le Père Couturier). It was, for instance, Couturier who directed Le Corbusier in 1953 to the twelfth-century abbey of Le Thoronet in Southern France, one of the finest examples of medieval Cistercian building, as a source for his design of La Tourette, and it was in the French journal, *L'Art Sacré* (edited by Couturier) where Le Corbusier's Ronchamp was featured on the cover in 1955 and where he published his designs for the Church of St. Pierre at Firminy-Vert in 1964 (completed after his death).

In fact, the evocative materiality of Le Thoronet was an influential source of intellectual and visual inspiration for a variety of French artists and architects in the post-war period, many of whom were associated with the journal *L'Art Sacré*. This circle included not only Le Corbusier and Couturier, but also the French-Hungarian architectural photographer Lucien Hervé, who collaborated with Le Corbusier, and the architect Fernand Pouillon, whose 1964 novel *Les Pierres sauvages* offered a fictional account of the history of Le Thoronet. To them, Le Thoronet represented an "architecture of truth, tranquility, and strength" where "the whole and its details are one" (in Le Corbusier's words[9]), which achieved such a purity of form that nothing could be added to it—just the kind of perfection he had described as eliciting the experience of "ineffable space." The elements of this perfection were celebrated as its economy of expression; a disciplining of the components of light, stone, geometry, and proportion; and a level of craftsmanship that contributed to a refinement of completion and finish. Described thus, Le Thoronet is something of a palimpsest of the concerns that radiate throughout this volume in considering the "construction of the ineffable." Not surprisingly, a similar concern for the ways in which an intense interplay between materiality and form can give rise to a sense of transcendence in built form is a recurring motif in the meditations collected in this book.

---

[9] Le Corbusier, "Introduction" to Lucien Hervé, *Architecture of Truth: The Cistercian Abbey of Le Thoronet* (London: Phaidon, 2001). A different version of Hervé's photographs was originally published in 1956.

[10] Rudolf Otto, *The Idea of the Holy* (London: Oxford University Press, 1923). Originally published as *Das Heilige* (Breslau: Trewendt und Granier, 1917). Second English edition, 1950, reprinted in 1958.

A touchstone for every one of the authors presented here, to one degree or another, is the sense that there is a hierarchy of space, in which there are some places (such as Le Thoronet) that uniquely communicate deeply of human emotion and aspiration. Such an idea is particularly reflective of the work of the Romanian scholar, Mircea Eliade (as evidenced by the number of essays that make reference to him). Eliade, extending on Rudolf Otto's concept of the holy as the numinous,[10] argued that a religious person

Revue Mensuelle

Le Père Couturier
9 - 10
Mai-Juin 1954

L'ART SACRÉ
Revue mensuelle

RONCHAMP
1-2
Septembre-Octobre 1955

L'ART SACRÉ
Revue mensuelle

Un projet d'église paroissiale de
LE CORBUSIER
3-4
Novembre-Décembre 1964

Covers of *L'Art Sacré*
(left to right) Le Père
Couturier (1954);
Notre Dame du Haut,
Ronchamp (1955);
Le Corbusier with model
of St. Pierre, Firminy-Vert
(1964)

[11] Mircea Eliade, *The Sacred and the Profane: The Nature of Religion* (New York: Harcourt Brace Jovanovich, 1959), p. 20.

[12] J. G. Davies, "Architecture," in Mircea Eliade, ed., *The Encyclopedia of Religion* (New York: Macmillan, 1987), vol. 1, p. 384.

[13] Eliade, p. 22.

experiences certain sites as hierophanous in ways that others are not:

> For religious man, space is not homogeneous; he experiences interruptions, breaks in it; some parts of space are qualitatively different from others. "Draw not nigh hither," says the Lord to Moses; "put off thy shoes from off thy feet, for the place whereon thou standest is holy ground." (Exodus 3:5) There is, then, a sacred space, and hence a strong significant space; there are other spaces that are not sacred and so are without structure or consistency, amorphous. Nor is this all. For religious man, this spatial nonhomogeneity finds expression in the experience of the opposition between space that is sacred—the only real and really existing space—and all other space, the formless expanse surrounding it.[11]

We see here that the quintessential example for Eliade of sacred space is Moses and the burning bush, which is the archetypal holy ground distinctive from all other spaces surrounding it. The spatial differentiation of religious man focuses on sacral or "real" space; all other space is regarded as formless and of less consequence. As the historian J. G. Davies puts it, this dualism of the sacred and the profane is inherent to the religious building:

"To speak of the sacred and the profane in this way is to refer to two antithetical entities. The one is potent, full of power, while the other is powerless."[12] Eliade thus provides us with an explanation for the existential necessity of this sacred space: "If the world is to be lived in," he writes, "it must be founded—and no world can come to birth in the chaos of the homogeneity and relativity of profane space. The discovery or projection of a fixed point—the center—is equivalent to the creation of the world …"[13]

At this juncture, however, it is perhaps important to note that within Eliade's conceptualization of sacred space there lurks a particular phenomenological stance that hides what others would emphasize as the historical basis of religious experience. For example, Steven Wasserstrom's study, *Religion after Religion*, has argued that Eliade (and his collaborators at Eranos) enacted a scholarly shift away from the traditional religious elements of law and ritual toward the mystocentric and mythocentric (influenced by Jung's theory of "archetypes"). Among other things, Wasserstrom argues that this shift came at the cost of a more robust account of the ethical dimensions of religion and its associated practices, presumably including architecture. Wasserstrom thinks that by relying on a phenomenological rather than historical approach to understanding the power of religious symbols, scholars such as Eliade, "divested symbols of their original embeddedness in some historical solidarity."[14] This shift continues to influence academic discussions of religion, placing a modern conversation—such as the one proposed here—about the nature of the religious buildings into what might be thought of as a distinctly non-modernist context. Ironically, in this framework the available vocabulary most naturally emphasizes non-rational concepts such as transcendence and sublimity.

Given Wasserstrom's critique, it is striking how readily the authors of this volume nevertheless appeal to ideas of the sacred that are given expression by Eliade. The question could be raised whether this invocation is essentially retrogressive or whether, in fact, it represents a rediscovery of the power of a concept such as hierophanous space to establish real alternatives to what is now commonly described as "junkspace" or "the generic city," that is to say, the proliferation of global cities marked by a dehumanizing homogenization and a loss of cultural identity and historical sedimentation. Seen through the absence of this layering, architecture may through the distinct otherness of sacred spaces continue to reach toward a hierarchical visualization of space. Thus, for example, the Swiss architect Mario Botta (who has designed a number of exceptional churches, chapels, and synagogues) has recently written: "Every so often there is a compelling need for sacred space even within everyday life, an incontrovertible necessity that has been confirmed over the centuries by sublime examples, and that has now re-emerged decisively, perhaps in an extreme attempt to respond to the incompleteness of the contemporary dimension."[15]

Yet, to invoke such a hierarchically conditioned concept as "sacred space" also runs the risk of skewing the discussion of religious architecture in a particular direction, naming only those works which have a certain formal intentionality behind their conception while ignoring the fact that spaces experienced as sacred by ordinary men and women are often quite improvisatory and non-descript. Thus, as David Morgan and Sally Promey have argued in their studies of the visual culture of American religions, the relationship of material things to religious building practice needs to be studied from the standpoint of asking how objects (buildings included) "interact with texts, theology, narrative, and ceremony, and serve thereby to naturalize theology."[16] That is to say, the experience of the sacred is not completely dependent upon the construction or creation of self-conscious material forms of its expression; rather, in many cases people bestow sacred value upon all manner of sites and objects, as for instance occurred in the impromptu memorials that sprang up in New York after the events of 9/11. Space may be hierarchical and non-homogeneous—indeed, the practice of architecture is premised upon that condition—but one cannot fully predict, based upon that hierarchy, how constructed spaces will be experienced or understood. Moreover, some would approach the question of creating sacred space with a much stronger programmatic concept in mind: How is it to function liturgically? Or how will it accommodate public assemblies? Either from the more common or more liturgical point of view, a preoccupation with the "ineffable" may seem unnecessarily esoteric and abstruse. This perspective surely presents one of the greatest conundrums faced by the interlocutors in this volume: to what extent is the ineffable the product of a deliberate intentionality, striving toward the revelatory perfection of which Le Corbusier spoke, and to what extent is it the product of the unpredictability of human activity and projection?

[14] Steven M. Wasserstrom, *Religion after Religion: Gershom Scholem, Mircea Eliade, and Henry Corbin at Eranos* (Princeton: Princeton University Press, 1999), p. 98.

[15] Mario Botta, "Sacred Space," in *Architetture del Sacro: Prayers in Stone*, Engl. trans. (Bologna: Editrice Compositori, 2005), p. 12.

[16] David Morgan and Sally M. Promey, *The Visual Culture of American Religions* (Berkeley: University of California Press, 2001), p. 16.

Louis I. Kahn, Mikveh Israel Synagogue, project, Philadelphia, Pennsylvania, 1963, drawing showing sanctuary interior looking towards the ark

[17] Ronald Chyi-Tung Lim, "The Politics of Architecture in Malaysia's *Masjid Negara*," a paper presented in the course, "Architecture, Religion and Modernization," at the Yale School of Architecture, Spring, 2010.

As the essays in this volume indicate, the difficulties of addressing the conceptual questions raised by the idea of the ineffable are only heightened by the communal expectation that sacred buildings reflect a moral and aesthetic imagination that is able to give expression to common ideals, memories, and hopes. These expectations become increasingly complicated and distorted when they are intermingled with large-scale political and nationalist agendas that quickly necessitate moving the discussion of sacred architecture beyond a focus on the isolated structure. One might think, for example, of the new Church of the Holy Trinity built in 2007 at Fátima by Alexandros Tombazis, where layers of Portuguese nationalism, Catholic piety, and historical tradition are interwoven into a gathering place larger than Saint Peter's Square for immense numbers of pilgrims. Or, to give another example of the complexities for religious buildings of a nationalist identity and its overlapping political agenda, one might look to the Masjid Negara National Mosque in Kuala Lumpur, designed in 1957 by a team of public works architects to memorialize the nation's independence, where a deliberate embrace of international modernism was meant to assert the country's new identity as a multi-religious, multi-ethnic and secular state.[17] More recently still, there is the Basilica of Our Lady of Peace in Yamoussoukro in the Ivory Coast (1989), commissioned by the country's president at the time as a monument in his birthplace, a new national capital, and now claimed to be the largest church in the world and deliberately modeled after St. Peter's Basilica.

Such expectations regarding the communal significance of sacred spaces might at one level be understood as an expectation of monumentality simply as a matter of scale. Yet the term was used in a more nuanced sense in the 1943 manifesto, "Nine Points on Monumentality," where Sigfried Giedion, José Luis Sert and Fernand Léger asserted that "Monuments are the expression of man's highest cultural needs. They have to satisfy the eternal demand of the people for translation

Le Corbusier, Notre
Dame du Haut.
Ronchamp, 1950–55,
entrance door

[18] José Luis Sert, Fernand
Léger, and Sigfried
Giedion, "Nine Points
on Monumentality,"
in Joan Ockman, ed.,
*Architecture Culture
1943–1968* (New York:
Columbia/Rizzoli, 1993),
p. 29.

of their collective force into symbols. The most vital monuments are those which express the feeling and thinking of this collective force – the people."[18] While the authors did not have religious architecture specifically in mind, their call for a "new monumentality" was tied to a sense of the need for a re-organization of community life through the planning and design of civic centers, monumental ensembles, and public celebrations which would serve as symbols for communities' "ideals, for their aims, and for their actions," inevitably including sacred buildings. Indeed, the essays of this volume often understand the religious building type in terms of this kind of monumentality, with the idea that its ability to evoke memory or enshrine conviction, even in secularized societies, fulfills an important social need for centers of reference.

Moreover, it might be argued that the religious building type (and its contemporary equivalents, the museum and memorial), have made their most consequential contribution to the evolution of modern architecture in relationship to the concept of the monument. At one level, this theme of a modernized monumentality is vividly represented by such vast projects as Sir Edwin Lutyens' design in the 1930s for the Metropolitan Cathedral of

Christ the King in Liverpool. Only the crypt of this project was built, but, had the proposed domed church been completed, it would have been the second largest Christian church in the world, again second only to Saint Peter's Basilica in Rome. Such a monumentality of scale is not unlike Auguste Perret's competition drawing for the votive church of Sainte-Jeanne d'Arc in Paris (1926), proposed as a tower of 670 feet, nearly two-thirds the height of the Eiffel Tower, and later adapted in his design for the Church of St. Joseph in Le Havre (1953–57). Similarly, one might also think of Paul Tournon's design for a vaulted cathedral built of reinforced concrete in Casablanca (1930); or his reworking of Hagia Sophia in his Église du Saint-Esprit, Paris (1928–35). Perhaps one of the most remarkable examples, still, of a linguistically layered sacred space on a monumental scale, is the integrative regionalism evident in Antonio Gaudí's Sagrada Família in Barcelona (begun in 1883 and still under construction), with its startlingly tall, 18 spindle-like spires which compete in height with Barcelona's famed Montjuic hill.

———————

The real contribution of sacred architecture around the theme of a new monumentality, however, was not just about scale: more importantly, it had a deep grounding in an aspiration toward the ideals of permanence and timelessness, forming "a link between the past and the future," as the "Nine Points" put it. So, for example, Louis Kahn's concern for the spiritual dimension of architecture focused him on the ruins of ancient civilizations as a source, an influence one can see especially clearly in the monumentality of his religious buildings such as the First Unitarian Church of Rochester (1959–1967); the unbuilt Mikveh Israel Synagogue in Philadelphia (1961–1972); and also the unbuilt Hurva Synagogue in Jerusalem (1968–

1973). As Kahn expressed it, "Monumentality in architecture may be defined as a quality, a spiritual quality inherent in a structure which conveys the feeling of eternity, that it cannot be added to or changed. We feel that quality in the Parthenon, the recognized architectural symbol of Greek civilization."[19] Indeed, Kahn's ambition to achieve such a "feeling of eternity" in his own work becomes a point of reference for a number of the essays in this volume.

The ideal of building an intentionally monumental sacred structure in the sense suggested by the "Nine Points," however, arguably puts the individual architect in a precarious existential position. This consciousness, which is repeatedly invoked by the contributors to this book, perhaps comes from the fact that there is in the task of sacred building a more strongly implied obligation than usual to accept the responsibility of a moral creativity conferred by the constraints of time, place, and culture. That is to say, in venturing to construct a building that alludes either implicitly or explicitly to the spiritual dimension of human life in community, an architect must necessarily attend to those longer trajectories of meaning that become muted in the face of functional efficiency and economic expediency. To name only a few illustrative examples of where this cultural sensibility is clearly in evidence, there is in the American context the Northern California Arts and Crafts ethos of Bernard Maybeck's First Church of Christ, Scientist in Berkeley (1910) or the carefully balanced masses of Eliel Saarinen's Midwestern modernism in the First Christian Church in Columbus, Indiana (1942). In Europe, one might especially name the Finnish organicism of Erik Bryggman's Resurrection Chapel (1941) and Alvar Aalto's Church of the Three Crosses (1955–1958), or the mystical investigations of the German Expressionist architects of the 1920s and '30s, especially the Lutheran theologian and

architect, Otto Bartning, and Dominkus Bohm. In Latin America, mention must similarly be made of the work of Felix Candela in Mexico in the 1950s and '60s, where he deploys a hyperbolic paraboloid shell of reinforced concrete, or the attention to the indigenous material of brick by the Uruguayan Eladio Dieste, as, for example, in the Church of Christ the Worker, Atlántida (1958–1960).

Collectively, these examples (and there are many others) of modern religious works inflected by a regionalist, organic idiom, speak of the complex mediating role that an architect faces in engaging the sacred. What emerges in the current collection of essays is a contrast between occasions where projects take on the question of spirituality in a more explicit manner, as is the case when they provide space for ritualized functions of a self-consciously sectarian nature, and those where the evocation of the transcendent is more latent and even secular. In proposing the tautology of a "secular spirituality" to describe the sacred architecture of Tadao Ando, for example, Kenneth Frampton raises a focal issue that runs throughout this volume, because it also reflects what he identifies as a "crisis that lies at the heart of a great deal of contemporary culture": How can architecture, or any cultural production, be unequivocally modern, yet in the face of the very relentlessness of modernization also be informed by modes of beholding that are more primordial and historically layered? To attempt to construct a sacred space today stands apart as a provocative— some would say anachronistic—assertion of meaning. Yet the distinctive narrative that sacred building has historically provided within modern architecture, suggests that even in environments that are predominantly determined economically and technologically, sacred building can take a critical yet precarious stance that says more, even, than the architect may at first intend.

[19] Louis I. Kahn, "Monumentality," in Ockman, p. 48.

PART I   ARCHITECTURE AND THE SACRED

INTRODUCTION

The essays in this first section sketch out varied approaches to the idea of the sacred, establishing the terrain upon which the rest of the book will unfold. Most importantly, these five essays collectively insist upon the multiplicity of ways in which the sacred has been conceived architecturally. Two foundational essays in particular provide the formative groundwork for much of the book: Vincent Scully's comprehensive overview, "The Earth, The Temple, and Today," exploring how the sacred has been embodied in built form from the time of the ancients to the present; and Karsten Harries' argument from a philosophical basis that "the sacred needs architecture if it is not to wither and that, similarly, architecture needs the sacred."

As an historian of architecture, Scully has had a lifelong interest in the anthropological implications of architectural form, including especially the relationship of the sacred to buildings. Over the course of more than sixty years of research and teaching, his work has grappled with the ways in which human explorations of the sacred—in whatever culture or religious tradition—are related to both the natural and built world. Thus, Scully's essay relates the topic of sacred architecture to its primal origins in the earth's landscapes, while also appealing to the heroic dimension of the human quest for meaning. He significantly relates these concepts to canonical works of modern architecture, implicitly making the argument that modernism is itself deeply influenced by transcendent ideals.

The philosopher Karsten Harries has also engaged extensively in discussions of the ethical dimensions of architecture and its relationship to the sacred. As a scholar of Heiddeger, Adorno, as well as the aesthetics of Bavarian Rococco churches, Harries' work has long been directed to addressing architecture's interaction with the limits of objectifying reason. In his essay here, "Untimely Meditations on the Need for Sacred Architecture," Harries argues that an awareness of the transcendent is a presupposition of human flourishing, so that if architecture is to address the whole human person it must itself engage at some level with the idea of the sacred.

The theologian Miroslav Volf extends on this argument with a reading of the ways in which contemporary market-driven society holds questions of meaning and purpose at arm's length. Volf's work is heavily influenced by his experience of growing up in the fragmented and often violent environment of Croatia. Drawing on the theme of memory, his writings have engaged issues of cultural identity and reconciliation in light of religious commitment,

setting up a context in which sacred architecture may be understood as a site of sacred memory. In this context, the monument and museum emerge as other types of sacred buildings, a concept represented later in the book by the work of architects Stanley Tigerman, Moshe Safdie, and Peter Eisenman.

The concern with the relationship between modernity and secularity also leads into Mark Taylor's essay, which raises the question of whether the contemporary "return of the religious" is not best understood as a postmodern reaction to modernism (rather than a return to pre-modern modes of thought), and whether secularity in this regard does not have to be understood as a type of religious phenomenon. Raising the question of the violent destructiveness associated with the sacred, he asks if in the post-Holocaust world the ineffability of the sacred may not lie in its provocation of a *horror religiosus.*

Enlarging the possible terrain of sacred building still further, the religious ethicist Emilie Townes calls our attention to more vernacular expressions of sacred buildings, such as the storefront and rural churches so important to the American religious landscape. Her evocative and even poetic text, based upon her own Baptist background, reminds us that the role of sacred architecture to provide a center (in Mircea Eliade's sense) is manifested in any number of building types, and in this way she offers a helpful correction to any overly rarified treatment of the sacred.

THE EARTH, THE TEMPLE, AND TODAY   VINCENT SCULLY

I dedicate this essay to my late colleague George Hershey, who loved Greek temples too.

Fifty years ago, an essay on religious, or perhaps we should say "sacred," architecture would have been much easier to write. We could have affirmed with some confidence that the role of specifically religious structures as embodiments of the sacred was dwindling, and that, while elements of the sacred might be perceived in many kinds of modern buildings, in fact the attainment of the sacred was one of the well-hidden agendas of canonical modern architecture as a whole, which its protagonists defended and continue to defend with a ferocity previously peculiar to religious experience.

Today, though, with the startling rise of aggressive fundamentalism in varying degrees in the Christian, Muslim, and Jewish communities, the issue has become more complicated and even dangerous, deeply affecting and perhaps threatening all our lives. So, with ever-increasing urgency we ask: What has been sacred in the past? What is sacred to us today? And how may it be embodied in architectural form?

top: Notre Dame Cathedral, Laon, 12th century

bottom: Frank Gehry, Guggenheim Museum, Bilbao, 1997

The problem of Modernism itself remains central; it is a question of meaning. In two contrasting images of the Cathedral of Laon and the Guggenheim Museum in Bilbao, we surmise that the cathedral is a sacred building because it is so different from everything else—different in scale, bigger, demanding, with the enormous rose window, the deep entrance, and the towers with their horned animals rising in the mist at the end of the city street. In the image of the museum in Bilbao, we see many of the same characteristics. There is the clear, dark, rational street, and then something that seems to have no connection with everyday experience, expressing something transcendental, a silver cloud at the end of the street that is delicately picking up the profiles of the hills surrounding the city. Indeed, the way we see it from the automobile bridge as we cross the river, it resembles a ship that has sailed up from the Bay of Biscay and crashed into the bridge. It is a nave, a sacred vessel swimming through the town, no less than Notre Dame through Paris. But in this case it contains not the host but a second-string collection of modern art from the Guggenheim basement and a few colossal objects run up for the occasion.

When I was there last time, someone whose opinion I respect felt there was a kind of satanic laughter in this: it pretends to be sacred, looks sacred, but what does it mean? This is a question that modern architects don't ask very often; they love forms no matter what they are for, no matter what they mean. Perhaps our cult of the museum—and this museum has probably done as much for the city of Bilbao today as a cathedral would have six hundred years ago—acting to serve aesthetic experience, represents the closest most people today can get to the sacred. The problem is still that Modernism and traditional religious experience have certain points at issue. So the questions remain: What has been sacred? What is sacred today? What is more than consumerism? What is more than satanic laughter?

Whole cities can be sacred, or can be intended to be. New Haven, Connecticut, for example, with its perfect nine squares—originally with a square meetinghouse in the center—was closely based on Villalpandus' 1604 reconstruction of Ezekiel's description of the ideal city that Jehovah shows him as a sanctuary for the refugees from Jerusalem (Ezekiel 48). Thus, the city was imagined as the new Jerusalem, the "new haven." Ezekiel describes how the twelve tribes of Israel hold the gates, with the Levites dividing the middle at the major intersections to protect the tabernacle. The tabernacle itself faces east, exactly as does the meetinghouse in all early maps of New Haven. And there is something more than this: Ezekiel begins his description of the ideal city by saying that Jehovah takes him to the top of the high mountain, "which is as a frame for a city on the south." For New Haven this is the outcropping of East Rock, actually north of the city and looming over the city's nine squares —red, like a butte from Arizona.

So, a sense that the earth is sacred runs deep in Ezekiel's prophecy. And if we look chronologically at the history of sacred architecture, we find that the first monumental sacred forms tend to imitate natural forms, or defer to them. It seems to be a worldwide cult. We find it at Teotihuacán, the most important ceremonial site in the Western hemisphere, where the long Avenue of the Dead leads to the Temple of the Moon, which echoes the shape of the mountain behind it, Tenan, "Our Lady of Stone." The mountain is conical, cleft at the summit, and running with springs. So the pyramid of the temple below it is striated horizontally to indicate pressure, as if from the mountain, forcing ground water out through it down to the fields below. The water goddess from Teotihuacán is exactly that. She wears a mask like the mountain on her head, and like Tenan it is cleft and its weight compresses her body, so that water is squeezed out of her hands. Another example is the temple of Quetzalcoatl at the entrance to the site, whose *tablero* construction squeezes water out like jets from a mountain: some are heads of the rain god Tlaloc, others of Quetzalcoatl, god of agriculture, the plumed serpent—the water from the sky and from the ground.

In classic Maya, in the Petén, where no mountains are close by, the temples themselves rise high into the air. They stand like the heroic Maya kings themselves in sites such as Tikal. In Temple I, the tomb of Hasaw Chan K'awil,

top: East Rock, outcropping looming over the city's nine squares, New Haven, Connecticut

bottom: Teotihuacán, Mexico, ceremonial site, city established c. 200 BC

102:—Empire State Building, New York.

above: Temple I,
Tikal, c. 730

above right: Postcard
of Empire State Building,
New York, New York,
1939

the king is still a mountain; he leaps up and his roof comb touches and echoes the shapes of the clouds and the little concrete cavern of the temple breathes out in the heat the chill rain breath of his companion clouds. Such temples become the first skyscrapers of the Americas, rising high above the houses of the towns. Temple I becomes a direct and well-documented inspiration for our most iconic skyscrapers, such as the upward-leaping temple of the Empire State Building in New York. It is touching in the picture postcard (similar to the one published by Rem Koolhaas) that it leaps to the sky to reach the dirigible, one of the new sky gods, and was built in good part by Mohawks from Caughnawaga. They had no fear of heights, full of confidence in the gods.

The image of the temple which rises in the middle of the city as a sacred mountain, existed three thousand years before the Mesoamerican temples in the ziggurats that towered over the cities of Mesopotamia. They were climbed by a priest-king, who sacrificed to his people's gods on the summit. The ziggurat of Ur, constructed in 2100 BC, was the first true ziggurat to connect the earth to the sky by a continuous stairway. But even 300 years before that, in Egypt, the sacred mountain had already been turned into pyramids of light at Gizeh, facing the rising sun and dedicated to the cult of Ra like obelisks buried in the sand, missiles aimed at the sun and all covered with blinding white limestone so that, when the sun rose, sheets of reflected light would sweep out across the delta of Egypt below them.

These examples are all sacred mountains built where no mountains were. But where the mountains existed, they were sacred themselves, as in Crete. Crete is a striking example of the continuation in very sophisticated forms of ancient stone-age traditions, especially the straightforward worship of natural forms. All the palaces of the kings there, like the palace of Minos at Knossos, are focused on sacred mountains. In this case it is Mount Jouctas, which is conical and cleft a little bit like Tenan, but steeper in profile and, like the

above: First Temple of
Hera, Paestum, 550 BC

above right: Temple
of Apollo, Delphi, 7th
century BC

goddess who occupies the cavern near its summit, conical and horned. This is where, in Cretan myth, Zeus was buried. At Phaistos, where Mount Ida opens, he was born.

Finally then, the Greeks inherit this entire tradition but change it forever by introducing into it the demanding, intractable image of mankind. Nature is still sacred. In Paestum in Southern Italy two temples of Hera as goddess of childbirth focus upon the conical hill just inland. But here the sacred building does not echo nature's shapes but contrasts with them, its muscular columns standing together like men in their compact phalanxes, the body of a divinity man-conceived, balancing, even confronting, the divinity embodied in the land. It is two alternatives as facts—nature's law and human wish—indeed an embodiment of the whole beautiful structure of Greek tragic thought. The two temples of Hera are together on the south facing the hill and the temple of Athena is to the north. The first temple of Hera is of about 550 BC; the second of 450 BC is a contemporary of the Parthenon. We can see how the Greeks developed the temple type, always the same type, to convey that sense of the building as the physical body of a divinity, as palpable as the forms of nature but embodying human character, as the Olympian gods all do.

For example, in the first temple the builders borrow from the Ionic temples of Eastern Greece, with nine columns across. That number demands counting. There must have been a high pediment above them, compressing the columns, squashing

the capitals, bulging the shafts. Hera's presence is heavy on the land, in this colony in Italy. In the later temple the columns are reduced to six, so we can see it all at once; we don't have to count. The body is compact. The columns get bigger and the pediment smaller. Instead of being a structural drama, like the first temple, it is a unified sculptural force of enormous power. Hera is there, the old goddess subjected to the Greek Zeus as wife. There is resentment in her, menace, awe, and terror in the columns. One of Hera's major myths is that of Cleobis and Biton, sons of a priestess of Hera, who drag their mother's chariot across the muddy plain of Argos to Hera's Heraion. In gratitude, the mother prayed to the goddess that she grant them the most precious gift any human beings could have, and Hera put them to death in their sleep. This is a very un-Greek myth, but there they are, like the columns. They are oxen, enthralled, sacrifices.

Athena, on her height at Paestum, is totally different. We see her from below; she rises. Her columns are slender. The point of entasis, of swelling, is high. They get very thin up above, with more space between them. It is the only pedimented Greek temple we know which never had a horizontal cornice. The heavy secret body of Hera now opens. Athena flourishes her aegis in front of the Italic mountains; Sophocles called her "our own dear *Kore* who is among us," and we can feel her openness, her receptivity. She is of 510 BC, and another temple of exactly the same date but in another place has a totally different kind of column. It is a monolith, not built of drums, and has no entasis whatever, with a purely conical section. It is a divinity who is neither compressed nor heavy on the earth, nor rising lightly above it, but one who is indomitable, immovable. It is Apollo at the Isthmus of Corinth. He stands there like a rank of Greek hoplites themselves, and he confronts all the images of the old goddess around him, especially the great looming rock of Aphrodite: Acrocorinth, the center of the worship of the goddess in Greece. And that is the way Apollo confronts, across the gulf, the most majestic image of the power of the earth: the great Horns of the Phaedriades at Delphi. The columns of the archaic temple were much like those at Corinth; the present columns are Hellenistic. They are taller, but have no entasis either. In that whole wild landscape, expressive of nature's terrible power, Apollo stands immovable, his columns like disciplined men, standing firm and confronting the old dominant force of the earth.

In the classic period following the Persian war, the mood changes. The first of the great classic sites is Olympia, where we find something totally different from Delphi. There are no savage horns of rock, only a gentle conical hill named, so Pindar tells us, by Herakles after his labors. He called it the Hill of Kronos, after the dead father of Zeus, whose *tholos* tomb it is. Pindar tells us that Herakles planted the trees of the sanctuary "to shelter the god from the sun's fierce glare." It is a quiet dominion, the dominion of the classic Zeus, as he is embodied in the bronze statue from Artemision. It is the Zeus to whom Aeschylus cries,

The Acropolis, Athens, 5th century BC

"Zeus, if this of many names to you seems good, Zeus, who taught men how to think." Long before that, Hesiod, in the eighth century, had said the most basic thing about him, writing in his *Works and Days*, that the animals and birds and fishes all eat each other, but for mankind almighty Zeus gives *dike* (which is law court justice): *dike*, so they can live together in towns, in *eunomia* (harmony), and *eirene* (civic peace). This is its first classic phase, looking backward to the past, to its origins in ancient law. And in this justice of Zeus there is none of the demand of the monotheistic religions to believe. Unlike the monotheistic divinities, not a single human being is ever butchered in Zeus' name. The Greeks found all kinds of reasons to kill each other, but never over the gods.

The second phase looks forward, embodying in Athens the pride of democracy and empire. The city of Pericles breaks with all the old ways. The buildings raised by him on the Acropolis are the result of his unilateral abrogation of a treaty with the other Greek states that no shrines that the Persians destroyed would be rebuilt. Pheidias oversaw it all, and the Parthenon stands out against the landscape, dominating it from the Acropolis' height, victor over everything. Beyond it, "violet crowned," as Pindar sang it, is Hymettos, the sacred mountain, with the cones of Aphrodite, Athena as mountain goddess, and the sanctuary of Zeus on the summit, all deploying before our eyes, as we advance toward Athens from the new war harbor at the Piraeus that Hippodamus of Miletus designed for Pericles.

Other things, too, happen on the Acropolis which lead on to Hellenistic architecture and to Rome. For example, the classic Propylaia looks straight down toward Salamis, the place of victory, and through it we mount the Acropolis height toward the Parthenon and the Erechtheum, setting up a perspective toward the altar of Athena near the crest with the horns of Hymettos which rise

Vaults of the Baths of Caracalla, Rome, 212–216

directly beyond it. And from the altar of Athena we look back down toward Salamis over the Propylaia. Le Corbusier once wrote that "the axis of the Acropolis runs from the sea to the mountain." That is true, though he misnames the mountain. It is the axis of victory, which is what the Acropolis is unashamedly all about.

I say that this axial organization leads on toward Rome, but there is a generic difference between Greece and Rome, and it is certainly this: the Greeks worshipped the body from first to last and the Romans from the beginning worshipped space. The old Roman word *templum* means a sacred space, not a building, and like us they make spaces that appear sacred, but were actually secular, like the great public baths—the baths of Caracalla, for example. Their vaults look like wind-blown canopies, held down by columns, not supported by them—a magical space, high above us, ennobling us all, great crowds of us.

When the Romans came to make the definitive temple, such as the Emperor Hadrian created in the Pantheon, it becomes the whole universe: a planetarium, with the planets standing around at the sides and the sun illuminating the Mediterranean

San Vitale, Ravenna, 526–547

with the Roman Empire surrounding it. Indeed it is so Roman that it is all done in a circle—a clear, classical shape enclosing everything, the whole Empire, the world. That form slips seamlessly into Christianity: all one had to do was eliminate the oculus, cut windows in the outer walls, have an ambulatory with a screen of columns curving back into it, so that we no longer know where the boundaries are. From a finite form an infinite one emerges.

So Ravenna's sixth century San Vitale is built in a very Roman way, but now completely logically in that the outside of the building means nothing. It is the inside that counts, the space. The exterior is simple, with no Greek columns, no portico, just doors and windows at floor heights, and a thin brick shell. The same is true in the other early Christian type, the basilica. Constantine's basilica of St. Peter in Rome is a card house, built as cheaply as possible because the space is everything. Totally unlike the Greek temple, the fabric of the building is no longer holy. The model is the Roman law court, but now there is an enforced perspective in one direction. It is the absolutism of monotheism, not the earth and the temple, only the altar.

At Hagia Sophia, the transcendental landscape is made by the square in plan which the pendentives turn into a circle so that the dome can be set upon it. But the dome seems to float above it. The windows and the mosaic dazzle our eyes. We have the long axis and the central dome as well. It is like the Parthenon, a union of two opposites, there Doric and Ionic, here the basilican plan and the central plan. But it is all space, and it is the first example I know of a truly big monumental building which wholly embodies the parenthetical remark by Vitruvius which later dominated western aesthetics, namely that the human form fits into the perfect shapes of the square and the circle. There are hundreds of drawings of this idea in the Middle Ages and the Renaissance, the best known by Leonardo.

Earlier, among the Greeks, there had been the recognition of two realities, equally divine and equally sacred: nature and the human will. Now it is all one way in the basilicas, enforced by the thinnest of architectural means, wooden-roofed, not vaulted, and this remains true in the big Ottonian basilicas along the Rhine from Charlemagne's time on, and in the Lombard basilicas in Northern Italy.

Finally, in a tiny, remote place of refuge in the Pyrenees, on Mount Canigou above Perpignan, someone decided right after the millennium (for reasons we don't know), to vault a space again, to make it permanent. Perhaps the builders felt that things were starting again, that the world was not going to end after all. So they start over from the beginning with a cavern, lovingly built, with a thick masonry barrel vault whose enormous weight is brought down through dramatic capitals to the thinnest of monolithic stone columns, all on this little mountain not far from the great prehistoric caves, which are, with their paintings, the oldest images of the human perception of the sacred that we have. Surely some deep passion created this wonderful thing that the French call the *premier art roman*, and out of it all the great sacred architecture of Romanesque France took shape.

At Vézelay, for example, we can't help but feel that both the fabric and the space are sacred. The special quality here, of course, is that created when the Gothic choir was added to the Romanesque nave. The choir was intended to be the image of heaven on earth, and the Gothic introduces a splendor of light that makes us feel such has to be so; we go from the darkness of earth to the brightness of heaven. Eventually, with the development of Gothic architecture through the twelfth and thirteenth centuries, all the fabric of the church is dematerialized at last into something like a growing forest. Everything is glazed between the branches—no wonder that the eighteenth century believed that Gothic architecture had developed

from the forests of the north. It does convince us that it is all as sacred as nature itself, both the fabric and the space.

But in Gothic architecture, as in Greek, there is also a political dimension, having to do with the *polis*, the state. Abbot Suger begins it all by building a new church for his king, and his Saint-Denis is the place where the kings of France were buried. The first new thing Suger does on his façade is to create a circle in a square. One doesn't know whether he did that by accident or through the influence of Abelard, who had been teaching Plato there in the

Abbey Church of Ste.- Marie-Madeleine, Vézelay, dedicated 1104, nave looking toward the Gothic choir

decades just before. But he uses it, the famous basic Vitruvian figure, so that the great rose window, the first of Gothic architecture, now brings a heavenly light into the chapel of the king, which is open to the nave beyond it so that the king stands out in the light from the west, far outmatching in radiance the Holy Roman Emperor on his western throne.

All this climaxes in the façade of the cathedral of Reims, where not only is the rose there, now lighting the nave, but everything is glazed between the skeletal structure. The king is crowned within, and he comes forth toward the west with all his kingdom in the capitals of the nave marching along with him, alive with the fruits and flowers and beasts of his realm, until he emerges in the light in glory.

Out in front of the church stands the nineteenth-century equestrian figure of Joan of Arc, the virgin who saved France after hearing heavenly voices like that of the carved courtly angel who speaks to the Virgin as a peasant girl on the central portal at Reims. The cult of the Virgin is the heart and soul of Gothic architecture. She shares the façade of Chartres with Christ, in the pediment of the southern portal, where as patron of the universities, she is surrounded by the liberal arts in the *voussoirs*, a goddess of wisdom like Athena and, like her, the guardian of the state. At Amiens, the Virgin comes down to the *trumeau* of the same lucky sunny southern doorway, but at Reims she inherits the whole façade, taking over the central *trumeau* and the statue columns around it, first as a peasant girl with the angel and then as a proud matron visiting Elizabeth, the mother of John the Baptist, and delivering the great speech Luke gives her which sums up all of France, medieval and modern, royal and revolutionary. She is greater than Athena, since she is the mother as well, but she is much in the same vein.

With the architects of the Renaissance, we begin to encounter for the first time that myth of the hero-architect that is so prevalent today.

The Vitruvian figure becomes their professional talisman; they know Vitruvius, they know they are right. Like modern architects, they have their own ideas as to what a sacred space should be. When Leonardo drew his perfect man in the circle and the square, I'm sure he had himself in mind as the heroic male figure standing in the center, and he designed scores of central plans, none of which were built. But this form is found everywhere. Brunelleschi's loggia of the Innocenti, at the very beginning of the Renaissance, is this: cubes of air capped by spheres of air shaped by handkerchief vaults. They are defined by the thinnest possible architectural elements; it is all drawing, the purity of the idea undefiled by matter. The architects love this purity, wherein the square and the circle are so clear. But the central form is awkward for normal ritual, making it hard for architects to get it built. A few of these churches did come to fruition around 1500, all dedicated to the Virgin, all outside cities in gentle landscapes, as was Santa Maria della

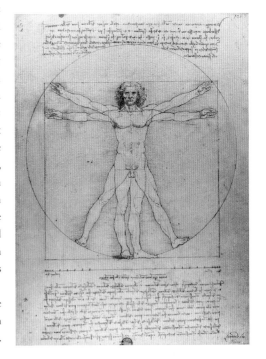

Leonardo da Vinci, Vitruvian man, 1485–90

Church of Santa Maria della Consolazione, Todi, dedicated 1607

Consolazione at Todi, where we imagine the pressure of the arms pushing the circles of the apses out, all clearly expressed on the outside. These are some of the most beautiful and touching churches—Greek in a fundamental way in the landscape—but all Roman, all space, all enclosed. They also form the basis for the first great icon of a new religious movement: the cult of the house.

It is Andrea Palladio who shapes that image best. He takes the square and the circle, the cube and the cylinder, and he makes the central plan house, as in the Villa Rotonda. But then he uses not Todi's gently rounded apse forms, but hard-edged Greek frontispieces on all four sides. So he, too, like the architects of the Parthenon and Hagia Sophia, is condensing two opposites: both the Christian church and the Greek temple front with its pediment.

But the fate of the central plan in Renaissance architecture is a wild one, because nobody likes it much except the architects and a few special patrons like Julius II. So the central plan of the new St. Peter's (imagine the power of the concept to replace Constantine's basilica, like Frank Gehry rebuilding the Capitol in Washington), that Bramante proposes and Michelangelo revises and enlarges, succumbs in the end to generations of pressure to add a nave, like the old St. Peter's. Now the nave protrudes and its façade does the thing all the Renaissance architects hated: it progressively masks the dome as one approaches it. So what does Bernini do? He pushes the oval of his great colonnade (pushes the crowd in effect) out just to the first point in space from which we see it all, shaping the urbanism of that part of Rome, the façade and the dome together.

Palladio too solves that problem (a very modern phrase to use: "solving a problem" in architecture) in Il Redentore in Venice, by controlling the approach to it. On the Feast of the Redeemer, a bridge of boats is built across the canal, and from there we see it all. As we cross the bridge, however,

above: Pieter Saenredam, *Interieur van de Nieuwe Kerk te Haarlem*, 1652, Frans Hals Museum, Haarlem

opposite: Frank Lloyd Wright, Unity Temple, Oak Park, Illinois, 1905, interior

the dome goes out of sight, and the big nave dominates the view. But that is acceptable because it is exactly what is happening inside. The nave is bigger, more consequential than the apse, which also has an open colonnade behind the altar. So when we enter, the altar is lost and what we feel is the width of the nave, which must have been wonderful for the Venetian antiphonal singing they loved so much. Of course the Catholic Church instantly moved to correct that effect and to focus on the altar once more, as in Rome's Il Gesù of 1600 by Maderna, the first Baroque church. Here he constricts the nave, brightens the altar, and makes that the enforced climax of the experience once again.

But the Protestants loved that dominant nave, that diminished altar. In the great paintings by the Dutch painter Pieter Saenredam of Catholic churches that had been taken over for Protestant worship, the altar indeed disappears; we often can't tell where it was. Preaching now is not down the length of the nave (which is irrational anyway, since that shape is not good for preaching), but across the axis where the congregation can be in a better relationship to the preacher's voice. That makes the New England meetinghouse: the preacher is all, there is no altar. People sit in pews, looking at him, and into each other's faces under the clear windows that bathe everything in Saenredam's bright, clear light. This cross-axial innovation culminates, we might say, in the secularization of Unitarianism, of which the great monument is Frank Lloyd

Wright's Unity Temple. We are in what Wright calls "a perfect cube" focused on the preacher, from whom all energy seems to flow.

The sacred building is now more rational, more secularized, and it emphasizes the word, the pulpit, not the altar. This may be why so many of the most emotionally transcendent monuments of the twentieth century, such as the great war memorials (and God knows the twentieth century was better at producing death than anything else), don't seem to have any directly religious connection. For example, in the great war memorial to the dead of the Somme by Sir Edwin Lutyens at Thiepval, he shows us a demon: the great open scream, the bulging eyes, the god of death who lords it over the dead, thin companies of men who nevertheless do not shrink from him. The French are on the right, facing the scream; the English on the left, all facing the emptiness, the pain, the overwhelming physical presence of war. Then Maya Lin, partly inspired by Lutyens and his list of names on the white slabs of the arch at Thiepval, herself has a wall of names at the Vietnam Veterans Memorial in Washington, D.C. She resisted the pressure of all the jurors, who had wanted her to have the names arranged alphabetically, which would have been a great mistake. Instead she made them chronological, so that those who died together remain together, but the wall dwindles away, getting smaller and smaller.

Another phenomenon is that so many really moving churches by great architects in the modern period have had a curiously primitive sense about them, evoking more primitive states of feeling like, for example, Gaudi's great Sagrada Família in Barcelona. This church is a ruin, begun in the 1880s and not yet completed. In Gothic Revival terms, Gaudi's motto was, "Build according to nature," and it is almost as if he is shaping one of the prehistoric caves, like the cave of Chauvet—not so far away—from 32,000 BC. We know from

the evidence of the walls and the floor that men and cave bears shared this space and occupied it at different times, and perhaps together, and the last layer of footprints are those of bears, not men. Men lost here. Before these people, these Cro-Magnons, Neanderthals had used bear bones too, for a kind of altar, like the bear's skull on the rock at Chauvet. This may be one of the first altars we know.

All that sense of the cavern, of the basic primitive experience of the earth, is what Edouard Trouin was engaging at Sainte Baume. He was a devotee of the cult of the three Marys, deriving from the legend that, after Christ's crucifixion, the three Marys (some say only Mary Magdalene and some disciples), moved to the south of France and lived in a cave, ending up with Mary Magdalene alone at Sainte Baume. Trouin induced Le Corbusier to create a great pilgrimage center around that cavern, based on an underground basilica that was supposed to be lighted by shafts of light coming through the rock and signaled by the great peak of the mountain. Of course the project fell through, but Le Corbusier built it nevertheless, in Notre Dame du Haut at Ronchamp. There is the peak, with the irregular holes in the rock to light the cavern within, but the body of the building is something more. Here again the Parthenon comes to mind; as seen from the southwest, it seems to swell and turn toward us from its nearest corner. Le Corbusier can't quite equal that in Ronchamp, but he does want the Virgin's pilgrimage church to turn like an active force, rushing open to the peak, invoking the horizon. He calls it a "bell," "*une acoustique paysagiste, prenant les quatre horizons à témoin.*"

We might say that in all his late work Corbusier consistently tries to evoke the sacredness of the body. In *béton brut*—as at the Unité d'habitation in Marseilles—he masks his glass surfaces, as in Greek temples with their peripteral colonnades. He tries to give the impression that the building is not

Le Corbusier, Notre Dame du Haut, Ronchamp,
1950–55, exterior showing the peak or "prow"

Le Corbusier, Monastery of Notre Dame de la Tourette, Eveux, 1952–60, altars under light cannons

primarily a container of space, but a sculptural body. He stands it on powerful legs, forms more primitive than those of any Greek temple. The building is a kind of ancient monster, a giant on the earth. The pilotis are essential, just as they were in his early days. Even in that period when he talked about a *"machine à habiter,"* the difference between his houses at Weissenhof and those of Gropius and Mies (which were simple slabs or boxes), is that they stood on legs. Buildings don't stand on legs; creatures do; human beings do; gods may. But Corbusier's buildings stand on legs however thin they are, however light the box they support. There is always that special aura, and this may be one reason why the followers of Le Corbusier have normally been so fanatic, perhaps because the sense of sacredness is somehow always in his work, early and late. And late in life he can take that box, and make a church with it, as at the monastery of La Tourette near Eveux. Inside there is primitive darkness. But on our approach to the altar, we see on the left, barbarously lighted by the *canons de lumière*, that the sacrifice is of the blood: rough concrete and blood-red tones tell us that it is nothing less. It can also remind us of the toughness of French Catholicism, its Jansenist side.

In his own way, Louis Kahn does much the same thing. In the Unitarian Church at Rochester, he takes what is apparently a very cheap set of materials and gives us cinderblock walls articulated by a stiff concrete frame supporting a rising slab. But then, clear silver light comes floating down from the corners of the building and the slab becomes the dark cloud over Golgotha,

right: Louis I. Kahn, First Unitarian Church, Rochester, New York, 1959–67, exterior

the darkness over Jerusalem rent by Rembrandt's silvery light that bathes the crucifixion down below. I don't know how a Unitarian would react to that iconic description, but we may legitimately guess that it was in Kahn's mind somewhere, because all his work is like this: somehow divine, somehow sacred. Kahn also inspired a fanatical devotion in architects and critics who actively disliked some close followers of his—Venturi, for example, who has always avoided this sacred effect. But already in Kahn's Art Gallery of 1953 at Yale, the ceiling slab is so ominous, so powerful, so physical that the space it makes comes to feel special, dangerous, an awesome presence. One reason that Kahn could do this was because his slab indeed had a sacred background in the pyramids of Gizeh, more critical to it than its debt to Buckminster Fuller. In fact, Kahn was doing his pastels of the pyramids when he learned of his commission for the gallery. He sees that they are creatures of light,

Louis I. Kahn, Yale Art Gallery, New Haven, Connecticut, 1951–55, interior ceiling slab with the architect

and he treats them that way, sometimes reflecting the desert, sometimes in black shadow, and then finally, climactically, reflecting the full blaze of the sun, as the pyramids, clad in shining white limestone, all did originally. All those conditions of light occur in the gallery slab in their tetrahedrons, sometimes dark, sometimes bright with the lights they contain.

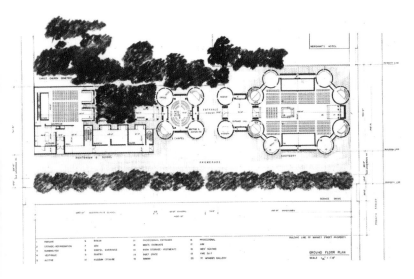

Louis I. Kahn, Mikveh Israel Synagogue project, Philadelphia, Pennsylvania, 1963, plan

Another sacred source for Kahn was the Kabbala's Tree of the Sephirot, hung with the bright characters of God, of beauty, power, and the rest. Kahn clearly uses it for the plan of his Mikveh Israel Synagogue, and its "Supernal Lights" suggested his use of perforated cylinders for lighting. But as soon as one tries to glaze those cylinders, the point is lost. Kahn clearly wanted it without glass, like the Roman ruins he loved. I think that's probably why it was never built: it was impossible to glaze. Kahn had a ruin in mind, with pure voids in solid masonry. He wanted a primitive condition.

Of course, Kahn creates that in the other great synagogue project of his, which was also never

built and mainly for the same reasons, the Hurva Synagogue in Jerusalem. Hurva, as I understand it, means ruins. Again we can see how it is based on Kahn's pastels of the pyramids: the hard edges, the angles, and the shapes of light or darkness so similar in both. More than that, the four piers, which are hollow, support four inverted pyramids expanding upward, but never quite touching each other or the Egyptian pylons that form the outer walls. So it has to remain unglazed. It's a shame that it couldn't be built, even that way; with its name, it would have been wholly of the place.

Indeed, Kahn shares with Le Corbusier a deep sense of the sacredness of all architecture, based on its primitive beginnings in the cavern, in savage sacrifice and demanding gods. By comparison, Abdel Wahed El-Wakil embodies a more gentle primitivism, something bright and clear. He built a beautiful series of mosques in Saudi Arabia in the 1970s and '80s, all out of traditional materials and in traditional, primitive ways: single bricks making the dome above the desert or the hot waters of the Gulf. He had offices in Constantinople, Cairo, and London; now he is a wanderer. He once said to me, "Before the Gulf War, it was mosques. Since the Gulf War, all they want is missiles." Thinking of that, one thinks also of El-Wakil's good friend, Aldo Rossi, and his little Teatro del Mondo in front of the Salute, a modest presence, calling up the grandeur of the sacred architecture of the past, but so gently, so sweetly, with an undying grasp, however, of the sacred type. One thinks of the relation between these two civilizations, these rivals in the Mediterranean, sworn enemies who yet share so much, especially a common heritage of the domes of Rome.

One thinks of what might have been, what could be, but that of course is not where the power lies. The power lies with the voice. The power derives from the pulpit, and with the rise of television and mass audiences, and the stresses

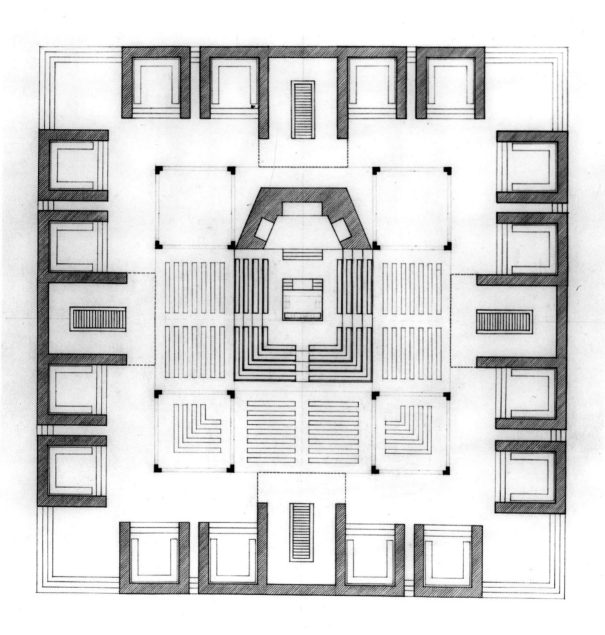

Louis I. Kahn, Hurva
Synagogue project,
Jerusalem, 1967–68, plan

above: Abdel Wahed
El-Wakil, King Saud
Mosque, Jeddah, Saudi
Arabia, 1987, exterior

right: King Saud
Mosque, interior of the
great dome, looking
through the hanging
chandelier

and strains of modern life, the preacher can become a kind of a rock star, as was the late Reverend Jerry Falwell in his Thomas Road Baptist Church. Again, Falwell preached across the axis, as in a Saenredam painting, now to 6,000 people crammed inside what is, in fact, a big box warehouse—all interior, a windowless theater deeply ceiled, with no feeling or care about traditional sacredness except for a movable altar and a couple of classical façades pasted on the exterior. This of course seems the opposite of Reverend Robert Schuller's Crystal Cathedral by Philip Johnson, where the preaching is also cross-axial but in a mountain of light. Yet it all opens to a parking lot, again, like Falwell's church, suggesting a profoundly secular model, though here an open and expansive one. But Falwell's effect derives from the stringent enclosure, banishing the sun. It is a pressure cooker enforcing its own homogeneity of belief.

In these circumstances, it is peaceful, even in hazardous old age, to get outside once again with the gods of things as they are, who promise no happy afterlife, no resurrection of the dead, but in whose presence things become at least reasonable. Even the sharp arrows of far-darting Apollo seem understandable to us and relatively humane, as does sad queenly Hera, mother and reluctant wife, and Athena, of whose Acropolis Le Corbusier wrote, "Nothing left but these closely-knit and violent elements, sounding clear and tragic like brazen trumpets"—Athena, goddess of human victory, who, under whatever name, has been a support to human political and intellectual life for many hundreds of years. Finally, and most of all, there is the justice of Zeus, who taught us how to think, *dike* and civic peace, *dike* and the sacred earth.

UNTIMELY MEDITATIONS ON THE NEED
FOR SACRED ARCHITECTURE

KARSTEN HARRIES

The title of this essay needs explanation. It is meant to recall Nietzsche, who wrote his four untimely meditations to challenge the dominant spirit of his age. He was not telling his readers what they expected or wanted to hear. This, to be sure, is not to say that he was not telling them something they needed to hear. In that sense, his untimely meditations were timely indeed.

What I have to say here may well seem similarly out of touch with the dominant spirit of this age, which has relegated the sacred to the periphery of our modern lives. This finds expression in the built environment. Just compare the way churches and cathedrals tower over medieval cities with the way they are usually dwarfed in our cities by other structures. Ever since the Enlightenment, the church and temple have ceased to be a, let alone the, leading building task. This reality does not mean that houses of worship, some of them architecturally significant, have not been built throughout the nineteenth and twentieth centuries, right down to the present. But it does not change the fact that, like the modern world, modern architecture has distanced itself from the sacred. Challenging that distance, I want to insist on the continued need for sacred architecture and this indeed in a twofold sense: I want to claim that the sacred needs architecture if it is not to wither, and that similarly architecture needs the sacred. Untimely as they are, both claims invite challenge.

To turn to the first: Does the sacred really need architecture? If a few persons gather in some shed to worship an invisible deity, is that not sufficient to sanctify that modest space, to make it sacred? What sanctifies the space here is not the work of the builder. All that is asked of him is that he provide a serviceable shed. What sanctifies the building is, rather, the activity it houses. The word *Gebetsscheune*, or "prayer barn," to describe the churches built by the preaching orders of the Middle Ages is of interest in this connection. So are the many simple meetinghouses built in this country. Does religion really have a need for what deserves to be called architecture? Is it not the quality of the inner life, open to a spiritual dimension, that transcends the sensible, that matters? Indeed, does the very transcendence of the sacred not demand that religion preserve its distance from art and architecture?[1] My claim that the sacred needs art, and more especially architecture, seems out of touch with the inwardness demanded by the sacred. Is it not the very dynamism of religious transcendence that caused religion to leave art behind? This is how Hegel understood the superiority of Christianity over Greek religion. He recognized that in the beginning of history, architecture and religion were inseparably bound together.

Architecture is, in fact, the first pioneer on the highway toward the adequate realization of the Godhead. In this service it is put to severe labor with objective nature, that it may disengage it by its effort from the confused growth of finitude and the distortion of contingency. By this means it levels a space for the God, informs His external environment, and builds Him his temple as a fit place for the concentration of Spirit, and its direction to the absolute objects of intelligent life. It raises an enclosure for the congregation of those assembled, as a defense against the threatening of the tempest, against rain, the hurricane, and savage animals. It in short reveals the will thus to assemble, and although under an external relation, yet in agreement with the principles of art.[2]

Architecture and, more generally art, are here assigned a place in the story of the Spirit's progress. This progress tends towards an ever more complete appropriation of the earth. This process has to break down the walls that separate persons, races, and regions, as it has to subject the earth to the rule of technology. As Hegel understands it, this progress also has to leave behind architecture, that "first pioneer on the highway toward the adequate realization of the Godhead," and finally all art that claims to express humanity's deepest interests. Do not science and technology provide us with a far more complete mastery of the earth than art can ever provide? And is it not reason alone that in the end should bind freedom? Has the Enlightenment not taught us that it is within ourselves that we must look for whatever can give meaning to our lives?

Let me turn to my second claim that architecture needs the sacred. How can such a claim be defended? Is it not sufficient to create a building that meets whatever function it is expected to serve and at the same time convinces us as an aesthetic object—however that is unpacked—to make it a successful work of architecture? That function may, but certainly need not be, religious.

A more promising approach to our topic would seem to be opened up by Nikolaus Pevsner, when he begins his *An Outline of European Architecture* with this often quoted and seemingly unproblematic observation: "A bicycle shed is a building; Lincoln Cathedral is a piece of architecture." Pevsner interprets this distinction for us when he suggests that works of architecture differ from functional buildings in that they are "designed with a view to aesthetic appeal": work of architecture = building + aesthetic component.

[1] Cf. Louis Dupré, *Transcendent Selfhood: The Loss and Rediscovery of the Inner Life* (New York: Seabury, 1976).

[2] Georg Wilhelm Friedrich Hegel, *Vorlesungen über die Äesthetik, Jubiläumsausgabe*, ed. Hermann Glockner (Stuttgart: Fromann, 1937), vol. 12, p. 125. Trans. F. P. B. Osmaston as "Selections from The Philosophy of Fine Arts," *Philosophies of Art and Beauty*, ed. Albert Hofstadter and Richard Kuhns (Chicago: University of Chicago Press, 1976), p. 439.

St. Mary's Cathedral, Lincoln, 1185–1311

Cesar Pelli, Petronas
Towers, Kuala Lumpur,
1992–1998

That he chose for his example a splendid cathedral seems unimportant in this connection. Would Cesar Pelli's Petronas Towers in Kuala Lumpur not have served Pevsner equally well?

How is what Pevsner calls "aesthetic appeal" to be understood? Alexander Tzonis and Liane Lefaivre give us a pointer when they insist, supported by a well-established tradition, going back at least to Aristotle, that the work of architecture, like every work of art, "is a world within the world, 'complete,' 'integral,' 'whole,' a world where there is no contradiction."[3] Given this conception of the work of architecture as a self-sufficient aesthetic whole, all "outside conditions" must be considered "significant obstacles." By its very nature, the aesthetic approach to architecture, so understood, knows nothing of sacred transcendence and is opposed to every contextualism. Like a framed panel painting, the work of the architect, although inevitably in some particular place, is, in its very essence spiritually mobile, without place, in this sense utopian. And is this not true of most modern architecture? Santiago Calatrava's Turning Torso in the Swedish Malmö can stand for countless other recent buildings. Does it belong to where it happens to stand? Does it remember the special history of that place? That such questions must be answered in the negative is suggested by the fact that not just one, but two Turning Torso towers are supposed to rise in the American Las Vegas, two more in the Turkish Istanbul. And there is no reason why this should be the end. Such buildings invite cloning.[4] In that sense they have a weak identity. They exemplify that loss of aura Walter Benjamin discussed as a mark of the work of art in this age of technical reproducibility—not only of art, but of just about everything. No longer belonging to a particular geographic or historical context, most modern buildings seem ready to travel.

And is this look of mobility not in keeping with the ever-increasing freedom from the tyranny of

place that science and technology have given us? Just think of how the progress of transportation and communications technologies has made us not just physically, but spiritually, mobile as never before. Is such mobility compatible with place-establishing architecture? To be sure, we still require physical shelter and buildings that meet that need, but do we still look to architecture for spiritual shelter?

Whatever we experience as sacred we experience as transcending our ability to produce or reproduce it. What Benjamin has to say about the way art must lose its aura in this age of its technical reproducibility, applies also to architecture. Here the way Benjamin links the aura of the authentic work of art to the way it is "imbedded in the fabric of tradition"[5] is significant. Reproduction is said to tear the artwork out of its historical context and thus to destroy its aura. By the same token, it has to destroy our experience of the sacred. The sacred, too, depends on history and memory. To experience architecture as sacred is to experience it as possessing an aura of transcendence. But what sense can someone truly of this modern age still make of such an experience?

What makes my claim that architecture needs the sacred untimely is thus at bottom nothing other than our modern understanding of reality. Key here is the Cartesian conviction that whatever deserves to be called real is, in principle, comprehensible. But we cannot comprehend what is fleeting and cannot be analyzed into simple elements, or represented by joining these elements. In this sense, we really understand something only to the extent that we can reproduce it. Descartes thus promised a practical philosophy that allows us to understand nature as distinctly as a craftsman understands what he is able to make. Understanding comes to mean know-how. It was no idle promise. The triumph of that promise in technology had to carry the loss of transcendence that is a presupposition of

[3] Alexander Tzonis and Liane Lefaivre, *Classical Architecture: The Poetics of Order* (Cambridge, Mass. and London: MIT Press, 1986), p. 9.

[4] See Jean Baudrillard and Jean Nouvel, *The Singular Objects of Architecture*, trans. Robert Bononno, with foreword by K. Michael Hays (Minneapolis: University of Minnesota Press, 2005), p. 4.

[5] Walter Benjamin, "The Work of Art in the Age of Mechanical Reproduction" [1936], in *Illuminations: Essays and Reflections by Walter Benjamin* (New York: Harcourt, Brace, Jovanovich, 1968), p. 223.

the conviction that human reason can encompass and finally reproduce reality back into our concrete lives. No surprise then that reality should be experienced ever more decisively as a reality without transcendence, a reality in which the sacred has no place: mere material for us to use and transform as we see fit.

There is a very different objection my introductory claims need to confront. I claimed that our built environment speaks of a way of life that has relegated the sacred to the periphery of our lives. But is ours not the most religious of all advanced industrial societies, as countless statistics and newspaper reports have documented, indeed the only developed country in which, in poll after poll, a majority of those polled say that religion plays an important part in their lives, that they believe in God, that they go with some regularity to church or temple? And has religion not strengthened rather than weakened in the last fifty years? Just look at the political arena and the role religion plays there today. Has interest in religion not been growing everywhere, including in our universities and colleges? To give just one local example: when I was a graduate student at Yale, Brand Blanshard, then the leading member of the philosophy department, could state without being challenged that it was impossible to be a good philosopher and to be religious. How things have changed.

But, the religiosity of this country invites questioning. How, for example, are we to understand that, according to one of these polls: "only 33 percent of the American Catholics, Lutherans, and Methodists and 28 percent of the Episcopalians agreed with the statement that Christ was without sin"?[6] Or that the vast majority of America's Lutherans, Episcopalians, Methodists, Presbyterians, and Catholics do not accept the doctrine that man is justified before God alone by grace, through faith in Christ's saving work, but believes that good works are sufficient? As Gerald McDermott, an Episcopalian, put it, "in the last thirty years, American pastors have lost their nerve to preach a theology that goes against the grain of American narcissism."[7] But are narcissism, which is self-centered, and genuine religion, which is centered on what transcends the self, not incompatible? George Gallup, Jr., supported by seventy years of Gallup family polling, points out that "Americans are largely ignorant about doctrine and lack trust in God."[8] How then are we to understand statistics that show that in the United States 85 or 90 percent of the population consider themselves religious, while 59 percent consider religion a very important part of their lives, making the United States the thought-provoking exception to the general rule that the higher the annual per capita income in a country, the less likely it is that religion will be considered very important?[9] That religion should flourish in countries where the quality of life makes it difficult to experience this earth as a home is hardly surprising. But how are we to understand the anomalous role of religion in a country with perhaps the highest standard of living? Do we too, despite our affluence, find the quality of life in some important way deficient and therefore look to religion for a spiritual supplement?

Despite what the statistics have to tell us, despite the obvious political significance religion possesses in this country, I do not experience this as an especially religious society. This raises the question: What does it mean to be religious? To be able to give an affirmative answer to some pollsters' questions: "Do you consider yourself religious?" or "Do you believe in God?" or "Do you go to church or temple with some regularity?" Do the results of countless polls refute the claim that our culture has relegated the sacred to the periphery of our modern lives? Could it be that our religious practices, too,

6 Barna Poll on U.S. Religious Belief—2001. http://www.adherents. com/misc/BarnaPoll. html

7 Ibid.

8 "God Important, Not Primary," Clergy/ Leader's Mail List, No. 0-003 (Melbourne, Australia: John Mark Ministries, c. 1995). http://jmm.aaa.net.au/ articles/46.htm

9 "Among Wealthy Nations ... U.S. Stands Alone in Its Embrace of Religion," Pew Global Attitudes Project (Washington, DC: Pew Research Center, 2002), p. 2. http://pewglobal. org/reports/display. php?ReportID=167

including the architecture that serves them, have increasingly lost sight of the sacred?

The very title of this collection of essays presupposes that we can speak of "Contemporary Sacred Architecture." It is indeed not difficult to come up with significant examples, as this volume demonstrates. But just what is it that allows us to speak of a "sacred architecture"? There is a ready answer: If "sacred" is defined, as it often is, as "dedicated to or set apart for the worship of a deity," there is no problem. That definition invites us to look for what makes a certain building sacred, not to the material object and its special aura but the use to which it is put. It is understood that there would be no very significant relationship between the sensible qualities of a structure and the sacred. The sacred is not thought to be present in the stones. Indeed, what sense does this make? Stones are stone, just stones. What renders some material object sacred, on this understanding, is the religious practice it serves. In this sense, to use an example given by Rudolf Schwarz, some simple shed serving a few people assembled around the Lord's table is rendered sacred by the activity.

And must something of the sort not also be said of Philip Johnson's and John Burgee's Crystal Cathedral in Garden Grove, close to Disneyland, an enormous glass tent that, since 1980, has been home to the Reverend Dr. Robert Schuller and his congregation (and, more importantly, to the television show, "Hour of Power")? This is a space that Judith Dupré calls in her book, *Churches*, "the first major structural expression of the fastest-growing segment of American religion— evangelical, multimedia ministry, characterized by vast congregations, state-of-the art ecclesiastical entertainment, utilitarian spirituality, full-service outreach programs, and no less than a fundamental rethinking of what constitutes religion."[10] This is a building that succeeds as a functional shed and at the same time presents itself to us as a

striking aesthetic object. But does this mean that we experience this architecture as "sacred"? The Crystal Cathedral certainly presents itself to us as a church, and it does so in a way that speaks of an increasingly important trend in contemporary religion that blurs the boundaries between religion, entertainment, and business. That its architect, Philip Johnson, should have pointed to both Sainte-Chapelle in Paris and London's Crystal Palace as precursors is significant, in that it places this architecture in a tradition that has seen a progressive secularization of the symbolism of light that has provided one key to what has rendered sacred architecture sacred from the very beginning. In this age of artificial light, light too has lost much of the aura of the sacred that once surrounded it. The Crystal Cathedral would indeed seem to have more in common with this worldly palace than with the medieval chapel. Is this "'super-studio' for televised Christian worship"[11] a convincing example of sacred architecture? Given the definition just given, the answer would have to be a clear "yes." This is architecture that very successfully answers to its intended religious function. But how is religion understood here? Does it remain grounded in experiences of the sacred? Could it be that in this age of the technical reproducibility of even religion, the objects that figure in the practice of religion, especially works of architecture, have similarly lost that aura of the sacred that once seemed essential?

What need does this age of the decorated shed have for sacred architecture? What do I mean by the expression "decorated shed," which I borrowed from the authors of *Learning from Las Vegas*, but am using here in a much broader sense?[12] A shed is a structure usually raised to meet a certain need; like a tool, it has a function. But, from the very beginning, human beings have demanded more of their dwellings and tools and indeed of their own bodies. The urge to decorate is as old as humanity.

[10] Judith Dupré, *Churches* (New York: Harper Collins, 2001), p. 136.

[11] Ibid.

[12] Robert Venturi, Denise Scott Brown, and Steven Izenour, *Learning from Las Vegas: The Forgotten Symbolism of Architectural Form*, rev. ed. (Cambridge, Mass.: MIT Press, 1977).

Philip Johnson and John Burgee, Crystal Cathedral, Garden Grove, California, dedicated 1980

Human beings have thus always demanded more of their buildings than that they provide shelter, storage space, or a functional frame for certain activities: they have demanded that they please in their appearance, in the way they present themselves to the senses, i.e., that they also give pleasure as aesthetic objects. But is this quite right? Should we not rather say: they have demanded that such objects provide, not just the body, but the soul, with shelter? At issue is once more the relationship of the aesthetic to the sacred.

Not only the body, the soul, too, needs a home. But how is architecture to build us such a home? To meet this need we moderns tend to look to the past, to its achievements, its values and ideals, to find there material that we can weave together to cover what an instrumental rationality has rendered mute. And can something analogous not also be said of our art, of what we call culture generally, and also of our religion? Do we not need what we have inherited to decorate a life that seems impoverished without such embellishment?

That there is tension in an understanding of works of architecture as decorated sheds, as functional buildings that should be appreciated also as aesthetic, culturally significant objects, is obvious. It is thus hardly surprising that, with the rise of the aesthetic approach in the eighteenth century, architecture, caught increasingly between the conflicting claims of the engineer and the artist, should have entered a period of uncertainty and crisis from which it has not yet emerged. The architecture world has thus tended to separate the engineer from the architect-artist, allowing the latter to claim his place beside the sculptor and the painter. With this, the architect's primary task is reduced to the creation of aesthetic objects that also meet whatever programmatic requirements are pre-given. The more pragmatic architects, concerned to stay within the limits of the available budget, are likely to think first of all of contour and applied decoration, content to clothe the body of the building in an aesthetically pleasing exterior, while the artistically more ambitious would transform the building as a whole into a kind of mega-sculpture, allowing the sculptural dress to bend and shape, perhaps smother the architecture beneath. In either case, the actual construction is entrusted to the engineer. In both cases the aesthetic component presents itself as a welcome, yet from the point of view of function, dispensable addendum, wherein the question, just why should such an addendum be welcomed, sometimes at enormous extra cost, demands an answer.

What this modern understanding of architecture leaves out is suggested by a work such as Lincoln Cathedral. Does Pevsner really do justice to it when he understands it as a functional shed that succeeds also as an aesthetic object? Nietzsche points to what has been lost:

> Originally everything on a Greek or Christian building had a meaning, with an eye to a higher order of things: this aura of an inexhaustible significance surrounded the building like a magical veil. Beauty entered the system only incidentally, without diminishing in any significant way the fundamental sensation of the uncanny sublime of what the proximity of the divine and magic had consecrated; beauty softened

Crystal Cathedral, interior

at most the terror—but this terror was everywhere the presupposition. What is the beauty of a building to us today? The same as the beautiful face of a woman without spirit: something mask-like.[13]

For the aura of the sacred we have substituted aesthetic appeal, beautiful or just interesting masks.

I do not deny that Lincoln Cathedral was intended to have a special aesthetic appeal. But we need to ask ourselves: just what does this have to do with its function as a church? Like Benjamin, Nietzsche recognized that the aura that still haunts such cathedrals is incompatible with the spirit of our modern world. And if auratic experience has indeed become untimely, as Nietzsche and Benjamin argue, so has my insistence on an

essential connection between art, more especially architecture, and the sacred, become untimely because of the way our spiritual mobility implies a fall out of history and a loss of place. Sacred architecture places us in both time and space.

What distinguishes Lincoln Cathedral from the more ordinary buildings that surround it is therefore not just the addition of an aesthetic component. That component here has a re-presentational[14] function: it invites us to look at what we see as more than just a building large enough to allow a multitude to assemble and that was considered important enough to expend the resources necessary to transform it into a remarkable aesthetic object. The cathedral, as a whole and with all its countless details, speaks of

[13] Friedrich Nietzsche, *Human, All Too Human* (1878), para. 218.

[14] On "representation" and "re-presentation," see Karsten Harries, *The Ethical Function of Architecture* (Cambridge, Mass.: MIT Press, 1998), pp. 118–33.

what those who built it thought to matter most profoundly in their lives; it speaks of God; also of birth and death; of genuine community; and of the promise of everlasting happiness. Into the ground of everyday buildings serving everyday needs the cathedral inserts a figure of utopia. The experience of the sacred is thus like a vertical intersecting our horizontal lives that opens them in this particular place to the transcendent. Once the cathedral thus helped gather individuals into an ongoing community by speaking to them of what those joined by this work thought to matter most. The approach presupposed by our architecture of decorated sheds substitutes the aesthetic for the sacred.

But is that quite right? Is there really a profound difference between a work of architecture such as Lincoln Cathedral and a modern high-rise building, say Pelli's Petronas Towers? Do these twin towers not very much evoke thoughts of a modern cathedral, a cathedral raised, to be sure, not to God, but to the power of capital? Both the enormous height, and the aesthetic sensibility that gave these glass, steel, and concrete commercial office towers their distinctive shape, capture our attention, invite us to look at what we see in the image of the sacred architecture of the past, as an up-to-date version of some twin-towered cathedral that once had the power to gather some city into a genuine community by providing it with its spiritual center. Why should modern architecture not be able to do the same? But, despite inevitable associations with the cathedrals of the past, lacking is the faith that built them. The power of capital cannot be put in the place of the now-absent God, for money has an essentially instrumental function. It is abused when its pursuit is made into an end. To be sure, the great architecture of the past—especially the sacred architecture of past centuries—remains available to architects who want to give their buildings an air of special importance. And it remains available especially to architects asked to build a church or a temple. But often, such use of the sacred architecture of the past and the associated meanings is itself little more than an aesthetic gesture. Nostalgic invocations of a past that has perished are insufficient to create what deserves to be called "contemporary sacred architecture." This is why Schopenhauer, writing in the nineteenth century, felt that he had to reject the neo-Gothic churches of his time as in bad taste, because born of bad faith:

> In the interest of good taste, I am bound to wish that great wealth be devoted to what is objectively, i.e., actually, good and right, to what in itself is beautiful, not to that whose value rests merely on the association of ideas. Now when I see how this unbelieving age so diligently finishes the Gothic churches left uncompleted by the believing Middle Ages, it seems to me as if it were desired to embalm a Christianity that has expired.[15]

Schopenhauer took the religion that finished these churches to be a religion in bad faith. Today we might say he considered such religion and its churches a form of kitsch. His words retain their relevance.

When I invite you to look at our age as the age of the decorated shed, I am thinking of something more essential than just the fact that "decorated shed" describes what works of architecture have to become in an age that understands works of art first of all as aesthetic objects, to be appreciated as such: the modern world itself, I would like to suggest, including many of its religious practices, invites understanding in the image of a decorated shed. As Wittgenstein knew, whatever can make life meaningful must be sought outside the reality that is presupposed by our science and technology. And do not beautiful fictions, which turn their back on this reality in which accident rules and which knows no higher meaning, furnish us with just such an outside by presenting us with creations in which

[15] Arthur Schopenhauer, *The World as Will and Representation*, vol. 2, trans. E. F. J. Payne (New York: Dover, 1966), p. 418.

everything appears just as it should be? And can something similar not be said of modern religion? Often it seems little more than a decoration of what our reason has created. But what we need is not a decoration of a reality from which meanings and values are excluded, but a window to what transcends that reality: a window to the sacred.

But, and this returns me to my first claim, even if the need for transcendence is granted, do we need sacred art or, more specifically, sacred architecture? If art, by breaking the bond that once tied it to religion, can be said to have purified itself, does religion not also have reason to welcome that break? From its very beginning biblical religion is shadowed by iconoclasm. Think of Moses smashing the golden calf. Israel's God is invisible. Such attitudes carried over into the early Church. "Do not make a picture of Christ," Asterius of Amasia warns us. "The humiliation of the Incarnation to which He submitted of His own free will and for our sake was sufficient for Him to endure—rather let us carry around in our soul the incorporeal world."[16] Does the religious life not require a movement of introversion, a turn away from the world, into the depths of the self? Such a movement is inevitably also a movement of self-transcendence, as suggested by the word "ecstasy." And, as the individual is cast back into him- or herself, that self loses the identity that only engagement in the world can give it. The dynamism of religious transcendence, especially when one adds the attribute "infinite," carries thus with it the danger of a radicalization of transcendence that threatens to so empty it and God of all definite meaning that mysticism and atheism come to coincide. As Kierkegaard knew, the experience of this empty transcendence does mean a new experience of freedom. But this freedom, acknowledging no measure, must degenerate into caprice.

But where is freedom to find a binding measure? The science that has shaped our world knows nothing of what might bind freedom, keep it responsible, and give weight and substance to our lives. This is to say that it has no room for the religious understanding of reality. Although the etymology that ties the word "religion" to the Latin *religare*, "to bind again," is not generally accepted, despite the authority of Lactantius, St. Augustine, and St. Thomas,[17] must a religious person not experience his or her freedom as bound by, and to, what is taken to matter unconditionally and most profoundly—bound, we can say, by what is experienced as sacred? The descent of the transcendent into the visible is a presupposition of successfully dwelling here on earth. One site of such descent is the experience of the other person; another is the experience of nature as a gift; a third is the experience of sacred texts and sacred art, more especially of sacred architecture. Is the task of architecture not to wrest place from space in order to provide not just the body, but the whole human being, with shelter? Neither instrumental thinking nor aesthetic invention are capable of providing this. That requires a binding back of aesthetic creativity to the sacred. That is why I claimed in the beginning that architecture needs the sacred if it is not to wither.

[16] Arnold Hauser, *The Social History of Art, Vol. 1—From Prehistoric Times to the Middle Ages* (London: Routledge & Kegan Paul, 1962), p.125.

[17] Lactantius, *The Divine Institutes, in The Ante-Nicene Fathers* (reprint, New York, 1899), IV, xxviii; St. Augustine, *The City of God*, trans. Marcus Dods (1st ed., 1872; reprint New York, 1948), X, iii; St. Thomas, *The Summa Theologica of Thomas Aquinas*, (originally published in English 1911; reissued New York: Benziger Brothers, 1948), II-II, Q. lxxxi, a. 1.

ARCHITECTURE, MEMORY, AND
THE SACRED

MIROSLAV VOLF

One of the most significant and likely most controversial dimensions in these essays consists in the use of reflections on the relations between architecture and the sacred to underscore a major loss resulting from modernity's banishment of the sacred from the center of human life. Take the sacred out and, in a culture of pervasive, instrumental rationality, things as well as people degenerate into tools and the sheds that house them—decorated tools and sheds, sometimes even beautifully so, but nonetheless mere tools and sheds.

Let me begin by saying that I am not entirely persuaded that the sacred needs architecture (as Karsten Harries argues), unless "need" is understood rather weakly. Take as an example Christianity, the faith that I know the best. Its triumphant first centuries, when it was arguably as vibrant as ever, saw it completely devoid of anything like sacred architecture. Then, the ordinary homes of Christians, in which they pursued the ordinary activities of daily life, served also as places of worship, thus, the emergence of the term "house church." Romans and Greeks had sacred architecture; Christians did not. And yet the Christian sense of the sacred did not wither. Rather, it flourished, and did so in highly contagious ways.

We can observe an analogous phenomenon in the Christianity of today. I am not referring to Christianity in the most religious of Western democracies, the United States. I am instead referring to the house-church movement in China. Many of the most vibrant churches in the world today are just those house churches. These groups' sense of the sacred, just like that of the first Christians, seems in no need of architecture. I surmise that lack of need stems not from the radical inwardness of house-church Christianity, but from house-church Christians seeing the sacred as incarnated in the mundane.

I do not deny that architecture can come to the aid of the sacred in significant ways. Yet even as architecture does so, it is not the case that we simply need to make a good window and then look through it. Unlike a telescope, a window on the sacred is not an instrument or tool; instead, it is more like a tenuous sacrament. The sacred is essentially non-producible by human effort, and just because the sacred is non-reproducible, the encounter with the sacred is non-producible, and non-reproducible as well. One cannot make it happen, so to speak.

In furtherance of this window-imagery, the perception of the sacred through a stained-glass window from the inside is dependent on the light of the sacred that is shining from outside. Even when architecture serves as more than mere decoration, its functioning as a window to the sacred depends on the unpredictable self-manifestation of the sacred. As Harries writes, summing up his position on the relation between architecture and lived reality: "What we need is not a decoration of a reality from which meanings and values are excluded, but a window to what transcends that reality: a window to the sacred."

From my standpoint, this assessment is right on target. In the wake of modernity, we have increasingly narrowed the scope of our vision

of the good. I shall illustrate what I mean by sketching briefly some key junctures in the history of the American dream, an endeavor that Andrew Delbanco has undertaken admirably in his little book *The Real American Dream*. It is a history of a disturbing shrinkage. From the "holy God" of the Puritan founders to the "great nation" of the nineteenth-century patriots, American hope has today become reduced to the "satisfied self" of the hippy/yuppy culture and its aftermath.[1] With some modifications, America may in this regard be representative of trends in most societies that are highly integrated into the global market system.

What happens when the "satisfied self" becomes our highest hope? The definition of flourishing as a human being shrivels to mean no more than leading an experientially satisfying life, cut off from any overarching account of reality and with no connection to transcendence. The sources of self-satisfaction may vary: power, possessions, sex, food, drugs, and, of course, religion, whatever. But what matters most is not the source of this satisfaction but the experience of it: my satisfaction. Everything—word, thought and deed, the material and the immaterial—morphs into a means of leading the experientially satisfying life.

The consequences for architecture? Architectural achievements become to us little more than decorated sheds devoid of deeper meaning. This reduction of meaning has not come about primarily from the intention of architects or the execution of their work, though at least some poverty of intention and execution may have contributed to their decline. Nevertheless, it has happened mostly because of the broad cultural conditions under which architectural works of art are created.

It may be, however, that under the conditions of modernity and the turbo-market economy, we are not merely decorating a reality from which meaning and values are excluded; we are doing so

[1] Andrew Delbanco, *The Real American Dream: A Meditation on Hope* (Cambridge, Mass.: Harvard University Press, 1999).

Maya Lin, Vietnam Veterans
Memorial, Washington D.C.,
1982, detail of names of the dead
inscribed on the wall

for people whose lives are increasingly marked by an "unbearable lightness of being," to use Milan Kundera's phrase (echoing Friedrich Nietzsche on "last men" in *Thus Spoke Zarathustra*). It may be that we are also creating pseudo-sacred architecture. That suggestion may seem strange, for, as Peter Sloterdijk puts it, modernity is an age in which only the world may be the case. But this observation does not mean that modernity is an age from which the sacred is altogether absent; it may be pseudo-sacred, but it is sacred nonetheless. Money is arguably a most powerful and jealous "god of this age." Not completely unlike the divine of classical religions, money seems infinitely multipliable and exerts immense power to draw us toward it. Might not the splendid Petronas Towers of Kuala Lumpur be a kind of cathedral to the false god of money, service to which offers forged meaning to the frantic lives of its feel-good-obsessed worshipers?

Given that the sacred comes in many forms, some of which have a dubious relationship to human flourishing, must we not speak of it concretely and pay attention to its specific content, not just to its ineffable numinousness? How would we otherwise be able to distinguish between more or less salutary or even toxic forms of the sacred? This very effort of distinguishing has led the great religious traditions to present the sacred, though ineffably numinous, not abstractly but concretely, and tied to an overarching account of reality. Which brings us to the issue of memory, sacred memories as well as ordinary memories.

Architecture is properly sacred, I want to suggest, only as a site of sacred memory. What is sacred memory? Again I speak as a person who studies Christianity (as inextricably related to ancient Jewish traditions).

First, sacred memory defines identity.[2] To be a religious Jew is to remember the Exodus of the people of Israel from slavery in Egypt. To be a

Christian is to remember the death and resurrection of Christ. Of course, Jews and Christians don't only remember; they also act in the present (for example, they seek to love their neighbors as they love themselves), and they hope for the future (for example, they hope for the just and peaceful rule of the Messiah). But take away the memories of the Exodus and Passion, and you excise the pulsating heart that energizes and directs the respective actions of these groups and forms their hopes.

Second, sacred memory is communal. In one sense, as Maurice Halbwachs has argued in his seminal work, *The Collective Memory*, all memories are communal. This point certainly holds true to an even greater extent of sacred memories. Individuals receive the content of sacred memories from communities rather than directly experiencing the events recalled, and these memories shape their identity not simply as individuals but also as members of the communities that share them. Religious communities sustain sacred memories and revitalize them in new contexts just as sacred memories define religious communities.

The third formal feature of sacred memory, also shared by Jews and Christians, is concern with the future, not only the past. The idea of remembering the future may seem strange. Normally, we remember the past and hope for something in the future; but memory and hope are not disparate phenomena that never interact with each other. Indeed, memories shape hopes and hopes influence memories.[3] So it goes with the memories of the Exodus and Passion. A religious person remembers, and looking at the past he or she sees the future. If the Exodus is her story, then she remembers deliverance not only as the past deliverance of her community, but also as her own and her community's future deliverance.[4] Similarly, if Christ's story is her story, then in remembering Christ she remembers not only Christ's past but also in a significant sense her future. In remembering Christ's death and resurrection, she remembers what

[2] In the development of the following features of sacred memory, I borrow heavily from my book, *The End of Memory: Remembering Rightly in a Violent World* (Grand Rapids, Mich.: W.B. Eerdmans, 2006).

[3] See Reinhart Koselleck, *Futures Past: On the Semantics of Historical Time*, trans. Keith Tribe (Cambridge, Mass.: MIT Press, 1985), pp. 287–88.

[4] See Franz Rosenzweig, *The Star of Redemption*, trans. William W. Hallo (Boston: Beacon Press, 1972), p. 295.

will happen to her and to her community, indeed to the whole world. The memories of the Exodus and Passion are, intrinsically, memories of the future. To use the terms coined by Reinhart Koselleck, for Jews and Christians sacred memory is not only a "space of experience" (the past made present in memory), but also a "horizon of expectation" (the future made present in that same memory).

Finally, sacred memory is, most basically, memory of God. In this way we add to the temporal repertoire of memory the remembrance of the present, in which God manifestly exists. We can understand such remembrance by analogy: when lovers part, they sometimes promise, "I'll always remember you," or plead, "You won't forget me, will you?" When we remember in this way, we make a future commitment to keep the object of our love present in our minds and hearts, to live in consideration of a relationship that matters to us.

At one level, the memories of the Exodus and Passion are memories of flesh-and-blood events in the history of Israel and the life of Jesus Christ. If you are a religious Jew, you remember a people eating the bread of affliction and passing through the Red Sea to reach the Land of Promise. If you are a Christian, you remember a man condemned, beaten, crucified, and then raised to new and immortal life with God. In all these events, however, God is remembered to have been at work in faithfulness to God's people. And it is on God that sacred memory zeroes in. God heard the cries of the Hebrews suffering under the yoke of slavery in Egypt; God delivered them with his outstretched hand. The same holds true of the Passion. "In Christ God was reconciling the world to himself," writes the Apostle Paul (2 Corinthians 5:19), and it is God who raised Christ from the dead (Acts 2:24).

So sacred memories shape identity; they are embraced and deployed in community; they define horizons of expectation; and in all their worldliness they primarily concern God. Such memories have many homes, many sites, material and immaterial. Sacred architecture is one of them.

But what do sacred memories have to do with ordinary lives? How do everyday memories and hope intersect with sacred memories? Briefly, whatever we do, we always act—at least implicitly—in a framework that includes four components: a sense of (1) who we are, (2) where we belong, (3) what we expect, and (4) what, or who, we ultimately trust. These four elements of the framework for acting represent abstractly the four marks of sacred memories as I have analyzed them above. In other words, sacred memories fit into a similar framework.

Sacred architecture, as a site of sacred memory, incarnates such a framework. As such, it helps people find meaning in the everyday experiences of their sufferings and joys, of their defeats and triumphs. It helps them transpose memories of their past experiences, as well as their fears and hopes about the future, into a new register by inserting them into the larger story told by sacred memories. A great cathedral, I think, does precisely this service (and more). Yet other examples of what may count as great architecture—in their own way and with different sacred remembrances—do so too, such as the multitude of memorials that have been constructed to the twentieth century's violent conflicts.

REVEALING CONCEALMENT   MARK C. TAYLOR

I would like to begin, and perhaps end, with the title of this book: "Constructing the Ineffable: Contemporary Sacred Architecture." This title—indeed, any title—marks a certain impossibility for thought. "Constructing the Ineffable" is impossible because the ineffable is precisely what cannot be constructed; nor can it be thought. To think this impossibility, however, might be to un-think thought and thereby approach something that might be named, improperly, the sacred. From title to subtitle: "Contemporary Sacred Architecture." Why *sacred* architecture, why not "religious"? And why sacred *architecture*, why not the architecture of the sacred? Finally, why contemporary? Is the sacred ever contemporary, or perhaps is the sacred precisely what is never contemporary but rather always past, like the future that is ever to come?

The timing of this book is not, of course, accidental. We all live in an era marked by what commentators misleadingly claim to be the "return of the religious." We are repeatedly told that it was not supposed to turn out this way. Modernity and secularity were declared to be inseparable: as societies modernize they become more secular and this process was supposed to be both inevitable and irreversible. This widely accepted point of view was always misguided because it rests upon an inadequate understanding of both religion and secularism. There has not been a return of religion because the religious never went away, nor has it exactly been repressed. This is not to imply, of course, that some of the current manifestations of religion were expected. What is signaled by the return of religion is not a reversion to pre-modern modes of experience, but is a reaction to modernism, modernity, and modernization, which—it is important to note—are not identical. This so-called return of the religious is, therefore, a distinctively *post-modern* phenomenon. Many defenders and critics misunderstand both religion and secularity. The religious and the secular are not opposites; to the contrary, secularity, especially as it has developed in the West, is a *religious* phenomenon. While I cannot trace the complicated interrelation between the religious and the secular in the Jewish and Christian religious traditions, it is necessary in this context to reach greater clarity about the meaning of religion. I am therefore going to ask a seemingly simple question, which, for philosophical, political, and ideological reasons, has been forbidden for almost three decades: What is religion? And I am going to be presumptuous enough to suggest a one-sentence answer:

> Religion is an emergent, complex, adaptive network of symbols, myths, and rituals that on the one hand figure schemata of feeling, thinking, and acting in ways that lend life meaning and purpose, and on the other

hand disrupt, dislocate, and disfigure every stabilizing structure.

This definition of religion identifies two closely related poles, which might be described as "structural" and "post-structural." Religion both provides structures that form the foundation of life and disrupts structures by subverting every foundation that seems to be secure. The former function is often, but not always, associated with God, while the latter is more closely related to the sacred. So understood, the sacred is—to use a Freudian term—the denegation of God and God is the denegation of the sacred. The concept of God is (unknowingly) constructed so that in it we are *not* to think of the sacred, which does not exist and yet is not nothing. The question then becomes: If the sacred cannot be thought, how can it be figured, in all senses of the word "figure"? Perhaps, I will suggest, the sacred can be figured only in and through a certain disfiguring. And this disfiguring, in turn, might trace the limit of the ineffable, which can never be constructed but only deconstructed.

What is the sacred and how is it to be distinguished from the religious? As I have noted, the sacred is implicated in the disruptive—even destructive—moment of the religious. To describe the distinguishing characteristics of the sacred, I turn to a book by Rudolf Otto, published in 1923, which, unfortunately, is not often read today: *Das Heilege*. The title of the English translation, *The Idea of the Holy*, is, for reasons that will become apparent, very misleading. Otto describes the holy as the numinous, which he defines as the *mysterium tremendum*. The holy—or, in my terms, the sacred—is an awe-inspiring mystery that is wholly other: *Ganz Andere*. This *mysterium tremendum* harbors a "surplus of meaning" which remains irreducibly inexpressible. The radically other provokes fascination, and, as such, is simultaneously attractive and repulsive.

Kasimir Malevich, *Black Circle*, 1913, State Russian Museum, St. Petersburg

Summarizing Otto's conclusions in his influential though controversial book, *The Sacred and the Profane*, Mircea Eliade writes:

> In *The Holy*, Otto sets himself the task of discovering the characteristics of this frightening and irrational experience. He finds the feeling of terror before the sacred, before the awe-inspiring mystery, the majesty that emanates an overwhelming superiority of power … Otto characterizes all these experiences as numinous (from the Latin *numen*, god), for they are induced by the revelation of an aspect of divine power. The numinous presents itself as something "wholly other," something basically and totally different.[1]

Accordingly, the sacred is the wholly other whose "presence" provokes both irresistible attraction and profound terror. Recalling Freud and anticipating Heidegger, Otto describes *Das Ganz Andere* as an "uncanny presence." But this is a strange presence. As that which is wholly other, the sacred is never actually present as such, but appears only by not appearing—revelation and concealment, in other words, are inseparable.

Much should be said about the sacred, but I must limit my comments. In particular, I would like to underscore the complex ways in which violent destructiveness is associated with the sacred. From Orphic rites and Mayan rituals to Christian crucifixion and Islamic suicide bombers, violence and the sacred have always been inseparable. The destruction associated with the sacred provokes a sense of terror, which, in turn, often leads to trauma. Far from finding such terror merely repulsive, we are, as Freud has taught us, compelled to repeat what we nonetheless want to avoid. This repetition compulsion is symptomatic of the death drive, which threatens to dissolve the centered self in the undifferentiated matrix from which it originally emerged.

In order to bring this discussion of the sacred to bear on the issue of violence, which is addressed by several of the projects discussed later in this book (such as the Holocaust memorials of Moshe Safdie, Peter Eisenman, and Stanley Tigerman), I would like to note the way in which Georges Bataille appropriates Freud's insights about the death drive in his discussion of sacrifice in his *Theory of Religion*. Bloody rites and violent rituals simultaneously express and displace the desire for death. Bataille contrasts the calculated utility of production to the incalculable gratuitousness of consumption:

> Sacrifice is the antithesis of production, which is accomplished with a view to the future; it is consumption that is concerned only with the moment. This is the sense in which it is the gift and relinquishment, but what is given cannot be an object of preservation for the receiver: the gift of an offering makes it pass precisely into the world of abrupt consumption. This is the meaning of "sacrificing to the deity," whose sacred essence is comparable to a fire. To sacrifice is to give as one gives coal to the furnace. But the furnace has an undeniable utility, to which the coal is subordinated, whereas the sacrifice is rescued from all utility.

Never simply a reassuring presence, the sacred provokes what can best be described as *horror religiosus*, which is ineffable. Such horror, Bataille explains, "is ambiguous. Undoubtedly, what is sacred attracts and possesses an incomparable value, but at the same time it appears vertiginously dangerous for the clear and profane world where mankind situates its privileged domain."[2]

What Otto, Freud, and Bataille (there are others) are suggesting is that, contrary to expectation, holocaust is nothing less than a "manifestation" of the sacred. This is, however, a paradoxical manifestation because it shows what

[1] Mircea Eliade, *The Sacred and the Profane*, trans. Willard R. Trask (New York: Harper and Row, 1961), pp. 9–10.

[2] Georges Bataille, *Theory of Religion*, trans. Robert Hurley (New York: Zone Books, 1989), p. 53.

cannot be shown. How, then, might the Holocaust be figured? How can unrepresentable horror, which might or might not be a *horror religiosus*, be imagined? What would it mean to memorialize absolute terror?

Here lies the dilemma: If the evil of the Holocaust is incalculable, then is it possible to account for it—or to establish the accountability without which there is no responsibility—in a building that can be constructed only with myriad calculations? Might the impossibility of calculation and construction be the deconstruction of the sacred? And is it not necessary to read the "of" in the "deconstruction of the sacred" as at least a double genitive?

Eisenman recognized early on that the issue of representation lies at the heart of modern and contemporary architecture and philosophy. To attempt to represent the unrepresentable through the absence of representation is to inscribe the very presence one is attempting to avoid. Rather than the absence of representation, what must be evoked is the failure of representation. This failure occurs in the gaps, faults, and fissures of structures. I would not be foolish enough to attempt to explain the ineffability of these voids, but will end with more questions. In the case of memorials of the Holocaust, what is being memorialized? What are we called to remember? What can never be remembered? Is the sacred immemorial not because it is eternally present, but because it is the unspeakable trace of what can never be present and yet is not absent? Is the sacred remembered by forgetting? Revealed by concealment? How can unspeakable terror be remembered? What does it mean to memorialize horror? If these memorials do not traumatize, do they actually repress the very memory they are constructed to recall? Might art be the sacrifice of sacrifice in which the sacred is refigured as the ineffable that brings us together by holding us apart? Is it any longer possible to hope, with the memory of the Holocaust and in an age of terror? If, as Adorno famously insisted, poetry is impossible after Auschwitz, then how is architecture possible?

CONSTRUCTING THE IMMATERIAL
IN SPACES LARGE AND SMALL

EMILIE M. TOWNES

for as long as i can remember, i have been intrigued with sacred architecture

at first, it was the names that drew me as a child because they helped me learn how to read as i noticed the plethora of worship spaces in the south of my childhood:

white rock baptist church

camp creek jesus only church

enigma united methodist church

back to jerusalem pentecostal church

asbury temple united methodist church

mother bethel african methodist church

the one true world of god's love tabernacle

greater allen african methodist episcopal cathedral

one way deliverance fire baptized holiness church of god

the fire baptized church of the emerging spirit of christ church

greater mount zion missionary baptist church (there was the original mount zion missionary baptist church. but with a church fight and the resulting schism, the new church is always "greater" than the original) and now where i live in new haven, connecticut:

walk of faith

victory temple

flock of god ministries

our lady of victory church

promise land church of god

greater mount calvary holy church

a whisper from heaven incorporated

joshua's temple of the first born church

christ deliverance church of god in christ

new flame restoration christian center church

grace and truth apostolic church incorporated

i grew up in an oral and aural world where the sound of things mattered as much as the look of things

and so it was not until i was in junior high school that i began to pay attention to the buildings that accompanied the names

some were storefront churches that did the heavy lifting of people's daily struggles to make it through another day in urban areas

or 10-pew churches in the rural south that grew to ten times their size on sunday mornings and wednesday nights with the sounds of folks straining into salvation as their eyes were watching god[1]

others were breath-taking cathedrals that shaped light and air and sound in ways that i'd never felt the holy, the sacred, before in my youth

and in all those places i also found what historian of religion mircea eliade calls "the center"

in thinking about constructing the immaterial, a question comes to mind from my experience of dwelling in sacred spaces, as i look for eliade's symbolism of the center:

how do we shape space, to signal the sacred

invite what some call the holy, the centered, the divine to touch us, to move us

where we find a place to worship or simply be

where we are called to deep within deep

and then do something with that which is more than an act of possession or acquisition?

for me, this question *is* about constructing the immaterial

exploring how the spiritual, unbodied, unembodied, disembodied, bodiless

speaks to us as people of bodies—flesh and blood

[1] Zora Neale Hurston, *Their Eyes Were Watching God* (Philadelphia: Lippincott, 1937; reprint Urbana: University of Illinois Press, 1978), p. 236.

and it can give us clues about our living and the deep substance of what our breathing in and out should be shaped by

eliade's center is every place that bears witness to an incursion of the sacred into profane spaces

and he notes that when ancient holy places, temples or altars "lose their religious efficacy, people discover and apply other geomantic, architectural, or iconographical formulas ... [that] represent the same symbolism of the center"[2]

the center can be the sanctuary that reproduces the universe in its essence—the meeting point of heaven, earth, and hell[3]

and as such it is multivalent as it can signal the difficulty of obtaining entry into a center

or the center can be accessible

for others, the way to the center is often sown with obstacles, and yet every city, every temple, every dwelling place for eliade "is *already* at the center of the universe"[4]

other traditions attest to our desire to "find ourselves at the center without any effort"

while others insist upon it being "difficult and a matter of merit"[5]

ultimately, for eliade, it is not only an "intimate interconnection between the universal life and the salvation of [humanity]"

but for him, "*it is enough only to raise the question of salvation*, to pose the central problem; that is, *the* problem—for the life of the cosmos to be forever renewed"

and for him, this mythological fragment "seems to show—death is often only the result of our indifference to immortality"[6]

it is extremely tempting for me to take eliade on here, but that would be appropriate for a different topic

i draw on eliade's understanding of the center as a helpful trope for responding to the theme of "constructing the ineffable" and the architects whose creative spark leads them to dare (or embrace) the world of sacred architecture

and therefore, into the ineffable

the work of rudolf schwarz is compelling in this regard as this devout roman catholic and architect was the director in charge of the reconstruction of the city of cologne for a time

schwarz gives an intense sense of the church in what he calls his "primer for church building" in his book *the church incarnate*[7]

indeed, this elegant book, whose poetic sensibilities are preserved in the english translation, with the subtitle *the sacred function of christian architecture*, brings the center to life in compelling ways as he moves from

sacred inwardness, sacred parting, sacred journey, sacred cast, sacred universe and ultimately the cathedral of all times: the whole

[2] Mircea Eliade, *Images and Symbols: Studies in Religious Symbolism*, trans. Philip Mairet (Kansas City: Sheed Andrews and McNeel, 1961), pp. 51–52.

[3] Eliade, *The Myth of the Eternal Return*, trans. Willard R. Trask (New York: Pantheon Books, 1954), p. 17.

[4] Eliade, *Images and Symbols: Studies in Religious Symbolism*, pp. 54–55.

[5] Ibid., p. 55.

[6] Ibid., p. 56.

[7] Rudolf Schwarz, *The Church Incarnate: The Sacred Function of Christian Architecture*, trans. Cynthia Harris (Chicago: Henry Regnery Company, 1958), p. 211. The original title in German was *Vom Bau der Kirche*, which translates "of the building of the church."

the sacramental sense of his understanding of the form and function of church buildings is steeped, to my eye, with a sense of ritual and the importance of ritual as the space must reverberate with salvation and invite, lead the worshipping community toward it—a lure

for schwarz, church architecture is eliade's center, it is "the representation of christian life, new embodiment of the spiritual"[8]

further, schwarz believes that the holy cannot be "derived" from contemporary art or aesthetic doctrines or social theories of cosmic myths

> no, for him, the church building is a work in its own right and meaning—it is exhaustive in and of itself

> it is not applied theology or the fulfillment of a liturgical purpose

> for schwarz, the church building is the "work which prays" and is "borne by the movement of grace"[9]

schwarz closes *the church incarnate* with moving language:

> "There is still something to consider. This need is sacred need. God effects even the forms of surrender. The first impulse to carry out the movement is given by [him], grace causes the first step, the second, the third, and finally the last. And that which comes there is not a world which has fallen away from God: it is [his] own holy child coming home to [him]."[10]

i am intrigued by a question raised by rafael moneo in his essay in this volume on his cathedral in los angeles: "what meaning does it have in architectural terms to shift the focus away from *civitas dei* to the world that contemplates the religious act as an intimate ritual in architectural terms?"

> and even more so, his answer: "the architect cannot rely on a shared vision but must risk his or her own version of sacred space"

again, eliade enters in a helpful way as moneo sought consciously to design the cathedral in such a way that those spaces could be understood as metaphors of religious experience—the series of metaphors function as the center

> as the site is chosen—the cultural axis of downtown

> as it has space to breathe

> as it is visible

> yet it has an autonomy to it such that it remains independent from other institutional buildings

i am struck by the deep aesthetic sense informing the design process moneo allows us to hear

> in taking in the complex as a whole, it brings to life the import of the cathedral being located on the highest part of the site, such that to enter it, worshippers and visitors must navigate the transitional space surrounding the cathedral and its sanctuary

> > these are echoes of eliade—noting that some centers make you work a bit in order to enter

as moneo blends the historical context of religious sites and their sacred character

[8] Ibid., p. 228.

[9] Ibid., p. 212.

[10] Ibid., p. 231.

African Zion Baptist
Church, Malden, West
Virginia, 1872

he pushes those who seek a more individualistic experience of the center back into the world around it

back into the *civitas dei*

back into the urban environment

back into the complex multilingual, multicultural, multiethnic communities of communities that make up the archdiocese of los angeles

in other words, for moneo the center does not provide an escape from the world, but a deep and faithful invitation to engage it

yes, perhaps through the lens of the culture and faith many bring with them to los angeles, but there, in that place, that cathedral, they engage the transcendent together as individuals and as members of a rich and complex city they now call home

the center, doing its work well

so, returning to the initial question, what have i learned as one who grew up with a church entitled the holy order of the cherubim and seraphim movement church (the glory of god), from a world of black church architecture that most often symbolizes freedom, progress, culture, and prosperity?

it is a deepening of eliade's symbol of the center and how it moves

part of what i have learned is that constructing the immaterial takes hard work and careful attention for it to fulfill its task

the work of listening with an aesthetic eye

the work of seeing with an ear trained to the ineffable

the work of feeling with a vibrant soul

the work of an artist, who may be invisible except as hand to eye as he or she does

the work their souls must have

many of the churches i grew up with did not have the space or monetary means to stretch into the center as described in the essays of this collection

so they did it and continue to do it with their names

in some ways, this is a conversation between the center as a large, transcendent space and the center as a smaller, immanent space

i remain curious about the ways in which this volume sparks our understanding of the immaterial

large and small

and i return to my opening question:

how do we shape space, to signal the sacred

invite what some call the holy, the centered, the divine to touch us, to move us

where we find a place to worship or simply be

where we are called to deep within deep

and then do something with that which is more than an act of possession or acquisition?

in doing so, i do what i often ask my students to do: offer some preliminary thoughts on how i might answer my own question

so i offer 3

first, the center, the sacred is saturated with power

architecture that remembers this aspect of the immaterial does not just sit there glorying in itself

it evokes or provokes or invites and not simply to get a reaction, but to respect the ways in which humanity looks for meaning and purpose and often finds this in pursuit of the sacred, the center

second, power often radiates from the center with centrifugal force, but it also returns centripetally

architecture that respects this dynamic recognizes the way in which the center is the locus for an axis between earth and sky

this can give it legitimacy, authenticity, and coherence as those who approach, enter, sit, or walk in sacred architectural spaces may also find meanings of power that do not rely on annihilation or mayhem

third, there is a certain ordinariness in the extraordinary

architecture that represents this acknowledges that much of the drama of humanity is the domestication of space in the building or the garden and spaces—in the worshipper or seeker

domestication is not necessarily a bad thing, but it is not the only thing

our ways of shaping the sacred in buildings can create a vibrant dialogue or even cacophony with other ways in which space and spaces shape our lives

and ultimately, for me, constructing the immaterial is very much like walking on the rimbones of nothingness[11]

i must leave for another time and place

the question: how?

[11] Hurston, *Their Eyes Were Watching God*, p. 143. This is a paraphrase of Hurston, who writes: "the rimbones of nothing."

PART II   **PRECEDENTS: SACRED SPACES**
           CONSTRUCTED AND IMAGINED

           INTRODUCTION

           The essays assembled in this section examine four distinct engagements
           with the sacred drawn from widely divergent contexts that serve as a
           comparative backdrop to the more personal reflections by practicing
           architects in the final section. Like the essays in Part I, those here begin
           with two more lengthy pieces, emphasizing in this case the importance
           within modernism of a concern for the spiritual as a parallel, alternative
           discourse to the dominant rationalism so often associated with the
           evolution of modern and late modern architecture. The first of these two
           essays is Thomas Beeby's exploration of the influence of Rudolf Schwarz's
           poetic treatise, *The Church Incarnate*, and its impact on the work of
           Mies van der Rohe, in particular his design for the campus of the Illinois
           Institute of Technology. Beeby's essay may be read as an extension of
           Fritz Neumeyer's classic study on Mies' philosophical underpinnings, *The
           Artless Word*, which in part documented Mies' relationship to the Jesuit
           priest, philosopher, and theologian, Romano Guardini.

The second piece, Kenneth Frampton's treatment of the architecture of the Japanese master Tadao Ando, proposes the idea of a "secular spirituality" as a paradox that is at the heart of contemporary culture (relating it again to the relationship of Mies van der Rohe, Schwarz, and Guardini). Frampton addresses the revelatory aspects of Ando's architecture, which is at variance with monotheism, looking, for example, at Ando's Japanese concept of the *shintai*, or body. His reading of Ando pays attention to what he sees as the architect's political intention to compensate for the banalities of a late-capitalist consumerist society in contemporary Japan. Ando's secular spirituality, Frampton argues, cannot be separated from a larger critical aim that seeks to transcend the reduction of contemporary culture to consumerism. In this regard, it may also be worth noting that Frampton has connected Ando's work to a similar critique of capitalist culture made by the Portuguese architect, Álvaro Siza, who has himself built notable works of sacred architecture, such as the 1996 Church of Santa Maria in Marco de Canavezes, Portugal. As Frampton puts it, these two architects are "the twin magi of the late modern movement," and they each "exemplify in their own way a critical culture of architecture that pertains to the distinct regions of the world in which they are predominantly active."[1]

If Frampton draws on Japanese terminology (*shintai*, *roji*, *ma*) to draw out the connection of architecture with the sacred, with the movement of the body, and with the natural elements of water and light, then in her essay Diana Eck brings to the discussion a distinct syntax drawn from the Hindu vocabulary (*tirtha*, *darshan*, *puja*, and *jyotirlinga*). Eck focuses on the theme of light in relation to the Hindu temples and landscapes of India. Yet, her discussion of the sacred city of Banaras also returns us to the theme of the city as an example of a sacred center. Elsewhere, Eck has described Banaras as an example of an "orthogenetic" city. Rome, Jerusalem, Kyoto, and Bejing are others, cities which, by expressing a moral order, are situated at the center of the reproduction of a cosmology that makes the sacred accessible on the human plane.[2]

In Jaime Lara's wry essay on a futuristic proposal for a chapel on the moon, he brings the discussion of the representation of larger cosmologies back to the issue of the individual architect's ability to communicate meaning in new and unexpected circumstances. In relation to the building and design of spaces of worship, Lara reminds us, the architect is often charged by religious communities to be a futurist and visionary, articulating communal beliefs and hopes. Lara points toward iconic examples of modern church architecture where, in fact, this type of visionary representation was realized by the architect, including Oscar Niemeyer's Metropolitan Cathedral in Brasilia, Marcel Breuer's St. John's Abbey in Collegeville, Minnesota, and the work of the Mexican architect Felix Candela. Lara likewise challenges the contemporary architect to respond to new spiritual needs and new spiritual territories. How such innovations might be achieved is explored by the architects' contributions in the final section of this book.

[1] Kenneth Frampton, *Labour, Work and Architecture* (London: Phaidon Press, 2002), p. 257.

[2] Diana Eck, "The City as a Sacred Center" in Bardwell L. Smith and Holly Baker Reynolds, eds., *The City as a Sacred Center: Essays on Six Asian Contexts* (Leiden: E. J. Brill, 1987), pp. 1–11.

RUDOLF SCHWARZ AND MIES VAN DER ROHE: THE FORM OF THE SPIRIT

THOMAS H. BEEBY

For what is right and significant for any era—including the new era—is this: to give the spirit the opportunity for existence.

Mies van der Rohe, from *Die Form* (1930)

Mies van der Rohe arrived in Chicago in 1938. He began his tenure as Director of the Architectural Department of the Armour Institute, later to become the Illinois Institute of Technology (IIT). His English was imperfect and classes began in German, translated by a handful of disciples. At that time, Mies' early work in Germany was obscure to most professionals in Chicago. Yet, within ten years, the influence of Mies in America had spread beyond IIT and Chicago to become the controlling idiom of Modern architecture in this country. The capitulation of other strains of competing European ideologies, as well as native American architectural traditions (represented by the Prairie School), must point to a compelling need within the American character of the period to embrace the architecture of Mies van der Rohe.

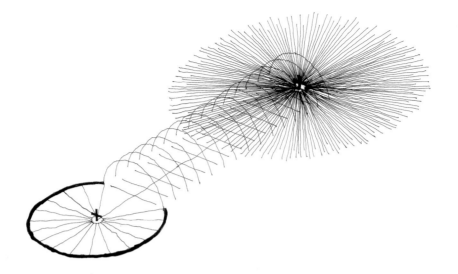

Rudolf Schwarz,
"The Cathedral of
All Times," redrawn
by Tom Beeby, from
The Church Incarnate
(originally published
in German in 1938)

In 1938, an intensely spiritual book written by
Rudolf Schwarz (1897–1961) was published in
Germany, titled *Vom Bau der Kirche*. Twenty years
later it was translated into English as *The Church
Incarnate*, and a foreword added by Mies van der
Rohe. Mies stated:

> This book was written in Germany's
> darkest hour, but it throws light for the first
> time on the question of church building,
> and illuminates the whole problem of
> architecture itself. Rudolf Schwarz, the
> great German church builder, is one of
> the most profound thinkers of our time.
> His book, in spite of its clarity, is not easy
> reading—but he who will take the trouble
> to study it carefully will gain real insight
> into the problem discussed. I have read it
> over and over again, and I know the power
> of its clarification. I believe it should be read
> not only by those concerned with church
> building, but by anyone sincerely interested
> in architecture, indeed it is one of the truly
> great books, one of those which have the
> power to transform our thinking.[1]

Schwarz was a German architect intensely
interested in the way the "sacred" forms of the
Catholic liturgy could best be accommodated
architecturally. Influenced by the theologian

Romano Guardini (an early pioneer in the
Liturgical Movement), his concern was that
worship should ultimately take place within living
individuals, not in the external forms of buildings
and images. For example, his revolutionary
Corpus Christi Church in Aachen (1930), which
was a single cubic volume of dazzling white with
black marble fixtures, emphasizes silence as the
most appropriate setting for liturgical action. In
The Church Incarnate, Schwarz describes the "way-
form" as the contemporary result of the evolution
of Christian history. The argument of this essay is
that this insight is the context that ultimately forms
the spiritual basis of Mies' work in America.

In a series of seven idealized plans that are
exquisitely delineated and poetically interpreted,
The Church Incarnate traces the development of the
forms of Christianity. Only at the end, at the last
plan, is the unfolding of his argument apparent:

> That building which summons all phases
> into structure at once, uniting time's entire
> flow within itself, is the cathedral of all
> times. Age-old it towers over the epochs,
> and in uniting them to one great form it
> adds something new, which none of them
> possessed: the completion, the whole. The
> cathedral possesses the fullness of time. In
> this cathedral time comes to an end ...[2]

[1] Rudolf Schwarz, *The
Church Incarnate: The
Sacred Function of
Christian Architecture*,
English trans. by
Cynthia Harris, fore-
word by Mies van der
Rohe (Chicago: Henry
Regnery Company,
1958). Successive
notes are all drawn
from this text.

[2] p. 194.

Three great elements go to make it up. The first and last are centric and between them the way takes its course. Where it leaves the one centric form and where it flows into the other arise situations of transition, situations of departure and of homecoming. Like two open harbors, the two end forms find each other, one the port of putting out to sea, the other that of putting into harbor, and between them stretches the path of life: this is the form at the root of sacred history.[3]

More literally, the plan could be interpreted in several ways. Schwarz explains the plan as a representation of Christ's life and, simultaneously, the history of the Christian church. It could also be seen as a representation of the Apocalypse of the Second Coming of Christ; closer examination of the elements of the plan supports this analysis.

As Schwarz interprets the history of the church, the Christian communities as described in the New Testament of the Bible portray a world of itinerant disciples of Christ preaching while on the move, transforming interested groups of listeners into converts who might further spread the word. As a fragmented and often persecuted church, they gathered in small groups not dissimilar to the idealized image of a small church so evocatively illustrated by Schwarz. The conversion of Constantine changed all that, however, giving imperial support to the church and transforming the basilica form of the Romans into large lineal churches built of rich materials with elaborate rituals to celebrate the sacraments of the church. The monastic orders were formed as an extension of earlier ascetic practices which have always been part of the Christian faith. The words of Christ suggest that worldly interests and material wealth were often confusing to genuinely devout Christians; reflecting this conviction, the tradition of utter poverty as a display of devotion was institutionalized and spread through the example of the mendicant orders.

As Christianity grew out from the Mediterranean world, its success in realizing converts produced a vast political and economic structure that became the most powerful force in all of Europe. Over time (as with all growing organizations), it lost many of its most intensely spiritual attributes in the face of compromises forced by the political realities of survival. The feudal period created a stable world of fixed relationships for all of society. The medieval towns that evolved into cities saw a rise in wealth and artistry which led to the creation of the great cathedrals in Northern Europe. However, the loss of spiritual direction within the church was attacked in Germany by Martin Luther early in the sixteenth century; his actions initiated the Reformation, an attack on the autonomous power of the Roman Catholic Church as well as an economic movement, resulting from the dissolution of Feudalism. This movement by the people to gain religious freedom simultaneously allowed the monarchy and aristocracy to usurp the power, land, and wealth of the Church. The lavish, ornamented edifices of the Roman Catholic Church became symbols of discontent, and in many countries were brutally stripped.

The Protestant Reformation demanded a sanctuary of a different, more abstract nature. The confrontation between two powerful Protestant leaders of the German-speaking world in sixteenth-century Marburg indicated the direction the Reformation would take—not only in relation to culture in general, but to architecture in particular. Luther's emphasis on scripture had reduced the number of sacraments from seven to two. He sanctioned Baptism and the Lord's Supper as essential to Christianity, for they were visible signs of an invisible grace. In Switzerland, on the other hand, Ulrich Zwingli had already taken the position that ritual would be cut from religious practice, by denying the mystery of transubstantiation. The Catholic Church and

[3] p. 193.

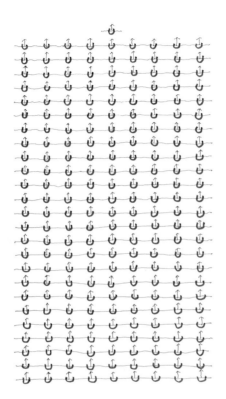

Rudolf Schwarz, "The Way," redrawn by Tom Beeby from *The Church Incarnate*

Luther maintained that, through the ritual of the Mass, the bread and wine of the Eucharist became the body and blood of Christ. Zwingli maintained that the elements of the Last Supper were mere symbols, draining the Mass of its supernatural power and reducing the communion to a memorial feast. At that moment, the unity of bread and the glorified body of the sacrificed Christ—word and deed, image and reality—were severed irreparably. Ironically, reality freed from symbol became more real; art freed from symbol, conversely, became more artistic. The least real of the arts, music, on the other hand, flourished; and the most real of the arts, architecture, was forever diminished as a vehicle for the expression of the full human condition. A totally transcendent God has no visible realm on this earth in a world where fact and spirit are decisively isolated, except in the perfection of nature. In a continuing assault on

the physical world as a proper medium for divine communication, all sacraments, images, and finally even music were disposed of. This culminated with the Anabaptists, for whom humankind stood alone in silent confrontation with God, and the only means of divine transmission was the familiar Bible. The church vanished as a meaningful physical entity, existing only in the minds of the true believers, the elect. God no longer had a dwelling place within this world. The Puritan settlers of New England and their descendants were the heirs to this tradition.

As described by Schwarz, this interpretation of Christian history could be understood by equating the "Sacred Parting"—or departure from the home sanctuary—with European history spanning the Reformation to the Modern period. It could be argued that Protestantism in Germany brought about the Modern World as we know it. Puritanical Protestantism set a course of an inner, worldly asceticism focused on the family, with political and economic institutions as the mediums of expression. The individual was stripped of the ritual of the church as an intermediary between God and self, and left in lonely confrontation with the eternal Judge and Redeemer. The individual believer was humbled by the condition of Original Sin that he or she was born into, and by a complete reliance on God. Yet, by being made personally responsible for one's own life and salvation, the individual's awareness of his or her own powers was increased, along with that personal isolation. Through the loss of the unifying force of the Roman Catholic Church, nations as well as people became isolated. Democracy, in its present form, arose during this period: the concept of religious liberty, separation of Church and State, limited sovereignty of the Church can all be viewed as resulting from the Reformation. Thus, the Reformation transformed Christianity, leading to the rise of secularization at the expense of organized religion. Industrialization exacerbated this transformation, resulting in the Modern Age.

The Church Incarnate, written in response to the modern condition, illustrates the central stage in Schwarz's description of the development of the church as the "Sacred Journey" (The Way). Critical interpretation of the modern world is the plan: Schwarz begins by describing the new Christian community as a people whose destiny is to be on a journey that is "the way." They are sent forth, knowing they come from somewhere, and are going somewhere, on a sacred way leading from God to God.[4] Schwarz then begins to describe the physical world that the modern Christian inhabits: each person a link in a chain, each chain a rank. All face the same way, looking ahead, each standing alone.[5] He then describes the relations between the members of the community, saying that any circuit of heartfelt communication or bond binding each to the other, is lacking: the people feel no warmth for one another, since the pattern has no heart.[6]

In modern Christian thought, the total transcendence of God shifts humanity's concern from the material world to the spiritual.

> Thus, the way-form is that form of the community which comes into being when the shared center of love flees into the infinite: … Any finite fulfillment is denied here, since the people share only the center outside and their common situation before the infinite.[7]

Schwarz then begins a detailed description of the perceptual and geometric characteristics of "the way." The people are organized into chains of individuals that are identical, constant—"endless monotony is the law of its formation."[8] A new link can be added, but does not alter the chain, for it becomes no better, no worse. He explains the nature of society in parallel terms, saying that as the individual is added to the field of the marching column, he or she feels nothing. The multiplication,

once begun, can be carried on endlessly, yet nothing new develops, "for the pattern itself, the number of people who are woven into it is without the least significance."[9] The bleak view of the world illustrated by the "Sacred Journey" is one vision of the modern world. It reflects an anonymous industrialized universe where the individual is lost within the whole. Its organization certainly suggests Germany during the Fascist period.

In the modern world, society is a net composed of chains made up of individuals that Schwarz characterizes in "the cross":

> The cross is the third element of form. The net grows together out of many small crosses, each of which marks a human place. Man's bodily structure is polarized; one axis runs vertically upward from below, one horizontally ahead in the direction of the way and the third runs at right angles to it in the direction of the shoulders. All three axes stand at right angles to one another … The cross form is spaceless. He who stands within it experiences the world as direction. His space-creating power is consumed in

[4] p. 114.

[5] p. 115.

[6] p. 116.

[7] p. 119.

[8] p. 120.

[9] p. 121.

Rudolf Schwarz, "The Cross," redrawn by Tom Beeby from *The Church Incarnate*

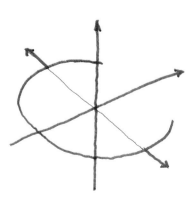

rendering the right-angled cross and so is translated into directed movement …[10]

Schwarz then alludes to the constructional possibilities of the people on "the way":

The net, formed by the individual crosses clinging to one another, is also a spaceless, linear structure, since in it, too, there is no spatial fullness, but only direction. World is experienced only as direction and as means in the net. The inner condition, however, can be compared to that of the "lattice-work" in an iron bridge or in some other "skeletal" structure: the power of the space has drawn together into a network of members and traverses the universe without expanding outward into it. And still this system has a kind of inner space: the tensions stream through the members and are interchanged among them, and in this way the form is made whole. The structure comes into being through simple accretion, yet each addition changes the inner tension in such a way that at each point the whole can be experienced inwardly. Since, in addition, the "lattice" is firmly welded together, the various intervals and extensions within it are precisely determined. The individual members are "located" in exact relation to each other and it is the feeling of location which is a metamorphosed feeling of space. The feeling is determined by the strange exactitude of the measurements. We know the feeling of desolation which overcomes us when we go through the streets of a city which is built according to a right-angled plan, but which has no center: much room, yet no space.[11]

Finally, after dealing with the structure of the space of "the way" and poetically relating it to an overall structural "lattice," Schwarz describes the difficulty of forming enclosure in this milieu.

In the earlier plans, the inner space of the people's ordering corresponded to the structure of the universe. When we rendered this inner space, through the use of the walls and the space of the building, we gave the world her form at the same time—from the inside to the outside, the structure was one harmonious composition of people and world intermingling.

Here it is not so simple. The way-form has no real, continuing space. Its knot-like structure interlaces a world which is traveled and yet not experienced, which completely loses itself in the uncertain. The inner "locating" in the way-form provides only a "relative-space"—what would correspond to it would be an unspanned skeletal structure. The best solution would actually be to give the relative shelter in just such an all-embracing grating.[12]

————————

With this description sketched out of Schwarz's concept of the "way-form," we can now turn to an examination of how it forms the spiritual basis of Mies' work in America, most evident in his earliest work on the campus of IIT. The Illinois Institute of Technology lies within the insistent grid of Chicago that runs from the Prairie to the Lake, where it dies with no compromise, never producing a center. Mies further subdivided this street grid down to a twelve-foot modular network that he placed over the entire site. Then, rather than embracing the nineteenth-century street façades, Mies turned his back on the surroundings by rotating the perimeter buildings perpendicularly to the surrounding façades, or setting them back from the edges.

In Christian ascetic communities, to separate the elect from the world, isolation from the surroundings is imperative. Although members

[10] p. 122.

[11] p. 123.

[12] p. 135.

right: Aerial view of the Chicago grid at night

below: Mies van der Rohe, Illinois Institute of
Technology (IIT) campus, 1939–56, construction

of the church are seen as missionaries within the
world, clear physical separation is maintained at
all times. This concept is also manifestly clear in
the plan of IIT: purity demanded isolation from
the world. Circulation of outsiders was relegated
to the perimeter, with a second internal system of
paths for the elect.

Within the IIT precinct, buildings are arranged
in an apparently informal manner, however right-
angle relationships are strictly maintained. All
column lines fall directly on the grid crossings at
twenty-four foot intervals. Individual buildings
are cubic volumes that display symmetry of

arrangement, yet axial development based on
that symmetry is carefully avoided. Hierarchy
of any sort is kept to a minimum, for the "way-
form" world professes equality, never significance.
Hierarchically important structures are sprinkled
randomly throughout the precinct, denying their
importance through careful disregard. There is no
central building as a focus; rather, a loosely formed
space occupies the central position.

The plantings are natural at IIT, returning the
site to a pseudo-wilderness. The plant materials
used are restricted to only those plants which
are local in derivation, and they are arranged in

Mies van der Rohe,
Crown Hall, Illinois
Institute of Technology,
1956

an ecologically pure manner. Joyful planting to please the eye is replaced by a "moral wilderness." Vines grow on the IIT buildings, dematerializing them at their bases and visually illustrating the transitory nature of construction. The ideal ascetic community is rural, preferably in undisturbed nature to ensure isolation. The planting at IIT creates a spiritual wilderness of the mind, edges unclear, for expansion has always been a primary goal of the missionary community. The IIT campus follows Schwarz's description of "the way" completely—from its position in the world to the development of its buildings.

The first campus buildings at IIT represent an apparent departure from Mies' early work in Germany. Gone is the virtuosity of Constructivist balance; in its place is an overwhelming plainness of uniformity as described by Schwarz. The dominance of the construction method over all other architectural considerations produces a severity of expression that fulfills the polemical drive against superfluity. The plans of Mies' buildings are all similar: a core contains all elements not easily placed within the surrounding, generalized space; service spaces become a dense mass rising through the regular framing members. This central mass

replaces the central void of inwardness found in the Pantheon. "All secular building about a center is work without hope ... Their space is forever the cave."[13] The abstract purity of the central core plan suggests a desire of Mies to produce a building type of such simplicity as to create a moral exemplar, as a reminder to the occupants of their place in an ordered world created by God.

In all cases, the partition lines fall on the supports as an obvious celebration of pragmatic concern. The result is a spatial envelope of absolute uniformity, with all parts equal in emphasis. The vertical circulation elements are utilitarian, exhibiting no celebration of passage familiar in the realm of high architecture. Openings are regular, governed by construction simplicity, and tend to be centered both in plan and elevation—only for specialized needs of light and entry are minor shifts from regularity allowed. The system is standardized, but altered enough to show the intentions of the builder to be utilitarian rather than formal. This avoids symmetry in the aesthetic sense, and replaces it with regularity as a method: the parts are always given precedence over the compositional organization.

Ornamental detail is kept to an absolute minimum, and centered on crafted elements,

[13] p. 54.

rather than decorative schemes. Mies focuses his decorative detailing on the structural display of joinery. Atypical, isolated wall sections in the core area are often locally symmetrical, with elaboration in treatment and material. The stair balusters and handrails receive special design consideration but the spatial configuration is restrained or minimal, avoiding spatial flow from floor to floor. Hierarchy as a major formal strategy is avoided: arrangements remain iconoclastic in their avoidance of figural expression in favor of an even display of the parts. Front-to-back differentiation exists in the IIT building systems, but elaboration on that theme is avoided. Mies desired to exhibit the structural frame in a manner similar to heavy-timber medieval prototypes, but code restrictions, as well as climate, forced him into a skin that concealed the structural frame. His celebrated corner treatments could be interpreted as a limited display of craftsman-like virtuosity based on artisanal pride, rather than connoisseurship.

The IIT buildings represent the conscious need to standardize construction in order to produce a large number of structures in a limited amount of time. The use of prefabricated elements in a regular manner produces a building type of a generalized, rather than particularized, nature. It also creates a plainness in keeping with the pragmatic, expressive needs of a puritanical Christian society. The almost complete lack of finish is offset by the ornamental use of natural materials in an unaltered condition. Formal manipulation is always avoided; and the simplest arrangement of pieces always chosen. Hierarchy based on functional need produces a series of building types articulated by distinctive structural treatment. Minimal use of material remains a major goal (in both the practical and spiritual sense, early Miesian buildings became lighter and lighter as the architect continually reduced the size of members for greater economy of means). All remnants of architecture's sensual

nature are suppressed, producing forms and spaces of such sparseness that they verge on meanness—this is repugnant to many in its destruction of sensual pleasure and spontaneity. Architecture is clarified to its simplest level of intent as a reflection of puritanical ascetic drive.

As pointed out by Mies van der Rohe in his introduction to *The Church Incarnate*, this book was written in Germany's darkest hour. If the diagram of "The Cathedral of All Times" is one that follows a millennial logic, certainly 1939 would be the apocalyptic year, for at that time the horror of the Nazis under Hitler was unleashed on Germany's neighbors, and Schwarz could only pray that a new world would replace the realities of a living Armageddon. Therefore, Mies' response to Schwarz at this time could be seen as a harbinger of a world to come, for his next buildings abandon the insistent regularity of "the way" for a more spiritual approach.

The presence of Crown Hall, which houses the School of Architecture at IIT, introduces a higher level of architectural intent than is present in the other structures on campus. The structural form is here changed from the earlier normative pattern to illustrate its transcendent use, and the original grid formulated by Mies is discarded in search of a more ethereal order. Recognizing this change in register, one can read Crown Hall as an Aesthetic Cathedral of German Romanticism, based once again on the observation that the prophetic images of Schwarz closely anticipate Mies' actual building. Describing the "Cathedral of All Times," Schwarz writes:

> It would be only a step to give up the fixed
> space entirely and to use the structure simply
> as a means with which to render, in free
> creation, the ever-changing space. Then the

liturgy would not be only a "cathedral" in its secret structure: every day the Whole would be visibly erected.[14]

This description offers the clue to capturing the entire history of the Church in one form—ever-changing and eternal. To suggest what it would mean to accomplish this in real material, Schwarz offers more detailed analysis. First, the relation of man to the land is explained as the age-old struggle between the organic and the inorganic.

The first uprising created the body. Its buoyant form contradicts for the first time the dumb heaviness of the earth, its tall growth the earth's unfathomable depths. The body stands erect, a contradiction in the midst of space. But in opposition the earth invents the vault. The vault overhead is again earth, earth which has closed over anew, burying the body once more in her womb. This is the answer which the body itself provoked by its uprising: the earth turns up her surface to form a vault, her depth becomes a cave and she clutches the mutineer still tighter, forcing him now into her innermost center. But for the second time he shatters the earthly fetters and frees himself forever into light.[15]

This passage can be interpreted as the evolution of the church freeing the Christian from the earthly, material confines of the Virgin Mary as descendent of the Earth Goddess, to rise into the light of spirituality. Schwarz continues:

If the form at the beginning was understood as cave, we understand the new form as landscape … An open valley lies beneath the sun and is bordered far in the distance by a remote range of mountains. But in the midst of the sheltered mead rises a high peak. The sunlight falls early upon it. Its summit is clearly aglow when the first light brushes the mountain tops and the valley lies in twilight.

On its slopes the light slowly sinks until it reaches the bottom of the valleys and gilds the whole sacred plain … Man stands erect in the center as mountain.[16]

The imagery is exactly that found in the paintings of German Romanticism, as for example the landscapes portrayed by Caspar David Friedrich. These sublime landscapes lie on the other side of the threshold separating "world" from "other world."

However, the history of the church denies the architect the opportunity to create a building as a cosmic analogy.

The world has undergone the great transformation. Her center of gravity has moved out into the eternal and all her forms are open … Hence what the artist has here to achieve is work which prays. Indeed a genuine likeness of the world but a world which is open to God and the forms which correspond to them are "open forms." They stand open ready to receive the Lord and in each of them is "threshold" and "emptiness."[17]

Schwarz then describes the solution adopted by Mies to bridge the gap between "world" and "other world," while still maintaining open form.

Only the architecture is valid here which takes the eternal rift up into its work and openly admits that here it is found wanting … Perhaps in this one single instance it is truly permissible to separate habitable structure from structure which is symbolical, to end the former on the threshold, and to continue the latter on beyond it. In this case we would close the gap in some imperfect way, using a substance which provides protection against the weather and which at the same time bars our passage—we could make the closing wall transparent, thus enabling us to see out, as it were, into the symbolical part of the building lying beyond. For indeed,

opposite: Mies in Crown Hall

[14] p. 198.

[15] p. 100.

[16] p. 101.

[17] p. 82.

Mies van der Rohe,
Chapel of Saint Savior,
Illinois Institute of
Technology, 1952

we can convey what lies behind the window only by illusion, by indication. To indicate a road means to point it out, to introduce it by intimation without transversing it: the pointing movement itself remains this side of the threshold.[18]

In Crown Hall the ends of the building are glazed with frosted glass, which allows vision only into the far distance and removes the middle ground of nature from view. The foreground of trees is set against the void of the sky. The partitions guide the space outward through the center parting of transparent glass into "infinity" and beyond. Structure is pressed beyond the glass line into the symbolic world. Thus, the relationship between the other world beyond the threshold and the built world is established.

By continuing the way on out to the horizontal edge of the world, we could even draw nature into this likeness. This would be possible where the window opens onto an empty landscape, which then lies between the threshold and the horizon, for example

on the shore of the ocean or at the edge of the desert or on a high mountain top.[19]

This is the space on the platform lying before the building, the empty plain viewed from the occupied space of the threshold. All these images are familiar to Romantic painting, the moment before the dawn of the Second Coming.

In all cases, however, the "image" behind the threshold would have to be blocked off unmistakably from the space lying in front of it, from the space in which we live. We might perhaps achieve this by the means of a pane of glass—glass is at once transparent and hard—indeed this image should mean "pathway which we cannot tread."[20]

The entry elaboration of the platform at Crown Hall is then interpreted as the beginning of a new age, as an exit from the sins of the past, rather than an entry. Here one can hesitate on the floating platform before setting out into the "other world." The building becomes transparent, opening up to the light of God. Denied the closed form of the Sacred Inwardness, the building must

[18] p. 85.

[19] p. 86.

[20] p. 86.

Caspar David Friedrich, *Der Wanderer über dem Nebelmeer* (The Wanderer above the Sea of Fog), 1818, Kunsthalle, Hamburg

name the presence of God, rather than reproduce a cosmology.

> Perhaps we may achieve this if we give, as it were, a silhouette of the sacred. A transparent representation can reveal in a most meaningful way. The great drawn forms then become at every part horizons, and in their infinite vista, that which is intended becomes visible: the creatures bathed in the light of God.[21]

> Within the building itself, the ambience is quite clear in intention: All these likenesses seek to say that God dwells in emptiness. They are good insofar as they succeed in bringing "emptiness" nearer the human comprehension.[22]

The luminous vessel of universal space in Crown Hall contains the sacred exhibition space as its open center, which is occupied by Mies as teacher. The closed core space, as shrine, contains the mysteries of the office of the director. Here, the relation of core to universal space is poetically interpreted as the "Cathedral of All Times," and is

condensed into a centralized image of density and power. The same centralized concentration is the dominant compositional device of the Romantic painters. As a representation of the material face of the world, Friedrich's images render the foreground in meticulous detail. A centered figure with its back turned faces distant eternity down "the way." The sacred landscape is portrayed with equal clarity in the distant horizon of salvation. Missing is the middle ground necessary to orient the viewer to naturalistic interpretation. Crown Hall exhibits the same qualities of meticulously rendered details set off against the void of the room. The emptiness produced by the lack of middle ground development, normally found in partitioning, allows the building to exactly match Schwarz's description of the renewed Christian world. Material elements are painted black to disappear. The luminous void expresses the world of a transcendent God.

The School of Architecture becomes the sacred center of the campus, displacing the cathedral in the hierarchy of significance. The actual "cathedral" is reduced to a single cell, a chapel, and is pressed into an insignificant corner of campus. This tiny structure is constructed as a brick load-bearing wall, the only one on the IIT campus.

Nothing can express the aim and meaning of our work better than the profound words of St. Augustine: "Beauty is the splendor of Truth."

Mies van der Rohe from Inaugural Speech, IIT, 1938

[21] p. 94.

[22] p. 86.

THE SECULAR SPIRITUALITY OF TADAO ANDO

KENNETH FRAMPTON

The tautology of a secular spirituality surely touches on the crisis that lies at the heart of a great deal of contemporary culture. The term would seem to be particularly pertinent in the case of Tadao Ando in that his work is imbued with the ethos of a rather primordial Japanese mode of beholding that—despite its unequivocal modernity—still seems to be informed by Taoism, on the one hand, and Shintoism, on the other. In the space of a brief essay, one cannot possibly elaborate all the ramifications of this assertion. All one can do is focus on the revelatory aspects of Ando's architecture and thought; the tropes that testify to his cosmogonic concerns that are at variance with the monotheistic Judeo-Christian tradition.

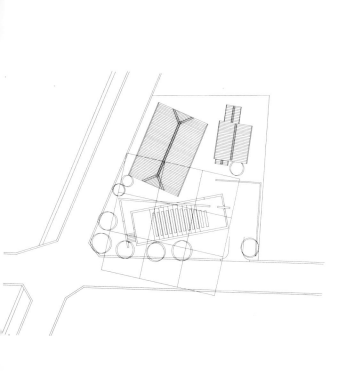

above: Tadao Ando, Church of the Light, Ibaraki, Osaka, 1989, site plan

above right: Church of the Light, interior

In this regard it would be hard to find a more existential point of departure than Ando's reflections on the Japanese concept of the *shintai*, the Japanese term for "body," that implies the inseparability of body-being that categorically transcends the split between body and soul that seems to be so central to the individualistic ethos of monotheism. Thus, of *shintai* we find him writing:

> Man articulates the world through his body. Man is not a dualistic being in whom spirit and flesh are essentially distinct but a living, corporeal being active in the world. The "here and now" in which this distinct body is placed is what is first taken as granted, and subsequently a "there" appears. Through a perception of that distance, or rather the living of that distance, the surrounding space becomes manifest as a thing endowed with various meanings and values .... Since man has an asymmetrical physical structure with a top and a bottom, a left and a right, and a front and a back, the articulated world, in turn, naturally becomes a heterogeneous space. The world that appears to man's senses and the state of man's body become in this way interdependent. The world articulated by the body is a vivid, lived-in space.

The body articulates the world. At the same time, the body is articulated by the world. When "I" perceive the concrete to be something cold and hard, "I" recognize the body as something warm and soft. In this way, the body in its dynamic relationship with the world becomes the *shintai*. It is only the *shintai* in this sense that builds or understands architecture. The *shintai* is a sentient being that responds to the world.[1]

It is evident that nature, including the *shintai's* sense of its own nature, plays a fundamental role in the experiential ontology of Ando's architecture, as he has made clear in countless texts; although, for him, it is the very transitory and haptic character of natural phenomena that serves to enliven and guarantee the spirituality of his architecture. It is, above all, light/wind, rain/snow, sun/shadow, water/ice, heat/cold, scent/sound, and vegetation/landfall that for him are the palpable constituents of nature as they mutually impinge upon both the body and built form.

Ever since the Tezukayama House of 1977, where an orthogonal frame precisely delineates from minute to minute the passage of the sun across its volume, the building as an azimuth has been a fundamental aspect of Ando's "self-

[1] Tadao Ando, "Shintai and Space" in *Architecture and Body* (New York: Rizzoli International, 1988), unpaginated.

enclosed" architecture. However, the use of light as both a volatile abstract figure and an ambiguous spiritual sign does not fully emerge in his architecture until the so-called Church of the Light at Ibaraki, Osaka, of 1989, where a slot window in the form of a cross extending over the entirety of the southern elevation creates an all-encompassing excised figure within, that changes its luminous configuration as the sun moves, cutting across the volume at an angle so as to be no longer legible as a cruciform. This is typical of Ando's ecclesiastical work in that the visual percept yields both the necessary Christian symbol and its simultaneous denial in favor of a cosmogonic spirituality. Such a spirituality is more profoundly grounded in nature, as revealed through the agency of his architecture.

This primal, non-animistic spiritual presence is also augmented by other means in this same building; most notable, surely, by the narrow *roji*, or threshold, triangular in plan, that must be traversed before entering the nave. Once within, a stepped, hollow wooden platform set within the concrete prism of the nave responds to the footfall of the congregation in terms of both sound and vibration, not to mention the smell of timber rising against the scent of concrete. Latent, ambiguous associations attend this sensuous conjunction, most notably the primacy of wood that has had a fundamentally spiritual significance in both occidental and oriental religious traditions. Despite these multi-sensorial nuances, it is light itself that is the phenomenon driving the conception of this church. This much Ando would abundantly make clear in 1993:

> Light, alone, does not make light. There must be darkness for light to become *light*—resplendent with dignity and power. Darkness, which kindles the brilliance of light and reveals light's power, is innately

a part of light …. Today, when all is cast in homogenous light, I am committed to pursuing the interrelationship of light and darkness …. Here, I prepared a box with thick enclosing walls of concrete—a "construction of darkness." I then cut a slot in one wall, allowing the penetration of light— under conditions of severe constraint …[2]

All of Ando's churches are imbued with this conjunction in which both Christian iconography and its Japanese "other" are simultaneously evoked, although the evocation of the divine depends on the revealed ineffability of nature rather than on the presentation of conventional symbolism. Thus, in the chapel erected on the top of Mount Rokko in 1986, we encounter a glazed arcade lined on three sides that alludes, however obliquely, to the tunnel of *torii* leading to the Fushimi Inari shrine in Kyoto. This reference is evoked analogically by a straight, single-story, concrete-framed corridor flanked on its sides by the large sheets of opalescent plate glass and covered by an equally translucent roof in curved glass. This glazed arcade, which slides past the building itself, ends in a staircase that cannot be seen since it descends abruptly, without any prior indication, to the concrete threshold of the chapel lying below the horizon. Thus, as one approaches, one sees nothing but open sky at the end of a translucent tunnel. By this device, the congregation is made aware at the outset of the latent void lying at the heart of Japanese cosmology; that is, one is confronted with the non-corporeal embodiment of *ma*, which may be characterized as a simultaneous presence and absence—as a hiatus even—between these two unstable conditions.

While the chapel itself assumes the discernible form of a diminutive basilica, complete with a discreet campanile, the disjunctive key established by the mode of approach pervades the entire

[2] Tadao Ando, "Church of Light" in Francesco Dal Co, ed., *Tadao Ando: Complete Works* (London: Phaidon, 1995), p. 471.

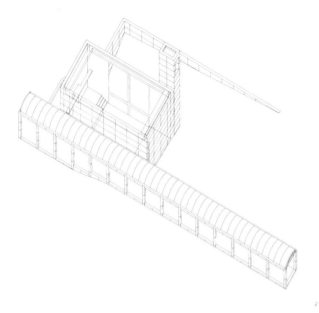

top: Tadao Ando, Mt.
Rokko Chapel, Kobe,
1986, axonometric

above: Mt. Rokko
Chapel, exterior

opposite: Tadao Ando,
Church on the Water,
Tomamu, Hokkaido,
1988, prism of steel-
framed plate glass,
interior

³ Tadao Ando, "Church
and Theater on the
Water," in Kenneth
Frampton, *Tadao Ando*
(New York: Museum
of Modern Art, 1991),
p. 42.

structure through one subtle contradictory gesture after another. Thus, while the nave is oblong and ostensibly enclosed on all six sides amounting to a double cube, in fact, its fourth wall is dematerialized for its full height and width by large sheets of inoperable plate glass held in place by a substantial concrete cruciform, and giving onto an embankment covered in gardenias. Here, nature is presented only too artificially as a permanently inaccessible inclined plane—as an anti-patio, in fact—the sole symbolic purpose of which is to remind the congregation of an ineffable presence of opposition to the Christian iconography of the crucifix, the altar, and the pulpit to which the small congregation, assembled for the purpose of witnessing the marriage, must ostensibly address itself.

This point and counterpoint, at once Western and Non-Western, Christian and Non-Christian, will be rendered in a more expansive, panoramic manner in Ando's Church on the Water, built at Tomamu, Hokkaido, in the Yubari Mountains in 1988. A laconic description, provided by the architect for the 1991 retrospective of his work in the Museum of Modern Art, New York, can hardly be improved upon.

The structure consists—in plan—of two overlapping squares: the larger, partly projecting out into an artificial pond, houses the chapel, and the smaller contains the entry and the changing and waiting rooms. A freestanding L-shaped wall wraps around the back of the building and one side of the pond. The church is approached from the back and entry involves a circuitous route: a counter-clockwise ascent to the top of the smaller volume through a glass-enclosed space open to the sky, with views of the pond and the distant mountains. In this space are four large crosses arranged in a square formation and almost touching. From this point, the visitor descends two levels to emerge at the back of the chapel. The wall behind the altar is constructed entirely of glass, affording a dramatic panorama of the pond with a large cross set into the water. The glass wall itself, spanned by a cruciform mullion, can slide to the side, like a giant *shōji* screen, opening the chapel towards nature.³

Once again, the approach to the liturgical space is via an ingenious hiatus that now assumes the form of a condensed labyrinth, with the subject passing through the blank perimeter of its concrete podium in order to arrive at an orthogonal prism of steel-framed plate glass. This virtual volume delineating the surrounding panorama is answered by an inner matrix comprising four concrete crosses that, square in section, are

right: Tadao Ando, Church on the Water,
axonometric

opposite: Church on the Water, exterior

above: Church on the Water, exterior from reflecting pool looking toward the chapel

below: Church on the Water, with glass wall behind altar open to the reflecting pool

articulated from one another at their extremities by an extremely narrow gap. As elsewhere in Ando's ecclesiastical work, the rendering of the crucifix as an abstraction is further desacralized here by the reiteration of the motif around the four sides of a virtual square treated as an inaccessible void. This void is further subdivided in plan by a cross of the same dimensions, the space between its arms being filled by a grid of sixteen squares of opalescent glazing, thereby affording zenithal light to the changing rooms beneath. The congregation ascends to the top of this belvedere via two short stair flights—one for each successive side of the inner square—whereupon they are constrained by both the glass screen of the outer perimeter and by the inner perimeter of the freestanding crosses. They have no choice at this juncture but to descend via two successive short flights into the main body of the church, where they see the body of the freestanding cross, standing within a seemingly infinite sheet of water. A large, steel-framed, sliding glass wall serves to close off the body of the church from the elements in winter. Reciprocally, this may be slid away in summer so as to establish a direct phenomenological link between the church and the expansive surface of the reflecting pool

beyond. This last is a three-tiered surface in which the water recedes from the church across two shallow weirs before eventually draining into a sump at the outer limit of the pool, prior to being pumped back to the base of the church to begin its descent all over again.

This is the first work in which Ando will employ water as the embodiment of the spirit, although here, as elsewhere, the manifestation of nature will be contingent on subtle climate fluctuations according to the time of day and the season of the year; the softly rippling sound of the water, its responsiveness to light and breeze, the relative humidity of the air, the presence of mist, frost, snow. All of these fluctuating conditions continually transform the site as experienced from both the threshold of the water and the belvedere above.

Nowhere, perhaps, in Ando's work has nature been more artificially contained and activated than in his Water Temple completed on Awaji Island in 1991 on the grounds of the existing Hompukuji Temple belonging to the Shingon Buddhist sect. Of his addition of a new temple within the compound, he writes of substituting the traditional Buddhist roof with an aqueous disk of lotus plants that stands in the midst of the site as the primary spiritual symbol. Ando bisects the elliptical reinforced concrete basin holding the water with a concrete stair descending to a temple set to one side of the undercroft beneath. Ando's description reveals all one needs to know about the elaborate landscape promenade that precedes one's final entry into the temple itself. He writes:

> The oval, manmade pond ... is placed on a bluff, and the temple hall underground, beneath it. The hall is composed of a round room, 14.0 meters in diameter, contained in a square room, 17.4 meters square. The round room is gridded with pillars, 4 meters tall and 21 centimeters square, set at intervals of one ken (a ken is a traditional Japanese module, equivalent to 1.8 meters).

> Walking over white sand, visitors ascend a path to the top of the hill and confront a long wall, with the infinite blue expanse of the ocean behind them. To the right, after passing through an aperture in the wall, is a constricted space that isolates a fragment of the sky between the 3-meter-high wall and a curved wall of equal height. Turning to the left, around the end of the curved wall brings one to the broad pond with its cover of green lotus plants. To enter the main hall, one descends a staircase penetrating directly to the center of the pond.

> The interior of the hall, and the pillars, are stained vermilion – this color becoming intense at the end of each day, as the reddish glow of sunset suffuses the space ...[4]

While this intense light effect does indeed occur at the end of each day, the temple itself, erected within the temple hall, will assume a traditional timber format and here, liberated from the constraints of Christendom, we are witness to the way in which Ando's abstract representation of the sacred—namely, a field of red pillars surrounding a statue of the Buddha—will not, in the final event, be accepted by the Shingon priesthood. They will, however, go along with an orthogonal gridding of the surrounding cubic volume that Ando finally handles as the converse of his original design, namely as a vermilion trabeated cage set within an equally red, reflective, cylindrical container. Either way, the diffusion of the light depends on louvered screens that Ando introduces into the space, a trope taken directly from the Mexican master Luis Barragán, by whom Ando has been subtly influenced throughout his career.

Beyond Ando's overtly religious buildings, however, there are other notable examples of what I have called here his secular spirituality. If one

[4] Tadao Ando, "Water Temple Tsuna-Gun" in Yukio Futagawa, *Tadao Ando, GA Architect*, vol. 2 (Tokyo: A.D.A. Edita, 1993), p. 157.

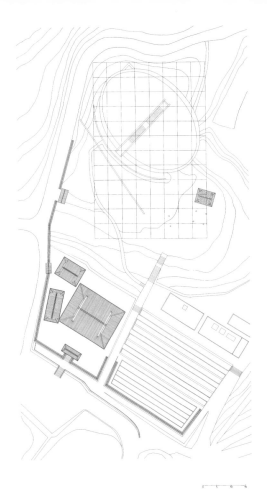

by shallow sheets of water running down the hill
in the opposite direction, on either side of the entry.
The intense kinesthesia of this mutual movement
is greatly heightened by the sound of the cascading
water and by the sparkling of the light bouncing
off its surface. The termination of this ramp in a
square viewing platform elevated above the water
induces another instance of *ma*—with the platform
serving as a gap or hiatus in the itinerary—as the
subject is momentarily suspended between the
nearby traditional dwelling of the writer Tetsuro
Watsuji, to whom the museum is dedicated.

With the Water Temple behind him, Ando
entered ever more fully into the orchestration of
landscape as the ultimate site for the evocation
of the spiritual. First among these topographic
interventions were two additional museum
complexes that Ando designed between 1989 and
1994: the Forest of Tombs Museum, Kumamoto
(1992) and Chikatsu-Asuka Historical Museum,
Osaka (1994). The strategy in both instances was
to create an acropolis-like belvedere that, in the
semi-subterranean darkness of an undercroft
gallery beneath, would engender the illusion and
atmosphere of being inside an actual tomb or *kofun*.
In each museum, the *parti* involved an elevated
viewing platform accessed by a broad flight of
steps overlooking a panorama of tumuli of various
sizes and shapes. Of the two, the Forest of Tombs is
not only far more intimate but more differentiated
sequentially: one passes from a parking lot through
a small forest into an ornamental court enlivened
by the presence of a wall-fountain (for the full
width of the structure), and then ascends abruptly
via a broad flight of steps to overlook the tombs.
In this instance, the viewing platform dissolves
into a circular spiraling pedestrian ramp that gives
access to the exhibition housed within the *kofun*
beneath. The artificial acropolis of the Chikatsu-
Asuka Museum is more monumental in character,
outstripping in scale the mounds themselves and

accepts that the museum is the surrogate religious
institution of our age, then Ando has surely been
privileged to pursue this secular substitute to an
exceptional degree, designing—if not always
realizing—well over twenty museums, large and
small, in the last two decades of his career. This
cultural production begins with two museums,
both erected in Himeji, in the Hyōgo Prefecture:
the Children's Museum of 1989 and the Museum
of Literature, realized close to the Himeji Castle
in 1991. Apart from being distributed across their
respective sites in an equally picturesque manner,
both buildings take their cue from the Church on
the Water by making an exceptionally animated
use of water across a large portion of the site: a
stepped fountain-cum-paddling pool in the case
of the Children's Museum that, while flaring the
building, fuses with the surface of a nearby reservoir
in such a way as to engage with the traditional
concept of borrowed scenery or "*shakkei*"; in the
Museum of Literature, by way of contrast, an
inclined pedestrian ramp rising towards the cubic
center of the museum is energized as an experience

above: Water Temple,
water basin, detail

right: Water Temple,
entry stair

set up as a continuously stepped theatrical space overlooking a small, irregular lake. This is, by far, the more topographically dynamic, since one's ascent up the stairs to the top of the acropolis form seems to be capable of energizing the area.

Ando's penchant for the use of shallow, cascading sheets of water—either in the form of serial weirs or as walls of water (both being landscape innovations)—attains its apotheosis to date in his Awaji Yumebutai development at Tsuna-gun, Hyōgo, realized between 1997 and 2000 and built as part of a comprehensive collective effort to reconstitute a coastal site badly ravaged, first by wholesale soil depletion, second by seismic damage inflicted by the Hanshin-Awaji earthquake of 1995, and finally by major arterial roads superimposed upon the site following the completion of the Akashi Kaikyo Bridge to the mainland in 1988. After participating in the earth replacement and the planting of some 250,000 trees, Ando added to this reforestation a "ruined" (that is, all but totally empty) Piranesian city-in-miniature, in which a heterogeneous juxtaposition of geometrical elements is combined with an interstitial stroll garden that is as much built as planted. The primary topographic focus of this complex is a concrete flower garden, stepping up the precipitous slope, to be paralleled by a water cascade that descends the same slope in steps to culminate in an aqueous plaza, animated by a lining of sea shells beneath the surface of the water. Among the finest cultural buildings that Ando has realized over the past twenty years, we see here the overall spirit of the place arising from the juxtaposition of the plastic intervention with the topography as found. This is made manifest through a contrapuntal formal presence operating over wide scalar range, passing from the close proximity of terraces, forecourts, and swimming pools to distant panoramic views of mountainous foothills or open sea.

In all of this, as William Curtis has pointed out, there is a latent political intention that seeks to compensate for, and even to overcome, the highly privatized consumer society that is as prevalent in Japan as anywhere else. In the last analysis, Ando's secular spirituality cannot be separated from a larger critical aim that seeks to transcend the reduction of contemporary life to consumerism, including, paradoxically enough, the consumption of mass tourism. Confronted with this nemesis, Ando strives to awaken society to a consciousness of its own past and an awareness of a topographic legacy that needs to be consciously cultivated if it is to be protected and maintained. As Ando has put it: "A site possesses its own physical and geographical character; at the same time it has layers of memory imprinted on it. I always listen to the whispering voice of a given place. I think of it comprehensively with all its forces – the visible characteristics as well as the invisible memories to do with interaction of a locality and humankind. And I try to integrate these into my building which shall carry that spirit to later generations."[5]

The most intimate and bucolic aspect of this newly found expressive spectrum is perhaps most evident in the Oyamazaki Villa Museum, Kyoto, of 1996, where a harmonious contrast is established between an arcaded walkway, a cylindrical gallery, and a preexisting Arts and Crafts villa from the turn of the century. A more cyclopean scale of interaction between building and topos seems to obtain in the Yokogurayama Natural Forest Museum of 1997, where a heightened interplay between the intimate and the panoramic asserts itself, as is also the case in the TOTO Seminar House at Tsuna-gun, Hyōgo, of the same year. As Ando expresses it, "The plan features an 8-layer terraced structure arranged along the natural topography, so that every room should open to the sea. The rooftop was to be covered by trees for the most part, to preserve the natural landscape as much as possible."[6]

[5] William Curtis, "Between Architecture and Landscape" in Yukio Futagawa, *Tadao Ando, GA Architect*, vol. 3 (Tokyo: A.D.A. Edita, 2000), p. 11.

[6] Tadao Ando, "TOTO Seminar House" in Yukio Futagawa, *Tadao Ando, GA Architect*, vol. 3 (Tokyo: A.D.A. Edita, 2000), p. 196.

All of these works exemplify what Ando has characterized as his "dialogue with geometry," designed to uncover and heighten the latent essence of a landscape. He writes, "My endeavor ... has been to engage the logic of nature and the logic of architecture in dialogue—not so that one might absorb the other, and neither so that they might obtain, as in the Japanese aesthetic, an ambiguous fusion—but in a manner by which their harsh confrontation will produce a place rich in creative resonance."[7] No one has perhaps written more perceptively of Ando's extension of his internalized architectonic discourse out into the landscape than Yuzuru Tominaga when he wrote of Ando's work in 1995:

> The Japanese word "*fukei*," derived from the Chinese, means "landscape," a compound of "*fu*" meaning wind and "*kei*" meaning sunlight. (It is also called "*fuko*"—wind and light.) "*Fukei*"/landscape implies natural things filled with wind and light; furthermore landscape (as *fukei*) is a humanized scenery, staged through wind and light, and not nature as matter itself....
>
> The new main hall of Honpukuji [Water Temple 1989–91] is located under a shallow, oval-shaped pond that is raised above the ground...."

Later in the same text, Tominaga continues:

> The highly developed architectural engineering of the end of the twentieth century is employed for the sole purpose of recalling the architectural history in man's memory and awakening one's perception; it does not show itself off. But on the other hand, it is this same technology that is being used to construct the extension of the new Honshu-Shikoku bridge which pierces through the whole island by cutting a narrow slit into a mountain and modifying the natural topography to the extreme.[8]

What I have alluded to as a secular spirituality crops up in Ando's work, irrespective of the subject matter, and never more surprisingly perhaps than in Ando's handling of overtly commercial commissions, as in two totally contrasting works dating from 1984: his Festival building in Naha City, Okinawa, and his "Time's" shops erected in two phases in the Nakagyo Ward of Kyoto. In both instances, we are witness to the serial accommodation of boutiques within an overall structural frame that – in a totally disarming and irrefutable manner – is enlivened by the constantly changing, animating presence of nature. In the first instance in Okinawa, we encounter the filtering of sunlight through grilled screens in such a way as to proliferate a continually shifting fugue of light and shade; in the second in Kyoto, we are confronted with a conscious manifestation of the *oku*. As Fumihiko Maki has written in his seminal essay on this theme: "*Oku* emphasizes the horizontality and seeks its symbolism in an invisible depth."[9] He goes on to argue that it often takes the form of a time-honored spatial crease in the landscape, a familiar route linking distant points.

Just such a "crease" lies adjacent to the site of the Time's shops in Kyoto, where it assumes the form of the shallow, channeled Takase River. This element, with its crystal-clear water, was sufficient to serve as a synthesizing concept for this otherwise nondescript aggregation of boutiques. After establishing the party wall boundary and stair slot, the difficulty became one of relating the three commercial floors to the water. Ando solved this problem through three riverside stairways and one long cascading stair, giving direct access to the stores at the rear of the site (cf. Ando's STEP, Takamatsu, Kagawa Prefecture, of 1980). The first of the riverside stairs, and the most expressive of the three, leads directly to a plaza close to the water's edge. The second, comprised of only four risers, leads up from the sidewalk to a wide gallery

[6] Tadao Ando, "TOTO Seminar House" in Yukio Futagawa, *Tadao Ando, GA Architect*, vol. 3 (Tokyo: A.D.A. Edita, 2000), p. 196.

[7] Tadao Ando, "In Dialogue with Geometry: The Creation of 'Landscape'" in Yukio Futagawa, *Tadao Ando, GA Architect*, vol. 2 (Tokyo: A.D.A. Edita, 1993), p. 25.

[8] Yuzuru Tominaga, "Reflections on the Architecture of Tadao Ando" in Dal Co, pp. 510–11.

overlooking the same plaza. From this datum, a third and culminating dog-leg stair connects to the top floor. In this way, all three levels are brought into contact with the water, and hence with its constant slow passage out towards the *oku*, towards a remote and unspecified depth.

In spite of the fact that Ando's work postulates the continued coexistence of the sacred and the profane in the later modern world, in most instances the secular character of his spirituality poses the question: How should we relate his all-but-animistic conception of nature to the institutions that continue to house orthodox traditional religious practices within contemporary Japanese society? This question evokes a similar spirituality that may be found in the work of Mies van der Rohe and in the relationship between Mies and the Catholic Reform movement in Germany during the Weimar Republic, as organized by Romano Guardini and Rudolf Schwarz. In Guardini (a Jesuit priest, philosopher, and theologian who undoubtedly exercised a crucial influence on Mies[10]), I think one may readily recognize the tenor of Mies's secular spirituality, as demonstrated in the following passage from Guardini's *Letters from Lake Como* of 1927, in which he writes:

> We belong to the future. We must put ourselves into it, each one at his station. We must not plant ourselves against the new and attempt to retain a beautiful world, one that must perish. Nor must we try to build, with creative fantasy, a new one that claims to be immune to the ravages of becoming. We have to formulate the nascent. But that we can only do if we honestly say yes to it; yet with incorruptible heart we have to retain our awareness of all that is destructive and inhuman in it. Our time is given to us as a soil on which we stand and as a task we have to master.[11]

As Neumeyer points out, it is obvious that Mies was profoundly influenced by this passage, for in 1930 he himself would write:

> Let us accept changed economic and social conditions as a fact.
>
> All these take their blind and fateful course.
>
> One thing will be decisive: the way we assert ourselves in the face of circumstance. Here the problem of the spirit begins. The important question to ask is not "what" but "how". What goods we produce or what tools we use are not questions of spiritual value. How the question of skyscrapers versus low buildings is settled, whether we build of steel or glass, are unimportant questions from the point of view of the spirit.
>
> Whether we tend to centralization or decentralization in city planning is a practical question, not a question of value. Yet, it is just the question of value that is decisive. We must set up new values, fix our ultimate goals so that we may establish standards.
>
> For what is right and significant for any era—including the new era—is this: to give the spirit the opportunity for existence.[12]

With this passage, of course, we may immediately return to Ando and to a similar but not identical kind of secular spirituality that may be detected in his work. Only now, this stoicism in the face of relentless modernization is overlaid with a subtle critical cultural discourse opposing the Buddhism and Shintoism of Japan with the still-extant Christianity of the West, irrespective of whether the church in question finds itself situated in the West or the East. We may say that Ando overlays these profoundly different ideologies with a symbolic nature worship that transcends their differences to embrace the predicament of modern man as a whole.

opposite: Water Temple, interior detail

10 Fritz Neumeyer, *The Artless Word: Mies van der Rohe on the Building Art*, trans. Mark Jarzombek (Cambridge, Mass.: MIT Press, 1991), p. 196.

11 Romano Guardini, *Briefe vom Comer See* (Mainz, 1927), p. 93, quoted in Neumeyer, p. 199.

12 Ludwig Mies van der Rohe, "The New Era" in Philip Johnson, *Mies van der Rohe*, 3rd ed. (New York: Museum of Modern Art, 1978), p. 195.

TEMPLES OF LIGHT   DIANA ECK

I should confess at the outset that I am an architect's daughter. I grew up in the mountains of Montana, and later on trekked into the Himalayas to visit its sacred shrines. The mountains give us a particular perspective on sacred space—its grandeur, its immediacy, and at the same time its transcendence of frame. I discovered early on the framing function of architecture: that it is often only through the lens of architecture that we are able to orient ourselves to the grandeur. It is through the windows that we are able to see in ways our unfettered gaze cannot comprehend. Architects do not, in that sense, construct the sacred. How could anyone do that? But they do enable us to see it, and in that sense architecture is a revelatory art. It is training the eye to see, training the soul to deep seeing. Of course, this is among the most important of religious disciplines, and architects and artists have always been visionaries. "Will God indeed dwell on the earth?" asks Solomon in I Kings. "Behold heaven and the highest heavens cannot contain thee. How much less this temple I have built. But your eyes may be open to this place and your name shall be there."

Waterfront of Banaras
(Varanasi)

Light has been architecturalized in many ways in shaping sacred space and invoking the ineffable. My own work has been on the sacred geography of India, looking at the places where the divine is said to be manifest, either by natural hierophany or by human creation and design. The Hindu vocabulary used to convey the intersections of life with the ineffable might be useful here. The term used in the Hindu context for what we might speak of as "sacred space" is *tirtha*, meaning "ford": a place where one crosses over from this shore to the far shore, from this world to the beyond. A *tirtha* might be a hilltop, or the meeting of two rivers, or a rock outcropping. A temple is a *tirtha* by design and construction. In visiting a *tirtha*, one might use a term like "worship," *puja*, but by far the more common term is one that would appeal to the soul of the architect, the term *darshan*, which simply means "seeing," beholding the Divine as present in that place.[1] One goes to a temple to take *darshan*, to see. In introducing the vocabulary with which I work, let me add a third term: the *jyotirlinga*, the manifestation of light, the hierophany of the

light that is so spectacularly demonstrated in the temples and landscape of India.

My work in India has explored the meanings of sacred space, beginning with the city of Banaras (also known as Varanasi), one of the most famous of the hundreds of thousands of *tirthas* of India.[2] Some of these places are, like Banaras, literally crossing places on the banks of rivers that have attracted pilgrims for hundreds of years. Pilgrims find there the quality of the luminous place, the place where the membrane that somehow separates us from the divine is thinner—there, prayers are more quickly heard, there the heavens are somehow more immediately accessible. The most important Hindu name for the city is Kashi, literally the "City of Light," the place where the light shines. It is one of the twelve *jyotirlingas* of Lord Shiva, or manifestations of divine light: the luminous emblems of the supreme Lord. Pilgrims also climb into the mountains for the *darshan* of Shiva at another of these *jyotirlingas*, Kedarnath, a stone temple open only a few months a year. While there is a Shiva *linga*, really a rocky outcropping,

[1] Diana L. Eck, *Darshan: Seeing the Divine Image in India*, 3rd edition (New York: Columbia University Press, 1998).

[2] Diana L. Eck, *Banaras, City of Light* (New York: Alfred A. Knopf, 1982).

in the inner sanctum of the temple, the *darshan* of Shiva is also in the surrounding landscape, where the five faces of Shiva are said to be manifest.

As Karsten Harries puts it in his essay in this volume, there is a kind of descent of the sacred into the visible, a descent of the ineffable into the world of nature. This is what is evoked in the landscape of India's *tirthas*. Actually, the obverse of the term *tirtha* is *avatara*, literally the "descent" of the Divine from heaven to earth. The River Ganga, for example, descends from the highest heavens into this world. As the river of heaven, she streams across the sky as the Milky Way, then plummets to earth, landing high in the mountains where Lord Shiva catches her in the tangled locks of his ascetic's hair. Even today, pilgrims make their way to Gangotri in the Himalayas, where the river of heaven is said to have her earthly source. A temple is there, to be sure. There is even an image of the goddess Ganga in the temple, but the profound sanctity of this *tirtha* is to be found in the water itself, its torrents carving and smoothing the stone of the mountain canyons. Here, at the time of the evening *arati*, when the lamps of offering are lifted to the Ganga, they are really lifted toward the river herself.

There are literally thousands of *tirthas* in India, many in places that do not have much of a built environment at all—like the great slab of Sharika Devi in Kashmir, where people affirm the power and presence of the Divine in this natural manifestation of stone. These places almost never stand alone, but are part of groups and networks of *tirthas* that cast a landscape of belonging, and create both regional and national identities. Among the *tirthas* I visited and studied in India are the previously mentioned networks of Shiva, the *jyotirlingas*, where the transcendent Shiva is said to be manifest of his own accord as a brilliant hierophany. On the whole these sacred sites are not the famous temple sites of India; not established

top: Sunrise over the River Ganga (Ganges) at Banaras

middle: Bather at the River Ganga

bottom: Gangotri in the Himalayas, origin of the River Ganga

by human hands, nor beautifully designed by the architect's imagination, nor supported by the patronage of kings. Rather they are said to be places of divine revelation, where devotees have evoked and experienced the blazing presence of Shiva. Even today, the question of whether the Divine is revealed, or can be revealed, in the modern world is simply not asked by the millions and millions of pilgrims who make their way to these places year after year.

Here, light is seen not as the ambience of seeing but as the icon itself. According to the Hindu myth, at the beginning of creation when the universe was only a quiescent potential, Vishnu and Brahma, two of the great gods, argued about who was the greater: the first, the true creator of all. Suddenly, between them, the ground of the cosmos opened up and a fiery shaft of light rose from the depths below, and extended upward through space as far as the eye could see. This was the *jyotirlinga*, the *linga* of light, a column of fire too brilliant to look at, inexpressible in its glory. The arguing gods were stunned into silence. Vishnu became a boar, and dug deep, deep, deep into the waters and into the mud beneath to find the root and source of this light. Brahma became a wild gander, and flew high up into the sky to find its top. For a hundred thousand years, they say, Vishnu dug down and Brahma flew up, but they could not find the extent of this shaft of light. No source was to be found; no top was to be found. It was truly immeasurable, ineffable. As they returned exhausted, the shaft of light opened and Shiva emerged, four-armed in the formless column of light. The other two bowed down to him.

The theological understanding of Lord Shiva here is the one who cannot be thought but is thought; who cannot be figured, but is figured. He is simultaneously called Nishkala, the one who cannot be seen or formed in any form, and Sakala, the one who emerges with form and face. This is

the play, moving back and forth between the an-iconic and the icon. The *linga* in the sanctum of the temple, they say, is the small representation of that inexpressible light. During the hours of worship in the course of a day, the plain and unadorned stone *linga* is honored by devotees. And then, a face is painted on its surface with sandal paste, eyes are placed upon it, and Lord Shiva is adorned with garlands of flowers and a crown of silver. Both moments of *darshan*—the faceless Shiva and the one who reveals a face—are part of the ritual of worship. While the highest heaven cannot contain Lord Shiva, even so Shiva's eyes are open here in this temple, towards those who would behold the face of the Divine.

Over the centuries, Hindu India has found a multitude of ways to express the language of the ineffable in ritual, thought, and architecture, and to invite us into the inner world of the ineffable. Almost three thousand years ago in the famous "Purusha Sukta," the Hymn to Purusha in the *Rigveda*, the hymnist conjectured that the universe we know is but a quarter of Reality. In another hymn, we are told that all human language is but a quarter of the language there is; the rest is beyond what we can know. There is much that is ineffable, and countless links that flow back and forth from this world to the beyond. In ritual, these links are evoked and enacted.

Architecture in India is a way of constructing and containing "what heaven and the highest heavens cannot contain." A temple, architecturally speaking, is a man-made *tirtha* laid out according to the geometric mandalas of ritual architects, like the plan of the great temples at Khajuraho. A temple is an embodiment of the Divine. The inner "womb chamber," the *garbha griha*, is where the seed, the *garbha*, the embryo of life, is contained. It is often likened to a cave within the mass of the temple. The vertical superstructure rises above it, as a mountain peak rises to the skies over a

Hindu Temple, Calabasas (Malibu), California, 1981

mountain cave. Indeed, the superstructure is called a *shikara*, which literally means "mountain peak." The exterior of the temple is often covered with forms and the *shikara* becomes a mountainscape of small *shikaras*, piled one upon the other, rising towards the heavens.

Inside there really is very little light, except from the entryway. Worshipers approach the inner sanctum through successive circumambulatories, where what light there is casts diffuse illumination. But always, the most sacred space is the dark *garbha griha*, where very little light can penetrate, and only at certain times of day.

While a *tirtha* can be self-manifested in nature, it can also be designed and made. Indeed, *tirthas* have become part of the architectural landscape of the United States. There is one right outside Boston in Ashland, for example, designed by ritual architects according to the architecture of the divine body. Laid out geometrically, it became Boston's first purpose-built temple, and was consecrated in 1990. One of the first in the country was the Sri Venkateswara Temple in Pittsburgh, dedicated in 1978, followed by a similar temple in Calabasas (near Malibu), built in 1981. Such temples begin with a ritual invoking the earth and laying out their orientation and cardinal directions, making them microcosms of the world.

The temple is consecrated by rites that take place at the very oldest of Hindu altars, the brick fire altar. Centuries before there was any such thing as a Hindu temple, it was the locus of worship. Here, fire is kindled and into its flames priests make offerings of seeds, fruits, oil, honey, spices, and other material representations of the creation. Fire, personified as Agni, is invoked through hours of Vedic chants, and that power transferred into hundreds of pots of water used to sprinkle the temple towers. After days of ritual work at the fire altars, the priests circle the temple bearing the water pots, ride the hydraulic hoist to the roof of the temple, and climb the scaffolding to pour the water over the temple towers. Having sanctified this architectural "body," they pour the sacred waters over the images of the gods within the temple sancta as well.

American Hindu temples have grown through the past three decades, and their structures gradually adapted to the American landscape and climate. The open-air circumambulatories of South Indian temples have yielded to fully enclosed temple spaces with occasional skylights. The transplanting of religious communities to the U.S. means transformation of memory, transformation of space, and the creation of new forms of sacred architecture. Scholars of architecture as well as religion must ask how traditions of constructing the sacred develop in a new place. Answers for such a fascinating study are to be found in the emergence of the new purpose-built American synagogues, Vietnamese Buddhist temples, Islamic centers and mosques, and Sikh *gurdwaras*.

A number of the projects discussed in this volume (e.g., Richard Meier's Jubilee Church, or Tadao Ando's Church of the Light, Church on the Water, and Buddhist Water Temple) each have a wide ecumenical sensibility that is not about the lowest common denominator, but rather the highest reaches of the ineffable. They play deliberately on light as an icon and image, though in different ways. Of course, the play of light and darkness has a long tradition of expression in the architecture of the Christian West. However, in the spaces we have explored here, light is not simply what illumines the cathedral interior, the icon, or the stained glass window. Light is itself the icon in a way that strikes me as remarkably similar to the iconic light of the great *jyotirlingas* of India. There is theological content here that is profoundly universal, drawing on the image of Christ as the light that the darkness has not overcome. In Buddhist terms, it is the light of enlightenment that makes us realize that we have been in darkness all along, and now we can see, as if for the first time.

It is little wonder that architects who work and play with the materialization of light have been some of today's real visionaries. If the Divine is everywhere, why build a temple at all? Why build a church? Light, too, is everywhere. It is reflected and refracted in a thousand vessels of water, for example. So why build a temple to refract the light of a thousand suns? But will that diffuse light, which is everywhere, kindle a piece of paper lying on the ground? No, it's only when the lens is ground and brings the light to focus that it leaps into flame. And so it is with any beautiful temple of light: through the creation of architecture, it becomes a *tirtha*.

VISIONARIES OR LUNATICS?
ARCHITECTS OF SACRED SPACE,
EVEN IN OUTER SPACE

JAIME LARA

There was but one universal feeling of surprise and alarm. Was it possible to go to the aid of these bold travelers? No! For they had placed themselves beyond the pale of humanity, by crossing the limits imposed by the Creator on his earthly creatures . . . Two hypotheses come here into our consideration. Either the attraction of the moon will end by drawing them into itself, and the travelers will attain their destination; or, the projectile, following an immutable law, will continue to gravitate round the moon till the end of time.

— Jules Verne, *From the Earth to the Moon* (1865)

Architects are a strange lot; they shoot for the stars. As an historian of architecture and art, it has always struck me that they appear to be preoccupied with the business of innovation and constructing the future. They aspire to be the high priests of Futurism, and of Progress writ large. One acute observer has called modern architects "seismographs of the yet to come."[1] Like the hero in Jules Verne's novel or the intrepid crew of the starship Enterprise, they desire, in terms of the built environment, "to boldly go where no one has gone before." But when it comes to the design of overtly religious buildings—sacred spaces as we call them—their challenges are astronomical. How can anyone in his or her right mind even attempt to construct the indescribable, the unspeakable, the unutterable, or the "ineffable," to use the enigmatic title of this collection of essays? Religious clients expect the architect to provide hospitable shelter and form for their worship experiences; they may sometimes ask for beauty in addition to utility, as illusive as that term is. But they often ask the architect to do even more: to be a futurist and a visionary, and to articulate their communal beliefs, audacious hopes, and deepest dreams as well. If so, then what are architects charged to speak, utter, or describe, if not that which most religious communities have come to define by the highly charged word "mystery"?

[1] See François Burkhart et al., "The Architect as Seismograph and the Mediation of Architecture" in *Sensing the Future: The Architect as Seismograph*, Sixth International Architecture Exhibition, Venice (Milan: Electa, 1996), unpaginated section.

right: Giovanni Battista Piranesi, *Carceri d'invenzione*, "The Smoking Fire," 1750

far right: Étienne-Louis Boullée, project for a cenotaph for Isaac Newton, 1784, night view, elevation

[2] My inspiration for this topic has been a seminal article by a mentor: John W. Cook, "Visionary Church Architecture," *Reflections* 81, no. 3 (Yale Divinity School, 1984), pp. 17–24.

[3] Christian Werner Thomsen, *Visionary Architecture: From Babylon to Virtual Reality* (New York: Prestel, 1994).

[4] The theological importance of the imagination is addressed in several recent studies, among them Paul Avis, *God and the Creative Imagination: Metaphor, Symbol and Myth in Religion and Theology* (London: Routledge, 1999) and John Pfordresher, *Jesus and the Emergence of a Catholic Imagination* (New York: Paulist Press, 2008), esp. pp. 1–77.

[5] The culmination of this mechanical interest is best represented by the dictum of Le Corbusier: "A house is a machine to live in."

[6] The author (presumed to be Francesco Colonna, a friar of dubious reputation) was obsessed by architecture, and the book's 174 woodcuts are a primary source for Renaissance ideas on both buildings and gardens. See *Hypnerotomachia Poliphili: The Strife of Love in a Dream*, trans. by Jocelyn Godwin (London: Thames & Hudson, 2003).

[7] Boullée's fellow countrymen, Claude-Nicolas Ledoux (1736–1806) and Jean-Jacques Lequeu (1757–1825), should also be considered in this visionary vein.

[8] See Stewart Johnson and Ray Leonard, "Evolution of Concepts for Lunar Bases," in *Lunar Bases and Space Activities of the 21st Century*, ed. by W. W. Mendel (Houston, Texas: Lunar and Planetary Institute, 1985), pp. 47–56.

One of the neglected themes in regards to the topic of sacred space is visionary architecture.[2] There is, of course, a long and noble tradition of visionary architecture. It is often unbuilt and sometimes unbuildable. One writer, for example, has been able to trace the origins of visionary architecture from the ancient Near East to modern computer-generated reality.[3] To be sure, all great architecture can be considered the result of a visionary experience in the mind's eye, the human capacity of the imagination—something that makes us distinct from other mammals on this planet. In theological terms, Thomas Aquinas, the thirteenth-century Dominican friar, defined the imagination as a divinely given "faculty of the human soul" with which the individual person is infused at conception.[4] But in the case of architectural visionaries, that soul-faculty appears to be frequently on overdrive.

Visionary architecture has been linked to the metamorphosis of the machine, in the widest sense of the word.[5] It could be said to have taken a significant step at the end of the fifteenth century with the mechanical dreams of Leonardo da Vinci, and with the publication of Francesco Colonna's *Hypnerotomachia Poliphili* with their fantastic pavilions and gardens of love.[6] But it exploded in the eighteenth century with the Venetian, Giovanni Battista Piranesi, and the Parisian, Étienne-Louis Boullée.[7]

It is in the visionary architecture of Étienne Boullée that we come closest to science fiction—indeed, one has to ask if his megastructures did not influence his fellow countryman, the sci-fi novelist Jules Verne (1828–1905). Verne culled the facts he needed for his writing from long sessions in the Bibliothèque Nationale, poring over various reference books, scientific magazines, and probably Boullée's otherworldly draftsmanship. In so doing, he came to envision the possibility of incorporating all this documentation into a new and innovative type of novel whose narrative format would simultaneously blend fiction with fact (like visionary architecture) and literary motifs with scientific data. In 1863 Verne's *Cinq semaines en ballon* (Five Weeks in a Balloon) appeared, the first of a series called *Les Voyages Extraordinaires*, and in 1865 his *De la Terre à la Lune* (From the Earth to the Moon) was published. Although fictional, this work is held to be one of the great imaginitive influences on the twentieth century's Space Age, and the rush by Americans and Russians to conquer outer space.[8] (Verne even predicted that the best place from which

Jules Verne, *De la Terre
à la Lune*, 1865

to launch his space projectile, carrying three astronauts like the 1968 Apollo Eight lunar mission, would be Florida.[9]) While Verne was no architect, his engineering creations do demonstrate his acute observation of the emerging technologies of the day and their association with utopian ideals.[10]

Such an extraterrestrial instinct has probably had some part to play in all visionary architecture, from the heavenward-looking ziggurats of Babylon to the cyber-spatial designs of today, and it manifests itself especially in utopian moments.[11] It is no secret, for example, that Futurism—as imagination, philosophy and creed—was a driving force behind the Space Race.[12] It also took popular and concrete form for the masses (and for Cold War world leaders like Nikita Khrushchev and Dwight Eisenhower) in Walt Disney's "Tomorrowland" in Anaheim, California, with its Monorail and Space Needle.[13] As construction began on Disneyland in 1954, the founding father of the theme park proclaimed: "Tomorrow can be a wonderful age. Our scientists today are opening the doors of the Space Age to achievements that will benefit our children and generations to come … The Tomorrowland attractions have been designed to give you an opportunity to participate in adventures that are a living blueprint of our future."[14]

Several architectural icons of Futurism followed closely on the heels of Disney's Tomorrowland, notably the Capitol Records building in Los Angeles (1956), the Theme Building of the Los Angeles International Airport (1961), the Trans World Airlines building at Idlewild (now John F. Kennedy) International Airport in New York (1962), and the Space Needle for the World's Fair in Seattle (1963). But no project was so completely futuristic and so totally surrealistic as the Federal District of Brasilia, Brazil (1960).[15] There, Oscar Niemeyer (1907–) used Antonio Sant'Elia's principle of oblique and elliptic lines to create a stunning Metropolitan Cathedral, a dynamic parabolic

[9] Jules Verne, *From the Earth to the Moon* (New York: Charles Scribner's Sons, 1890), chapter XI.

[10] See the many articles in *The Jules Verne Encyclopedia*, ed. by Brian Taves & Stephen Michaluk, Jr. (Lanham, MD.: Scarecrow Press, 1996).

[11] See Thomsen, *Visionary Architecture*; and Neil Spiller, *Visionary Architecture: Blueprints of the Modern Imagination* (London: Thames & Hudson, reprint 2008).

[12] Spiller, *Visionary Architecture*, pp. 70–97.

[13] In one of the more surreal moments in the history of the Cold War, Soviet leader Nikita Khrushchev exploded with anger when he learned that he was barred from visiting Disneyland on September 19, 1959, during a tour of Los Angeles. He was particularly interested in seeing Tomorrowland.

[14] See Greil Marcus et al., *The Architecture of Reassurance: Designing Disney's Theme Parks* (New York: Abbeville Press, 1997). Several of the architects who attended this conference have done work for Walt Disney Enterprises.

[15] Architects for the projects: Capitol Records, Welton Becket; Theme Building LAX, James Langenheim; TWA building, Eero Saarinen; and Seattle Space Needle, Victor Steinbrueck and John Graham. On Brasilia, see Richard J. Williams, *Surreal City: The Case of Brasilia, Surrealism and Architecture* (New York: Routledge, 2005), pp. 234–48.

Disneyland, Anaheim, California, 1955, entrance to Tomorrowland

tent of concrete, cables, and stained glass.[16] Four bronze sculptures of the Gospel writers, each three meters high, greet the visitor and direct a path to a hidden portal. The building is partially buried in the earth, and the entrance ramp takes one down to a dim subterranean narthex, which then transitions to the light-filled, submarine-like experience of the circular nave. Blue, aqua, and brown glass membranes hover overhead via tension cables which add stability to the ninety-ton ribs forming the hyperboloid tent. Other cables suspend three bronze archangels above the worshipers.[17] The Brasilia Cathedral is one of the few true icons of twentieth-century sacred space.

Niemeyer's visionary design was aided by the engineering experiments of Frei Otto on lightweight structures and tensile architecture.[18] In the 1950s and 1960s, Otto and his colleagues at the Institute for Lightweight Structures in Stuttgart were experimenting with parabolic, tent-like canopies stretched on steel cables—much like the Mexican, Felix Candela, who was then building churches with thin hyperboloid roofs of reinforced concrete.[19] During the same decade, Marcel Breuer followed in Candela's footsteps with the soaring, concrete bell-screen of St. John's Abbey, Collegeville, Minnesota (1953). And Buckminster Fuller was showing off the technology of the geodesic dome and developing his concept of "Spaceship Earth": the world as a limited machine with limited resources.[20] Fuller's space-frame engineering breakthrough allowed Philip Johnson to use the technology to maximum advantage in the Garden Grove Crystal Cathedral of 1980. It is no wonder then, that when it came to religious buildings, visionary architects of the second half of the twentieth century gave us nontraditional forms as they pondered the future of sacred space, even to the point of designing a chapel for *outer* space.

The November 1967 issue of *Liturgical Arts*, an avant-garde journal that propagated the religious

[16] A *New York Times* article of December 12, 2007 by Tom Dyckhoff called Niemeyer "the king of curves."

[17] Niemeyer's influence (at age 103) continues in the twenty-first century as younger architects such as Frank Gehry and Norman Foster stretch their buildings into ever more mind-binding shapes.

[18] See Frei Otto, ed., *Tensile Structures: Design, Structure, and Calculation of Buildings of Cables, Nets, and Membranes* (Cambridge, Mass.: MIT Press, 1973), vol. 2, pp. 15–89. One of the early proponents of tensile architecture was Eero Saarinen.

[19] Candela was born in Spain, but was nationalized in Mexico.

[20] Fuller's most notable building was the glass hemisphere for the United States Pavilion at the 1967 Montreal World's Fair; Frei Otto's German Pavilion, a tensile structure, also debuted there. On Fuller's "Spaceship Earth" concept, see Ian Tod and Michael Wheeler, *Utopia* (London: Orbis, 1978), pp. 146–47.

above: Oscar Niemeyer, Metropolitan Cathedral,
Brasilia, Brazil, 1960, exterior

left: Metropolitan Cathedral, interior

Roy Scarfo, "Colony on the Moon,"
Liturgical Arts, 36/1, 1967; Mark
Mills' Doman Moon Chapel is at
center of colony at 8A

works of architects like Breuer, Le Corbusier, and van der Rohe among progressive Christians, was dedicated to the theme of space exploration and religious art.[21] (In the same year, 1967, Oscar Niemeyer's Brasilia Cathedral was finally consecrated, and Buckminster Fuller's geodesic bubble appeared at the Canadian Expo.) Two years before NASA's Apollo Eleven mission landed on the moon, and Neil Armstrong announced "one giant leap for mankind," a young architect from California by the name of Mark Mills designed a chapel to be built under the lunar crust by the year 2000.[22] The ideology of the proposed project was further developed in the same journal by the Reverend Terence Mangan, who saw a future moon base as the perfect form of contemporary monasticism. The project was named after the Prior of the Camaldolese monastery near Monterey, California, Father Emeric Doman, a friend of the architect.[23] (The late Mark Mills was a follower of Frank Lloyd Wright at Taliesin. He left Wright's employ, together with Paolo Soleri, and the two later cooperated on vernacular commissions in California where they often employed thin poured-concrete shells, like those of Felix Candela.)

In Mills' design, within a concrete manufactured cave, a tent-like structure would be suspended on cables from a ring set in the moon's crust, defining sacred space and providing visual privacy. The moon's gravity is one-sixth that of Earth, but the engineering principles of a tensile structure there would be practically the same.[24] An alternative to traditional compression structures is to build with flexible materials and the force of tension, rather than compression; and the simplest of these is the membrane structure. Tents, of course, are an ancient form of human shelter, and they cross all geographic and ethnic lines, appearing on all continents.[25] They also have particular importance to Jews and Christians, because they appear so often in the Bible.[26] The patriarchs lived in tents, as did the wandering tribes of Israel after the Exodus; even God himself dwelt in a desert tabernacle for forty years like a great nomadic sheik. Saint Paul was a tent-maker by profession and supported his ministry with that trade; and the opening lines of the Gospel of John imply that the incarnate God continues to be a tent-dweller on the move: "In the beginning was the Word, and the Word was with God, and the Word was God . . . And the Word became flesh and pitched his tent among us." (John 1:14)

In early nineteenth-century America, Methodists developed the classic tent-meeting revivals. "Tenting Tonight on the Old Camp Grounds," originally a Civil War song of soldiers, was adapted to be used on those evangelistic occasions in the woods.[27]

In the same century, a new religious utopian group arose, the Latter Day Saints. The Mormons attempted to erect a Canvas Tabernacle in Nauvoo, Illinois, in 1844, but were prevented from doing so by persecution.[28] They were finally able to construct a huge wooden, lattice-trussed tent, known today as

[21] Terence J. Mangan, "The Doman Moon Chapel," *Liturgical Arts* 36, no.1 (1967), pp. 3–9. The issue also contained an editorial on the subject (p.1), and related articles: Clifford Stevens, "The Cosmic Adventure: A Challenge to Theology," p. 10; Constance Parvey, "Moon People's Liturgy," pp. 11–12; T.W. Adams, "The Impact of the Space Program," pp. 12–13; and a musical setting of Psalm 19 by Johannes Somary, p. 14. Sadly, the journal *Liturgical Arts* is now defunct.

[22] Mills developed his project from an earlier master's thesis by William R. Sims at Princeton University; Sims later joined Walt Disney Imagineering as Vice President of Architecture and Facilities Engineering. On Mark Mills, see the *Journal of the Taliesin Fellows*, no.10 (Spring 1993), and http://www.janeybennett.com/taliesin.html (last consulted 11/08). His domestic projects are covered in Alan Hess, *Forgotten Modern: California Houses 1940–1970* (Layton, UT.: Gibbs Smith, 2007).

[23] The Camaldolese hermits are part of the Benedictine family of monastic communities. They became independent from the Benedictines at the turn of the first millennium. In the United States their motherhouse is at Big Sur, California.

[24] As point of fact, NASA is now testing inflatable buildings for a moon base which are based on the pneumatic structures that Frei Otto designed in *Tensile Structures*, vol. 1. See http://www.universetoday.com/2008/02/09/building-a-base-on-the-moon-part-2-habitat-concepts/.

[25] On the history of tensile architecture, see E. M. Hatton, *The Tent Book* (Boston: Houghton Mifflin, 1979), pp. 3–112.

[26] On tents in the Bible, see Hatton, *The Tent Book*, pp. 5–10.

[27] The hymn, by Walter Kittredge, first appeared in the *Union Songbook* of 1861.

[28] Joseph Smith, Jr., *History of The Church of Jesus Christ of Latter-Day Saints*, ed. B. H. Roberts, 2nd ed. rev., 7 vols. (Salt Lake City: Deseret News, 1932–1951), vol 6: p. 302. Four thousand yards of canvas were purchased for the roof, which was to be approximately 250 feet long and 125 feet wide. The fabric did not go to waste; it was used for tents and covered wagons during the exodus of the Mormons westward.

The Tabernacle, in Salt Lake City (1864–1867); its original purpose was as a meetinghouse.

For Roman Catholics, the theological notion of the Church as the People of God on pilgrimage through time and space was very current at mid-twentieth century, and officially articulated in a doctrinal decree at the Second Vatican Council.[29] Oscar Niemeyer's concrete-and-glass Catholic tabernacle in Brasilia is an outstanding example of that tenting theology in stone.

———————

The lunar colonists of the future were envisioned as modern Bedouins caravanning about the bleak, desert-like moonscape on mechanical rovers and mining equipment[30]; but the proposed religious edifice would have classical references as well. In Mills' chapel, the ring and its oculus act as a solar eye filtering the only natural (sun) light into the worship place. Like the solar oculus of the Roman Pantheon—which was consecrated in 610 CE with little change as the church of Santa Maria Rotonda—the diaphragm and sweeping interior of the tent pulls the eye of the worshipper sunward and points the way home.[31] The lens permits "observation of the celestial bodies [which] reminds man of God's spatial infinity in contrast to the moon's ghetto environment."[32] Pressure, temperature extremes, and the elements do not exist here. The chapel, a film-sheathed tent defining sacred space in a subterranean space in outer space, provides visual privacy in a communal cavern where little privacy exists. Floors, ramps, and monastery mezzanine are of reinforced concrete or hardened moon dust (called regolith).

The Moon Chapel is similar in some ways to Oscar Niemeyer's cathedral for Brasilia, not only in its conical-elliptical shape, but also in the fact that the chapel's footing is recessed six feet into the cavern floor.[33] Here it permits spaces between the load-bearing piers to be left open and provide views into a terraced garden. A plant-covered bank provides visual privacy within the chapel and mutes outside noises, that is, those of the moon laborers. Above the chapel, a freestanding mezzanine provides living space for the staff. The mezzanine is accessible by a bridge over the chapel entry ramp.

This sacred space, complete with baptistery and confessionals, would be staffed by contemplative monk-psychologists. These clergy, who would have exchanged their habits for space suits, were to live in the adjacent monastery and its subterranean cloister and offer psychological counseling for those under lunar stress. They and their troglodyte parishioners would be space pilgrims with a sense of a larger journey through time and the heavens. The companion articles in this issue of *Liturgical Arts* also included examples of lunar art that might be created for the chapel, like a lightweight cast aluminum sculpture: "Our Lady of the Moon."

———————

How things have changed since the 1960s! We might look back on those Vietnam Era dreamers as lunatics. Our world is vastly different from that day in 1968 when Neil Armstrong planted the first footprint on lunar soil. In the Kennedy Years it was still a male-dominated world, where space*men* were envisioned as interplanetary conquistadors, oblivious to the ecological damage of strip-mining outer space. What would ecological groups like Greenpeace make of the destruction of such virgin territory now? What would today's secular-scientific community make of such an ecclesial enterprise?[34] What would the religious leaders of Jewish, Islamic, Buddhist, Hindu or Bahá'í communities make of a Christian chapel on the moon—and not only a Christian chapel, but a chapel of one particular denomination of

[29] See *Lumen Gentium*, chapter 9. It was earlier articulated by Pius XII in his Apostolic Constitution, *Munificentissimus Deus*, 1 November 1950.

[30] See Isaac Asimov, "Is 'Space 1999' More Fi than Sci?," *The New York Times*, Sept. 28, 1975, sect. 2: p. 1. The graphic artist was Roy Sarfo.

[31] Presumably, the chapel would be constructed on the near side of the moon which, although it rotates, always faces earth. The oculus would receive sunlight during the brighter phases of the moon.

[32] Mangan, "The Doman Moon Chapel," p. 5.

[33] The Metropolitan Cathedral was already seven years old.

[34] Unbeknown to the general populace is the fact that Buzz Aldrin, a devout Presbyterian, took Holy Communion along with him on the historic first moon landing in July 1969 and received it there in a private religious service. See Buzz Aldrin, *Return to Earth* (New York: Random House, 1973), pp. 232–33.

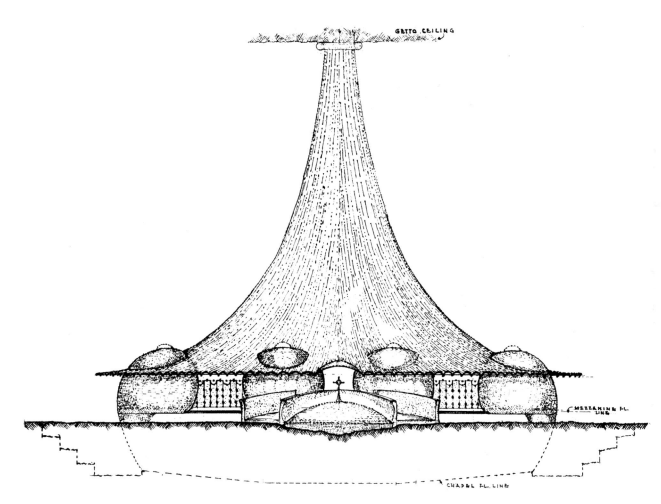

Marks Mills, Doman
Moon Chapel, 1967,
elevation

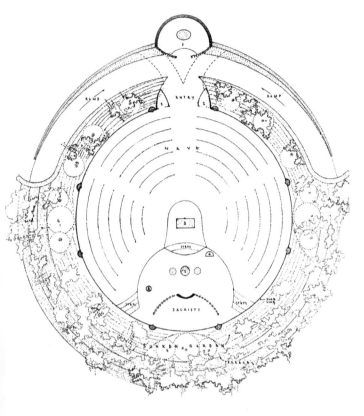

Ground floor plan

1 Baptistry
2 Confessionals
3 Altar
4 Lectern
5 Celebrant's chair
6 Tabernacle

above left: Doman Moon
Chapel, ground floor plan

above right: Doman Moon
Chapel, mezzanine plan

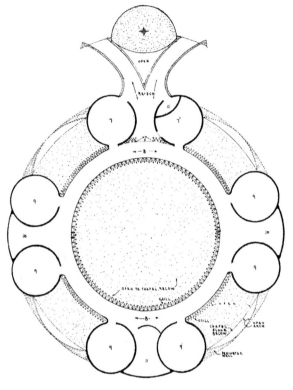

Mezzanine

7 Kitchen, dining space and conference room
8 Gallery
9 Cells for community
10 Studies and library
11 Bath

Christianity at that? Indeed, times have changed and, by implication, architects have to address that changed, and rapidly changing, world.

And yet, the call of the numinous remains. It may no longer be the mysterious face of the "man in the moon," or the pockmarked green cheese of its topography. In sacred buildings, architects are charged with the ineffable task of articulating "mystery"—we could say "Ultimate Mystery." Few faith communities have specified what that means for the built environment, but one particular religious body (the Roman Catholic Church) has attempted to put this into words in its guide for architects and designers:

> The experience of mystery which liturgy offers is found in its God-consciousness and God-centeredness. This involves a certain beneficial tension with the demands of hospitality, requiring a manner and an environment which invite contemplation —seeing beyond the face of the person or the thing, a sense of the holy, the numinous, a sense of mystery .... One should be able to sense something special—and nothing trivial—in everything that is seen and heard, touched and smelled, and tasted in worship.[35]

The preoccupation of twenty-first century architects—either the "grand masters" or the emerging voices—is intimately tied up with the health of our global environment and the fate of humanity. Whether moonstruck or not, they are more than problem-solvers, rather seekers addressing the potential of architecture to answer new spiritual needs, to enter new spiritual territories, and to sense the ineffable in our midst. Their concern is not to explore *outer* space, but rather the *inner* space of twenty-first century pilgrims on planet Earth, answering the call of Ultimate Mystery. As Terence Riley has put it:

> A century or two centuries from now our complex times will, rightly or wrongly, be remembered in much reduced terms. The artists and architects who will be considered as having been true sensors of the future will be those who, for reasons which are unverifiable today, were most correct in evaluating the political, cultural and economic factors of this historical moment. That we cannot really know, ultimately, whether we are moving forward or backward does not in any way diminish the necessity for the artist and architect to declare a position beyond the fashions of the day, whether it be motivated by a rational analysis, intuitive conviction or, even, a gambler's sense.[36]

The pressing question is, in the realm of religious buildings and sacred monuments, will architects be mere weather vanes of taste or seismographs of deep rumblings and things to come?

"Space: the final frontier . . ." Sacred Space: the ultimate frontier.

[35] *Environment and Art in Catholic Worship* (Washington, D.C.: Bishops' Committee on the Liturgy, 1978). Proceedings from the National Conference of Catholic Bishops, para 12.

[36] Terence Riley, "Of Seismographs and Weather Vanes," in *Sensing the Future*, un-paginated section.

PART III

PERSPECTIVES: CONTEMPORARY EXPRESSIONS
OF THE INEFFABLE

INTRODUCTION

With the more conceptual and historical essays of the previous two sections
in the background, this third section gathers reflections from contemporary
architects on their own engagement with the challenge of constructing sacred
space. The responses are remarkably self-reflective, expressing both the sense
of personal responsibility the architects felt in receiving a commission for such
a work, and the struggle to develop an adequate response to it.

Several themes stand out. First, the projects discussed here represent a clear diversity of perspective on what may be considered "sacred" and, by implication, what is or is not "profane": religious buildings (of course) are considered as sacred, but also museums, memorials, and even an eco-resort. In some cases, the cultural significance of the project evokes real doubt on the part of the architect, or a deep search for the means of connecting to the affective side of human experience. Some essays remark on the essentially personal nature of symbolic associations, which resists the enforcement of any particular narrative of sacrality that the architect might try to impose. As a result, many essays appeal to the abstractions of light, emptiness, and silence as the only effective media through which to explore the sacred. In some instances, the architect feels a deep personal, even existential identification with the intention of the project, while in other cases the architect acknowledges an emotional or intellectual distance.

Throughout, there is an implicit dialogical relationship with the client, for beyond any defined liturgical or representational program, a work of sacred architecture challenges the architect to render in plastic form that which cannot be conceptually described. Within this dialogue, many of the projects explore ways of rethinking traditional building typologies, inverting and subverting many common assumptions about the nature of sacred buildings. The relationality between client and architect also occasionally spills over to the relationship between architect and worker in the constructional act itself, when they are together conscious of seeking a transcendence that exceeds any individual's imagination of it. In this regard, the constructive materiality of these projects becomes a focus of great concern, as questions of continuity and rupture, technology and craft, temporality and permanence enter into the totality of the creative enterprise. Moreover, many of the projects are overt interventions into the situational environment in which they are located, whether urban centers, suburban developments, or college campuses. In these instances, the architects are keenly aware of the impact that the project is intended to have beyond its specifically sacred identity in shaping larger social groups and communities.

All of this is to say that the reflections in this section collectively offer a complex portrait of what might be called (after the literary critic Edward Said)[1] the "working reality" of the architect: the practical and theoretical competence through which one approaches a task as laden with contradiction and abstraction as constructing the ineffable.

[1] Edward Said, "Conrad: The Presentation of Narrative," in *The World, the Text and the Critic* (Cambridge, Mass.: Harvard University Press, 1983), p. 90.

THE TRIBE VERSUS THE CITY-STATE: A CONUNDRUM FOR THE JEWISH PROJECT

STANLEY TIGERMAN

The millennium arrived and so did a commission to design a three-part museum, memorial, and education center for the Holocaust Memorial Foundation of Illinois. My own memory of the Holocaust is from a time when I was growing up in Chicago, having neither the capacity to process the information nor an identity sufficient to contend with the reality of what was happening in Europe. I was fourteen when the death camps were liberated, and yet all I did was to distance myself from what I saw in newsreels and read about in newspaper articles, treating the information much as I did other information by which I was educated.

One is told that a professional needs distance to perform professionally; I prefer John Hejduk's contention that "architecture is a passionate pursuit." When I have seen elderly Holocaust survivors tear up as they witnessed the Illinois museum's construction—especially on the day that the German WWII boxcar was brought to the site—I have empathized, but I can never entirely comprehend the resonance of that response. Nonetheless, I felt the need to embed as much content and syntax as possible into the work, as if I had personally witnessed the unspeakable horror firsthand, so as to reach out to others who will one day visit the museum and who, like me, can only be secondhand witnesses.

Stanley Tigerman, Illinois Holocaust Museum & Education Center, Skokie, Illinois, 2009, showing vintage 1934 German boxcar held within the cleave of the building

I was not the only one who felt the need to present thematic materials powerfully. In discussions held with Holocaust survivors, their determination not to gloss over anything that might otherwise be presented in its most direct, albeit brutal, form astonished yet gratified me. Whether it was the exposition of orthotic or prosthetic devices, or even the display of human hair, the survivor community expressed great courage in demanding that the Holocaust be presented precisely in the way that they had experienced—and survived—it.

Paralleling the eight-year effort that it took to build the museum, I refreshed my memory about the many ways the Nazis conspired to relieve Europe entirely of Jews and their culture, as well as the Jews' history from those countries controlled by the Third Reich. During my research, I came across literature that addressed the synapse between Jewish tribal customs and European nationalism.

In particular, I was intrigued by Robert Pinsky's 2005 treatise, *The Life of David*, on King David's impact not only during his own epoch, which is recorded in the Bible, but on how he influenced modern life as it segued from nomadic tribal customs to systems elaborating on the idea of the City-State. Pinsky discusses David's initiation of a census and conscription, both of which frightened tribal constituencies. He writes about "measurement," and he raises questions about the shift to tribal coalition as a result of David's envisioning the First Temple and the City-State that followed it.

Measurement comes about as a result of "counting" (the work of the devil, since it was Satan who incited David to do it). King David focused on this so that he could produce a census, the fear of which was related to tribal anxieties about taxation and conscription and other strictures that might

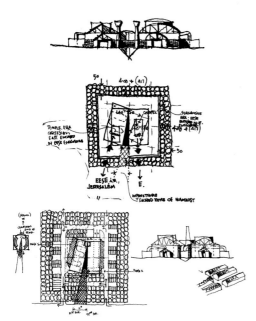

above left: Conceptual sketch

right: Study model

institutionalize and complicate nomadic life. Even in the New Testament (Luke 2:1-5), Joseph and Mary were reluctantly counted for purposes of taxation. Taxation notwithstanding, by first counting the foreskins of his vanquished enemies, King David initiated other acts of quantification so as to effectuate his dream of transitioning from being the perpetual "outsider" to that of an "insider," by envisioning a Sacred City: a home.

Fast forwarding to the twentieth century, with its increasingly migratory population and in the context of the fate of European Jews, I thought it necessary to reassess temporality in order to probe deeper into the Holocaust. After all, my architectural assignment was to address in built form the agony of a constituency that was subject to an evil of such a magnitude as to be virtually indescribable. Since buildings, like bodies, begin to die at birth, the Holocaust Museum could be understood as a metaphor of the transitory condition of life.

If one thinks about the several ways that inertia presents an impasse to building, then concocting a building that is present and accounted for using actualization as a means of measuring accomplishment can be understood as an act of bravery. To conceive of a structure that is not quite so present, and for which there is no accounting, is only more so. My work on the Holocaust Museum is as close as I've come to addressing the slippery quality to which I am alluding.

Denial and *orientation* both played pivotal roles in the biblical tale of the Jews. In Genesis 3:24, for example, we are told that God *denied* Adam and Eve's reentry into the mythic Garden of Eden. The two were repelled by a pair of flaming, sword-wielding *Cherubim* "placed at the East," which is the direction towards which the Bible's first couple are said to have been expelled, and the direction from which a Messiah was expected to emerge. According to Deuteronomy 34:4, Moses led the tribes to the "promised land" in the West, where he was *denied* entry to it himself, finding only death in that direction. The site of Jesus' crucifixion is thought to be in "Golgotha," the site of the Church of the Holy Sepulchre, west of the Temple Mount. Samuel 7:9 states that when David envisioned a "permanent" Temple for the Ark, God *denied* him the opportunity to actualize his dream. Only later would David's son Solomon fulfill his father's vision, according to I Kings 8:18 and 8:19.

The God of the Jews had sent forth his offspring in a particular direction for a purpose, repulsing their many attempts to return West to the comforts of the only home they knew in the Sacred Garden. The only home the Jews would find there was death. The Hebrew phrase *Lech L'cha*, or to "Go Forth" towards the East—towards life—signifies an act of separation as a means of testing one's faith. It strikes one that a Divine Message was being

above: East elevation showing the dark and light buildings and the columns named Jachin and Boaz to represent the columns of the Temple of Solomon

right: Main floor plan

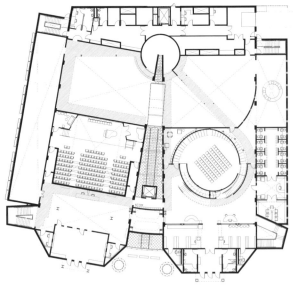

delivered: the God of the Jews didn't countenance a "permanent" home for Himself.

Treated as aliens and ghettoized to make their outsider label permanent, nomads behaved accordingly, clannishly adhering to rituals handed down from earlier eras. The Third Reich interpreted that clannishness as a threat to the German City-State with its unrelenting regulatory systems favoring the Teutonic over the Semitic. As in the time of the inquisition four centuries earlier, there were European Jews who attempted to assimilate into the dominant culture only to find that being counted revealed their religious preference and did them in. An architect commissioned to contend with such a poignant problem by producing an empty vessel to house Holocaust artifacts might understandably go beyond his charge by creating a symbolic container.

———————

The Holocaust Museum & Education Center is an expression of this lack of permanent rootedness in which slippage, or conflict, comes about in the context of a program where poignancy is the overarching theme. This conflict stems from the tribal otherness that came into conflict with the German City-State, whose ethnic cleansing laws reinforced centuries-old antagonism towards a constituency stigmatized as "outsiders" by a particular insider status quo. Those who came to power in Germany in 1932 loathed the minority they considered inferior to their Nietzsche-inspired concept of the "*Übermensch*," and set them up as scapegoats.

Primary among the factors underpinning the Holocaust Museum's conceptual slippage are the two discrete directions that define the cleavage between the Eastern orientation common to agrarian societies (Egyptians, American Indians, and Jews) whose belief in the rising sun is reinforced by a belief in a vision of a Temple, "in anticipation of a Messianic Age" (Ezekiel 43:2), and the rabbinic orientation that situates belief in a location other than the one in which the faithful are situated. For the Muslims, that site is Mecca. For the Jews, it is the Western Wall of the Temple Mount in Jerusalem.

Jerusalem is 5.9 degrees South of East from Skokie, Illinois. The significant otherness, in which one's object of desire is located elsewhere, is akin to a post-structural condition wherein signification is ostensibly absent, but because it pulsates with desire, is virtually if not actually present.

The cleavage that comes about as a result of the two geographically differing orientations produces an *unheimlich*, an uninhabitable space. For the Holocaust Museum, that space is hinged at one end by the skylight-flooded cylindrical Book of Remembrance that lists the names of those lost to the Holocaust. The Book of Remembrance sits above a deportation chamber utterly bereft of light. On the left side of that hinge, one descends downward into the windowless, increasingly darkened museum, which is spanned by raw, clear-lacquered steel sections composing warren trusses. On the right side of the hinge, one ascends into the light of the Education Center, which is open to the rising sun in the East and is spanned by white-painted bowstring steel trusses. Marking that cleavage on the exterior of the museum are palimpsests of Jachin and Boaz, the two columns of Solomon's Temple described in I Kings 5–9, which was evacuated when the Sacred Text was removed from Herod's Temple

With respect to the Eastern, or Temple, orientation, there are two challenges to that ancient focus facing the rising sun. One challenge is theological, the other nationalist. The theological challenge is expressed by the occasional American Reformed Rabbi who holds that an Eastern orientation in anticipation of a Messianic Age is "a

bankrupt concept," in other words, that a perpetually immanent state is pointless. The nationalist challenge held by the occasional Israeli scholar posits that *Messianic Immanence* "denies the existential fact of Jerusalem," as if the Sacred City was itself a Messianic replacement, or perhaps displacement.

In addition to slippage, I felt it necessary to organize the museum visitor's progression throughout the building sequentially, so that there would be no turning back. Virtually every building is entered into and exited from the same location. Thus, one perceives everything first in one direction, and then afterwards in the reverse direction. Not so the Holocaust Museum, where everything follows that which preceded it chronologically so that, as in real time, you exit at a location other than the one you entered. Just as for the victims of the Holocaust—or for that matter, Judaism itself—there is no return, just forward movement towards an unknowable end. In the case of the Holocaust, death (either in the form of death camps or death marches) represented that destination. In the case of Judaism, death—or in Hebrew, *Sheol*, which lay in the West, without the promise of return—awaits the end of life.

With respect to unitary measurement, the secular biblical cubit (nominally eighteen inches)

Hall of Reflection with 18 windows containing *Yahrzeit* candles: the number 18 in Hebrew is *Chai*, which means life. The 12 1x1x1 cubit benches represent the 12 tribes of Israel

Reflecting pool surrounded by plaques honoring the "Righteous," Gentiles who risked their lives to rescue the Jews during World War II

represents the incremental dimension that I used to measure, to internalize, the building. The biblical cubit is in conflict with American or European constructional conventions which are measured in an entirely different way, producing yet another sign of slippage or conflict, which helps to confirm the ambivalent, uneasy state in which a building such as the Holocaust Museum exists, in a culture detached from its mythic biblical origins.

Architecture, as the mother of the arts, is intrinsically abstract. However deeply one may feel about a program, architecture resists emotionally charged values that might otherwise call upon metaphor or metonymy for reification. The nature of the mass that defines architectural space does not suggest something other than what it is, in and of itself. Timber, concrete, metal, and glass do not conjure up forms that are a priori either comforting or confrontational. Thus, even when designing a building like the Holocaust Museum, where the poignancy built into the program is so dramatic, one still must build.

At another level, I chose to expose material and joinery each in its natural, undecorated state. As opposed to the deception employed by those who were responsible for the Holocaust, it seemed important to me to be transparent, to reveal all constructional materials. Thus, the building has the *industrial* look institutionalized by Modernism that expresses (but does not celebrate) structure, ducting, piping, and conduit. The methodology harkens back to an era when industrialization was still novel, establishing the uncompromising look of, among other structures, those six undecorated death camps in Poland: Auschwitz-Birkenau, Belzec, Chelmno, Majdanek, Sobibor, and Treblinka. Given the industrial aesthetic, the choice of materials was necessarily rudimentary, while the near-Baroque spatiality of the museum addresses the yearning of those absent souls whose life was prematurely and abruptly terminated.

above: Detail of dark and light building and one column named Jachin

right: West elevation

opposite: Two stairs around the Hall of Reflection

After eight years of being denied permission by the Village of Skokie to build on one site and then planning and fundraising for a different location, the building is at last finished. The shell and core were completed in early November 2008, coinciding nominally with the seventieth anniversary of "*Kristalnacht*," those late autumn nights in Berlin when Nazi stormtroopers shattered glass storefronts owned by Jewish proprietors, and torched synagogues. As the countdown to completion proceeded, however, attrition relentlessly reduced the Holocaust survivor constituency in Skokie. Finally, the museum opened in April 2009.

In his 2002 book *Abraham*, Bruce Feiler refers to the father of the three Western religions as being "the perpetual stranger in a strange land, the outsider who longs to be the insider, the landless who longs for land, the pious who finds a palliative in God for his endlessly painful life." The tribal nomad, the wandering Jew, who in the twentieth century wandered into a Holocaust of unimaginable proportions by denying the realities of one increasingly unsympathetic City-State, would have been better off to remain an outsider.

JUBILEE CHURCH
(DIO PADRE MISERICORDIOSO), ROME

RICHARD MEIER

In the Book of Genesis, Light is the first of God's creations, after his creation of the heavens and the earth. The hierophany of light is evident in the modern sacred spaces of our time, in Le Corbusier's Notre Dame du Ronchamp, Philip Johnson's Crystal Cathedral, Alvar Aalto's Church of the Three Crosses, Frank Lloyd Wright's Unity Temple. As a student and practitioner of architecture, Rome has always stood for me as a mecca for the most powerful spiritual relationships created by form and light, from the Pantheon to the works of Bramante, Bernini, and Borromini to the sheer mastery of Michaelangelo's *Moses*.

In Rome during the last century this continuum lost pace. The mid-twentieth century saw a massive influx of people relocating to Rome from various parts of the world. This rise in population gave way to the introduction of dense apartment complexes in the 1970s, most of them purely functional and without much aesthetic distinction. The somewhat depressed fringe areas of Rome were overtaken by these complexes, leaving little room for community life, including active churches.

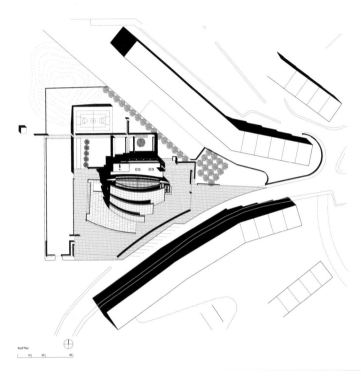

Roof Plan
| 10 | 20 | 40 |

To address this issue, the Vicariato di Roma, the Church of Rome, began an initiative in the mid-1990s known as the "New Evangelization," intended to revitalize parish life in these dormant communities. The plan called for the building of fifty new churches, with attendant community centers, by the year 2000. Two sites in particular were flagged to inaugurate this movement: a church in the Dragoncello district of Acilia, twelve miles southwest of the city's center, and one at Tor Tre Teste, six miles east of Rome. Tor Tre Teste would be a textbook example of one of these languishing exurban pockets of Rome. Settlements arrived in the area in the fourth century CE; the ruins of the Alessandrino Aqueduct frame the site on the south end. In the 1970s a master plan was executed, with apartment complexes occupying two distinct footprints. The two buildings fan out from the triangular site chosen for the new church and community center, creating a frame for the church to anchor the area. In addition, there was a smattering of office buildings, retail spaces, and one supermarket. As the Church of Rome put it: "The location for this church is in the outer periphery of the city where there is an urgent need for welcome from the point of view of the urban landscape, the sociological condition and the pastoral situation. The area is degraded, but could be ennobled with a new edifice, a place of welcome, a place of 'Church' in the fullest sense of the word."

After a discouraging national competition, it was decided that the timeline for these churches would be expanded, and Camillo Ruini, Vicar General of His Holiness for the Diocese of Rome, instructed Monsignor Luigi Moretti to see what interest there might be among distinguished international architects in building churches in Rome. Moretti's inquiries met with a positive response and, at the same time, the dynamic of the "Jubilee Year 2000" brought a new dimension to the development plans. As Pope John Paul II had built

opposite, top: Richard Meier, Jubilee Church, Rome,
Italy, 2003, roof site plan

opposite, bottom: West elevation

above: View of the front façade looking northwest

Nave looking west toward main altar

an extraordinary reputation for outreach, making pilgrimages to churches and faiths throughout the world, the new millennium was marked by the Roman Catholic Church as a time to shift the focus back to Rome, which had been neglected by the papacy for some time. This was a turning point of sorts, which added significant weight to the new project at Tor Tre Teste. The Jubilee Year was to be "virtually a reversal of the apostolic pilgrimages of Pope John Paul II. Instead of the Pope visiting the Churches scattered throughout the world, the Church of Rome will welcome those Churches to itself."

Cardinal Ruini initiated an invitational competition that included six architects: Tadao Ando, Günter Behnisch, Santiago Calatrava, Peter Eisenman, Frank O. Gehry, and Richard Meier. Of these six, only one, Calatrava, was Catholic, which was taken by many as a sign that the Vicariate's initiative for the church at Tor Tre Teste was not only a global endeavor, but also one that carried forth the progressive intentions of Vatican II. None of the six invited had a reputation as a church architect, though Ando had designed a church. Regardless of my Jewish religion, I was honored beyond measure to be chosen as the architect for the Jubilee Church, and to be given the opportunity to create a place of clarity and peace to usher in a new era for the Church of Rome.

The significance of the competition was perhaps never as apparent to me as it was when I was called to the Vatican during the design process to present the project to Pope John Paul II. We shipped over the model, and I had an appointment to meet with the Pope on a Wednesday at eleven a.m., directly after his weekly nine o'clock mass. This to me was no ordinary client meeting, so I arrived three hours early to make sure everything was just right. When I arrived, the model was sitting in the corner of a

very dark, windowless room, so I asked the Swiss Guards if they could arrange for some lights. They disappeared for what seemed like an eternity, and the mass was winding down, as I could see on a TV monitor while I waited. The guards returned five minutes before 11 o'clock with no lights, and I began to panic. My own *meshugaas* determined that the Pope should not see the model in the dark. I entreated them again to find some lights, but they just picked up the model and moved it to the door so the Pope would not have to walk so far to see it. At that moment, His Holiness arrived with a corps of TV cameras, and suddenly the model was awash in light. I tried to explain how honored I was to present the design to him, saying that I could only imagine how Michelangelo must have felt when he brought the model of the dome of St. Peter's to Pope Julius II. We walked around the model, and he was very gracious as I explained the design.

The ideas guiding the design were clear from the beginning. This Jubilee Church would offer a confirming sense of place for the community and the people who came to worship inside its walls, an expression of aspiration, hope and belief, as well as openness and transparency. Other than specific instructions regarding the materials for the altar, guidelines for the ambo and president's seat, the program set forth by the Vicariate in light of Vatican II was deliberately broad, requiring only that:

> The architect propose a space that bespeaks welcoming, assembly and Church. This is the only limitation imposed. It is left to the architect's imagination and design to realize this meaning … [The architect] is gently asked to represent in his work the timelessness of beauty … This is not a plea that the church change the society around it but rather that the church provides a place, a space of welcome, where human engagement

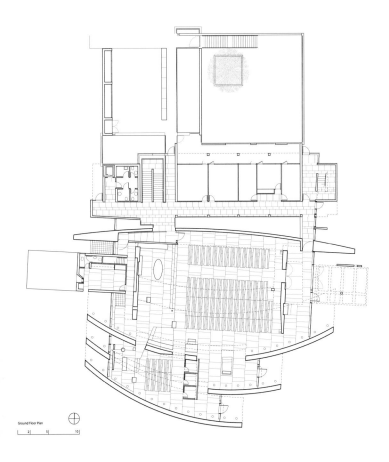

2 5 10

above: Ground level plan

opposite: View of the south side of the church
looking northeast

and religious activities take place. The space
is meant to ennoble those who enter it, both
in terms of the structure and in the activities
that take place within and around it. [It is to
be] a community space and liturgical space,
distinct but related to each other.

The fan-shaped site is approached from the
east across a travertine-paved entrance piazza,
which extends as a base to the church on the south
and west of the precinct. The church building,
in essence, combines curvilinear and rectilinear
shapes, making the distinction between the sacred
space and the secular, or community space. Three
large shell wall planes of varying height curve
over the traditional nave, altar, baptistery, side
chapel, and confessional booths. These shells, built
of twelve-ton blocks of precast white concrete,
are essentially elements of a half sphere, each
independently supported in a feat of engineering
that is deceptively simple to the eye. To mount
these sails, Italcementi invented a huge skeletal
machine that moved on rails as it gradually lifted
the blocks into place. It took enormous effort to
create what today looks so simple.

The curved walls, linked by glazed skylights
and a glass façade, create the effect of soaring over
the spaces of worship, lifting the eye skyward
and holding the occupant in the space. Bathing
the space in natural light creates ever-changing
patterns within this sacred space; the forms serve
to highlight the importance of looking up and out,
thinking beyond all the things that seem important
in our daily lives. A deliberately restrained palette
was taken in the materials of the interior spaces: the
floor, the altar, the priest's chair, and the ambo are
all executed in stone; only the pews are furnished in
wood. I had designed, initially, an abstract stainless
steel cross to hang over the altar, but the diocese
made it clear that the crucifix must feature a figure
of Christ. I suggested, as an acknowledgement of
the history of the Roman Catholic Church, that

left: Exterior detail

right: Chapel, view towards altar

the Vatican retrieve a seventeenth- or eighteenth-century crucifix for the altar. The pieces were deemed too valuable, so, as a compromise, a nineteenth-century papier-mâché crucifix was donated to the space. The organ and choir loft at the east end of the nave, and the sanctuary with the sacristy "tower" at the west, rise towards a translucent roof of clear glass superimposed with light-diffusing louvers.

A spine wall to the north of the concrete shells anchors the main space of the church and marks a separation from the adjacent community center and the bell tower, separate but connected with the church by a passageway. The tower, containing five vertically placed bells, stands perpendicular to the vertical spine wall, drawing a distinct frame for the L-plan, which houses the community center. The community center, comprised of four levels with attendant balconies around a sunken courtyard, is linked to the northern side of the church by bridges to the atrium, sanctuary, organ loft, and sacristy. Upper levels include the parish priest's offices and catechism rooms. The second floor houses the pastor's residence and kitchen, with a brick hearth and fireplace. Adjacent to the courtyard is the basement, holding the primary meeting hall. The skylighting and outdoor gathering places across both the church and community spaces make the roof part of the experience for the nearby residents, as they can see the activity from their apartment balconies. This component gives life to the idea of a "community church."

The main approach from the piazza is through the narrow, inner portico-cum-conservatory separating the church from the community center. The courts are designed to accommodate a broad range of informal and formal communal assemblies. The recreational court may be used by gatherings of adults or by children at play, while the enclosed lower court can function as a setting for the Blessing of the Palms or for the formation of the various processional assemblies that are an integral part of the annual church ritual. Thus, the entire complex has been conceived as a site for both formal and informal festive celebration, where symbolic remembrance is enacted through prayer and the orchestration of human movement.

In an age of pop-up iconic buildings, the Jubilee Church was a modest project. It is a community church that holds around 300 people at a time. There is no exterior mark or sign that would indicate that this is a Roman Catholic church, or any place of worship, yet its identity is clear. In this instance, the intention was simple, yet monumental: light itself is the icon, the medium that allows the architecture to be silent, but ultimately revelatory.

ARCHITECTURE AS A VEHICLE
FOR RELIGIOUS EXPERIENCE:
THE LOS ANGELES CATHEDRAL

RAFAEL MONEO

In the Middle Ages, the building of a church was based on an unassailable architectural principle: one was building the House of God. Thus, the homogeneous character of the medieval society led a critic like Erwin Panofsky to establish a parallel between the Gothic cathedral and scholastic logic. With the Renaissance, religion relinquished its absolute dominance and unquestioned system of values to the newfound importance gained by the individual and, consequently, the private realm. At that time, the hope of being able to build a kind of machine conceived from the perfect image of God was lost. From the sixteenth century on, Christians—or Catholics and Protestants, to speak of two opposing currents—have been more focused on realizing the fullness of the individual, than in perfecting the structure of society. What meaning does this have, in architectural terms, this step from the world understood as *civitas dei* ("City of God"), to the world that contemplates the religious act as an intimate ritual? To my understanding, it means that the architect, facing the challenge of building a church or a temple, cannot rely on a shared vision, but instead must risk offering his or her own version of sacred space.

When I began to work on the Cathedral of Los Angeles (Cathedral of Our Lady of the Angels), I did not feel capable of projecting a transcendent space able to incite a sensorial experience in the individual—as might be the case with the Rothko Chapel in Houston—nor did I expect to build a perfect machine like those I mentioned from the cathedral builders of the Middle Ages. The alternative was to design the cathedral conscious of those spaces which could be understood as metaphors of religious experience.

In the Cathedral of Los Angeles there are present many of those spaces which evoke a sense of the sacred for me: Byzantine and Romanesque churches, on the one hand, and Gothic cathedrals and Baroque sacred spaces on the other. Much of my experience as an architect is not so far removed from my education with the Jesuits. It was this formation that made me feel quite connected to many of the things of which Cardinal Mahony spoke (the Archbishop of Los Angeles with whom I worked on the project), but at the same time it also justified my fears, for it made me conscious of the great responsibility that was being entrusted to me as an individual.

All my work on the cathedral is marked by the simultaneous presence of my interest as an architect to build a cathedral and my fear at the assumption of such a responsibility (knowing the Church as well as I do). Perhaps for the others on the Cardinal's shortlist—Robert Venturi, Thom Mayne, Frank Gehry, and Santiago Calatrava— these aspects were not an issue. But the difficulty, in ideological terms, implied by building a church always weighed on me, converting itself into a palpable doubt and leading me to undertake every effort to do my best. I have always felt that it was a work destiny brought to me, not one I sought; I felt it was a work that had been put before me and that I had resolved, at least from my point of view, with a certain dignity.

The commission took place in June 1996, and, in principle, the new cathedral was intended to be built adjacent to the old Cathedral of Santa Vibiana, built in 1876. But this older cathedral, seriously damaged in the Northridge earthquake of 1994, was determined to be of historical significance, thus heavily conditioning the new project. Many of the important benefactors supporting the project did not wish to commit to such a costly restoration, thus leading to the decision to relocate. The new location was undecided, although all agreed it should be in "downtown" Los Angeles, an area of special importance in a city so centrifugal. Among the sites available to the Church was one situated on the perimeter of the city center, between Temple Street and the Hollywood Freeway, and between Hill Street and Grand Avenue. There were many reasons favoring this site, including its location on Grand Avenue along the cultural axis of downtown that includes the Disney Concert Hall, the Museum of Contemporary Art (MoCA), and the library. Set atop Bunker Hill, the site offered a dominant physical setting over downtown Los Angeles.

Another appeal the site had was its accessibility: it was easily reachable by bus, the Metro, and car. In addition, it was ample with more than 400,000 square feet, allowing for a comfortable resolution of the program without a need to crowd the parcel's limits. It was also notable for its visibility: the Hollywood Freeway is one of the city's most important arteries, and Angelinos are constantly passing through downtown. And, lastly, it was a site with a certain autonomy: the fact that it was in the heart of the city did not keep it from being isolated and independent from other institutional buildings.

The decision to relocate the cathedral was finalized in September 1996, and it was then that the purchase of the land was negotiated with the city, marking the beginning of the formal design process. Without question, the change of site transformed the basic terms of the project. The new location allowed for a complex of several elements, including the Cardinal's residence, a community center for the parish, a parking structure, and a public plaza. The dimensions of the site led us to understand the program and its elements in a way similar to the first missions built by the Franciscans, which were similarly diverse programs composed of many elements. And so the project of the complex as a whole took priority over the singular piece of the cathedral. In a meeting with Cardinal Mahony in Rome in

Rafael Moneo, Cathedral of Our Lady of the Angels, Los Angeles, California, 2002, the apse seen from the lower plaza with the steps to the main entrance to the left

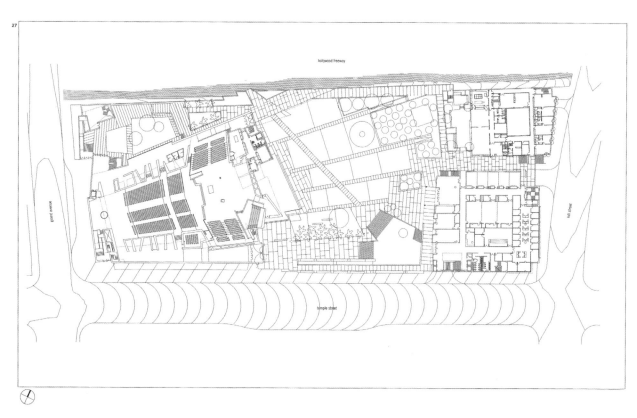

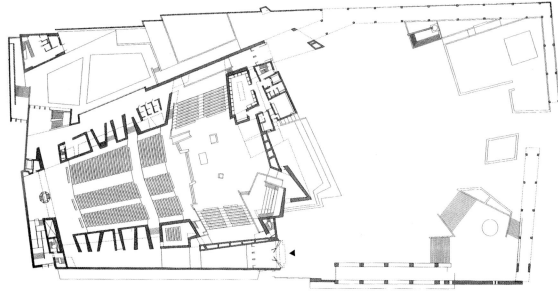

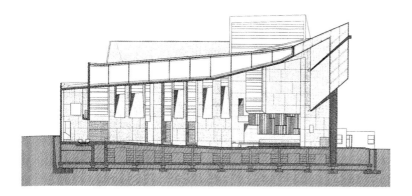

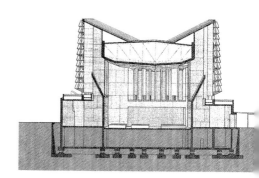

opposite, top: Site plan of the cathedral complex as an "autonomous precinct" including plaza, parish center, and portico, framed between main city arteries and the Hollywood Freeway

opposite, bottom: Ground floor plan

above: Sections

right: Site model with campanile on right

Cathedral seen
from across the
Hollywood Freeway

to the greatest advantage, along with two other fundamental convictions, provided the basis of the plan. Although some might find the decision arbitrary, one conviction was the orientation of the cathedral: the apse itself should look to Rome, as was traditionally the case in churches, emphasizing the importance that the ecumenical view has for Catholics. The other decision was the intent that the cathedral have a cruciform plan, since Christian temples had assumed the shape of the cross since their very beginnings. These two points reflect my historical conscience, and my desire to emphasize the religious rites in a historical context as part of their sacred character. These principles, applied literally to the site, meant that the apse of the cathedral should sit adjacent to the plaza and therefore contiguous with the entrance of the church.

This orientation, in turn, created what is perhaps the most distinctive feature, from a typological and architectural point of view. One passes into the church from either side of the apse, through two different doors leading to the ambulatories onto which a series of chapels opens, turned away as they are from the nave. In this inversion—the entrance at the apse, the chapels away from the nave—there is a certain typological innovation, since these elements are not habitually arranged in this way. The chapels, capable of assuming various uses in response to the needs of different ethnic communities within the Archdiocese of Los Angeles, mix with the path that leads to the baptistery, culminating finally in a broad view of the nave, down to the presbyterium, which is presided over by the illuminated cross.

The nave can be understood as the heart of the church, as a space capable of offering the essential solitude of the individual, as well as the celebration of collective ceremonies. While both ambulatories offer a gentle and measured access to the nave, each has a distinct character. From the small plaza at the Temple Street entrance—a plaza characterized by

November 1996, the general layout for the project was established, based on a small model.

The premise was clear from the outset: the cathedral would be located on the highest part of the site, dominating the plaza whose perimeter would be defined by the residence and parish center overlooking Hill Street, and by a portico along Temple Street and the Freeway. Below the residence and the parish center would be the parking lot, taking advantage of the descent between Grand Avenue and Hill Street. As such, the complex built around the cathedral was created as an autonomous precinct, making the access to the cathedral slightly more remote, and creating a transitional space between the daily life of the surrounding city and the interior of the church.

These first decisions related to the organization of the site were decisive in the design of the cathedral plan itself. The use of the site's topography

above: Cathedral nave
looking toward main altar

left: Cathedral
presbyterium and
nave seen from the
left transept, with the
inverted walls of the side
chapels on the far side

the carillon and pedestrian access to parking—we can follow two directions into the church. Taking the stairs parallel to the street, we find the bronze doors that lead to the south ambulatory. These monumental doors of bronze, topped by an 8-foot-tall sculpture of the Virgin represented as a young girl with mixed ethnic features, speak to Mexican-born sculptor Robert Graham's desire to relate to the entire community of Los Angeles. The doors lead the visitor past the Chapel of the Holy Sacrament and five other chapels, each illuminated by reflected light. A Spanish Baroque reredos situated at the back of the church leads the faithful along the corridor, offering glimpses of the nave. The wall that runs along it is poised to receive a historical narrative, in words and images, recounting the history of the parish. Taking the other steps from the lower plaza and crossing the main plaza towards the shrine of the Virgin of Guadalupe, one enters the north ambulatory. Just beyond the threshold, one comes into contact with the open garden, of a pantheistic origin if you like, but also valid for Christians who understand the natural world to be reflective of God. The confessionals are located along this ambulatory, lending it a more intimate character with its own spiritual life.

The inverted orientation of the chapels in plan was going to have an immediate effect on the section of the cathedral and, as a result, on the definition of the atmosphere of the architecture. In the section, one can see two generous clerestory windows to the north and south of the church illuminating the nave and the chapels together. The light that penetrates filters through large alabaster screens, throwing light on the inclined ceilings of the chapels, which then reflects its glow in the ambulatories lighting the pathways into the church. But this light that gives life to the ambulatory also passes through the vertical structural elements supporting the nave's ceiling,

and illuminates this space. The central nave is, as a result, contained and defined by a system of vertical structural elements and bathed in an indirect light, one that, entering powerfully through the curtain wall, reaches the nave after being filtered by the alabaster panels. The architecture of the nave appears set in a luminous atmosphere that leaves one remote from the exterior world and becomes a metaphor for the religious experience.

The cathedral also reflects my particular attitude about the role of construction in defining the character of the building. I did not want technological innovation to become a fundamental issue in the building of a cathedral, as it was, for example, in the Middle Ages; rather, I sought a direct, solid, rational construction and a careful selection of materials that would be the keys to defining the character of the building. Integrally colored concrete, alabaster, cherry wood, limestone, and bronze were the materials selected. From the outset, it was clear that building the church in concrete would help to resolve many problems. The color itself diffuses the strong Los Angeles sunlight, while offering continuity between exterior and interior.

Light is of paramount importance in the cathedral. On the one hand, light reflected by the ceilings of the chapels orients the ambulatories leading to the nave, a light not very different from that found in Romanesque churches. On the other hand, light filtered through the alabaster creates a diffuse, luminous atmosphere and enclosure in which the built work floats, providing sensations akin to those experienced in Byzantine churches. The architecture of the interior of the cathedral shows with clarity its source of light, as does a project like the Kursaal Congress Hall I did in San Sebastian, Spain. Finally, the cross clerestory presiding over the apse, through which sunlight filters, offers light as a mystical metaphor for the manifestation and presence of God. It would not

Detail of the cross clerestory above the main altar

be difficult to compare this type of architectural experience with those so often used by the architects of the Baroque period.

The ultimate symbol of the Church, the cross, is felt in the plan of the cathedral and openly manifest in both the presbyterium and the apse, as if it were a gigantic suspended reredos, given the dimensions of the church. The cross itself culminates and closes the system of folded walls which convert themselves in the key, or cornerstone, explaining how those complex planes of concrete meet the oblique planes of the roof. The fact that the cross is present in both the interior and the exterior needs explanation, for this architectural element appeared as a premonition in the first phases of the project and during the selection process itself.

When the committee decided on a short list of five architects, they asked us all to present, for a better understanding of our working methods, drawings and models for a small sanctuary to honor the memory of Fray Junipero Serra. The proposals of my colleagues corresponded to the quality one would expect from each of them, as well as their particular aesthetic-ideological criteria. Conscious of the fact that Junipero Serra is seen from very different perspectives (for some, he is the apostle responsible for evangelizing throughout the Californias, while for others he is simply another colonizer at the service of a foreign power), I located his figure following the image of the mounted equestrian statue of Cangrande in Scarpa's Castelvecchio Museum in Verona. Those who see Fray Serra from outside the shrine would recognize him as a historical figure, and those who see him from inside the sanctuary, framed in the opening of the window, would understand the statue as an object of veneration. This duality, this desire to give the cathedral a meaning for all Angelinos, Catholics or not, also explains the different modes in which the cross is incorporated into the architecture,

and how it became present from the very first moments of the cathedral's design.

The discussion as to what role art and liturgical elements could play in the new cathedral was the focus of many long committee sessions led by Cardinal Mahony. At one time I wrote an essay in which I cited a number of artists whose work I would have liked to have seen incorporated with the architecture of the cathedral. In it I spoke of the sculptors Joel Shapiro and Martin Puryear, and of the painters Agnes Martin and Susan Rothenberg, and I even suggested that it would have been possible to work monographically with someone as renowned and intimately associated with Los Angeles as David Hockney. My proposals were not taken into consideration; in fact, no contact whatsoever was made with these artists. In their place, artists were chosen by virtue of being members of the various communities represented in the Archdiocese. More than that, they were artists who do not surprise or challenge, but rather fulfilled the expectations of those in the congregation who did not share a vision with more adventurous artists. It was determined that the art of the cathedral should not be in any way elitist, and so an opportunity was lost for the Catholic Church to approach those aesthetic grounds defined by contemporary art. The alternative was a conventional historical art form, such as the tapestries representing the Communion of the Saints. This pragmatic, easygoing approach is what determined the selection of the Texan architect J. Stuart Todd for the mausoleum, another opportunity lost to establish a coherent language for the different facets of the cathedral.

Returning to the exterior, the space of the plaza acts, on one hand, as a filter to protect one from the exterior world, and on the other as a point of departure towards the ambulatories. It is here where we first encounter the heart of the Christian faith, the image of the cross. The plaza is a space dedicated for rituals and processions in which the apse of the church and the reverse face of the cross play an essential role, as does the buzzing of the Hollywood Freeway, revealing what the role of the *civitas dei* is in today's world. The plaza is meant to receive any and all; it is a public space in Los Angeles at its most urban, in the "downtown."

The Cathedral of Our Lady of the Angels is conceived as a home to all, and perhaps especially those who have left their own country behind, maintaining the culture and faith they brought with them. Seen this way, nobody would deny the important role played by the cathedral in a complex city like Los Angeles. As an architect, I would say now that these complex architectural problems that arose in the cathedral project, such as maintaining the identity of a building type we know well, and helping people formulate transcendent questions about their existence, can only be taken up with an architecture that history has taught us over the years.

Detail of the clerestory on the exterior of the Cathedral

FAITH AND FORM: CONTEMPORARY
SPACE FOR WORSHIP AND PILGRIMAGE

FARIBORZ SAHBA

In 1976, as a very young architect participating in an international competition, I was awarded a project that I found most challenging. I was to design a very special temple which the Bahá'ís of the world wanted to build in New Delhi, India. I say "a very special temple," because it had to welcome to worship people from every religion, race, or caste, as one human family, to pray to one God, the creator of humanity.

The *Encyclopedia Britannica* describes the Bahá'í Faith as the youngest of the world religions, with six million members who come from all corners of the globe. Bahá'u'lláh, who founded the Bahá'í Faith in the nineteenth century, designated Houses of Worship as spiritual places for prayer and meditation and envisioned that these temples would be surrounded by social, humanitarian, educational, and scientific institutions. The first of these Houses of Worship built on each continent were designated as "mother" or principal temples, and at that time six of these had been erected in Africa, Australia, Europe, the South Pacific, and North and Central America. I was asked to design the mother temple of the Indian subcontinent in India, where one of the largest national Bahá'í communities resides.

Of course, one can choose to leave the door of any building open to all, and they may, or may not, enter as enthusiastic visitors. It would be another challenge to make them recognize it as a sacred space, as their own temple, their own sanctuary, within which they could take refuge from the day-to-day, wild, material life in an immaterial world or space. So, my first challenge was to define *sacred space* for myself. As I traveled from the north to the south of India, I found this a most fascinating quest, in particular, in the land of mysteries, India.

Sacred space, space for meditation and prayer, immediately relates to the definitions of meditation, prayer, and symbolism which are associated with the very foundations of the Indian religions. Hindu temples are complicated, dark, and adorned with thousands of ornaments, statues of deities, images of religious metaphors and tales from their holy texts, while mosques are geometrical displays of brilliant tiles, mirror works, and calligraphies. No statue can be placed in them. In the same way, a Jewish synagogue, a Christian church, and a Zoroastrian fire temple each has its own definitions and functions. Prayers are a public affair in some religions, such as Islam, while in the Bahá'í Faith they are private and individual. Devotions might be a combination of performance and dance in one religion, social and political lectures in another, or purely a study of Holy Scriptures in yet another.

From another point of view, nowhere in the world could one observe such distinct differences and the importance of symbolism as in the religious buildings that exist in India. It has been said that if you take the hand of a blind person to a temple in India, on arrival he will be able to recognize to which religion it belongs, be it by touching a wall of the temple or smelling the fragrances of the plants of the temple.

While visiting a Hindu temple under construction in the South of India, I asked who was the architect of the temple. I was told that temples are designed by devoted high priests who, after a lifetime of meditation, contemplation, and spiritual journey, may develop a vision of a temple. The higher the spiritual encounter of the priest, the more complicated and elaborate the design of his temple. It is believed that the first form which comes to the mind in this spiritual journey is a bubble, and that is why mosque domes, in the view of a Hindu devotee, are not considered a sufficiently sophisticated spiritual design. I do not intend to evaluate the authenticity of such statements but simply to demonstrate how religious symbolism is used to draw boundaries around followers of different religions, making it hard for an architect to create a contemporary space that might be considered sacred by all people, irrespective of religion.

So how could I design a building in India, a country known for magnificent temples found at the top of nearly every hill, that would be accepted as a sacred place at once by a Hindu, a Muslim, a Christian, and a Zoroastrian? Wasn't this the dream for the greatest Akbar Shah of India, as recorded by Alfred Lord Tennyson?

> Well I dreamed that stone by stone I rear'd
> a sacred fane,
> A temple, neither pagoda, mosque,
> nor church,
> But loftier, simpler, always open door'd
> To every breath from heaven, and truth
> and peace
> And love and justice came,
> and dwelt therein.

I was to build a contemporary temple for the Bahá'í religion, and as such, I tried to understand my challenge from the perspective of that religion. The Bahá'í Faith teaches that this is the time of unity: the unity of God, the unity of religion, and the unity of humankind. Bahá'u'lláh wrote, "The tabernacle of unity hath been raised; regard ye not one another as strangers. Ye are the fruits

Fariborz Sahba, Lotus Temple, Delhi, 1986, front view showing garden pathways leading to the main hall

left: Interior, central hall of the temple with people at prayer

below: Interior looking up toward the apex with crisscrossing ribs and shells

Aerial view from the East showing the nine surrounding pools and gardens which help to ventilate the building

of one tree, and the leaves of one branch … So powerful is the light of unity that it can illuminate the whole earth."[1] Bahá'ís maintain that all the religions of the world believe creation was made by one Creator. If so, we are all children of one God, irrespective of our religion. By "unity of religion" Bahá'ís do not mean that all the religions are the same, rather that there is only one religion and all the Messengers of God have progressively revealed its teachings. So, in essence, the religions cannot contradict one another. Rather, they are complementary and progressive, based upon the degree of understanding of humanity at a given place and time. By "unity of mankind" Bahá'ís mean that if we are children of one God, although there may be a great deal of diversity, there can be no differences between us due to race, color, sex, or religion—no differences in shared humanity, dignity, and honor among us as human beings. Differences, if any, can only be due to the degree of our service to humanity. Based on this description, sacred spaces are those inviting all people to enter. No lecture, talk, or performance is allowed, but all are welcome to read from the holy scriptures of any of the religions of the world.

I often used to think to myself, "What is it that makes the Taj Mahal so mysterious, so loved by the people, that hundreds of thousands of Indians,

having seen it several times, still continue to visit it?" The Taj Mahal was constructed by an Iranian architect during the Safavid period, but it does not exhibit the same perfect geometry and proportion found in other Islamic structures of this period, some of which far surpass its geometry and beauty. How is it then, that this structure is dearer to people's hearts than all the others?

One morning, when I first journeyed to India and was occupied in studying the architecture of that country, I set out at dawn to visit the Taj Mahal. The air was enchantingly fresh and fine. Being the rainy season, the heavens were all in motion and presented a stirring array of vivid and ever-changing colors. Always, when one visits historical sights in India, one attracts a train of followers bent on offering their services as guides. On that occasion a poor, bare-footed man had fallen in behind me and was insisting on showing me around the Taj Mahal. For a time I resisted his entreaties, but finding my repulses of no avail, I finally permitted him to do as he proposed. After a short preamble reviewing various circumstances leading to the construction of the Taj Mahal, he spoke of the love of Shah Jahan for his wife, Mumtaz Mahal, and then her sudden death. He was so moved that his voice was breaking with emotion. I was filled with astonishment that such a person, who in all

[1] *Gleanings from the Writings of Bahá'u'lláh*, trans. by Shoghi Effendi (Wilmette, Ill.: Bahá'í Publishing, 1952), p. 267.

probability had repeated this narrative hundreds of times, should yet be able to discourse about the Taj Mahal with such ardor and passion, and feel so intimately connected to the building as to regard it almost as a living being. My guide's narrative was not precise, but to me the true significance of his words lay in the sensation they conveyed: that this building had a special place in his heart, and was in a manner connected to him. It came to me that architecture is not simply a question of beauty, proportion, and function, but rather of a direct connection with the human heart.

This question of establishing a direct connection with peoples' souls and spirits is, I believe, that which constitutes a sacred space and a sacred monument. I do not think it is the geometry, material beauty, or grandeur of the Taj Mahal that has made it so special to people, whether a Western tourist or an Indian villager of Rajistan, rather it is the building's story, mystery, and aura which have made it a sacred edifice. There is a fifth dimension in the space beyond length, width, height, and movement; it is a dimension of inherent relation in the essence of things, the realities of things. There is a mystic relation between the Taj Mahal, Shah Jahan, Mumtaz Mahal, the Ganges River, and the majestic sky of Rajistan, and all of them, with the visitor. This relation is so delicate, so special. And this is what makes it sacred.

And so I said to myself, "I need a story, a mystery, a reason, for my temple to establish why it should be in that form, and why it should be there, a building with five dimensions." It is interesting to point out that in the Bahá'í Faith love is defined as an "inherent vital relation and bond in the reality of things." Defining and understanding this vital relation is the main purpose and function of religion, as well as art and science. It was in this context that I took the journey through India to Sri Lanka. I visited hundreds of temples not for architectural guidance, but to discover a concept that would integrate the spiritual heritage of this subcontinent. I was looking for a concept and a form that would be acceptable to people of all religions. I wanted to design something new and unique, and at the same time familiar and intimate. On the one hand, it should be contemporary and reveal the freshness of the Bahá'í revelation as a new, independent religion; on the other hand, it should show respect for past religious beliefs and act as a constant reminder that the principles of all the religions of God are one. It should be as familiar to people as if they have seen it in their dreams, but now it is realized in material form right in front of their eyes.

Through this quest, I found the concept of the lotus. In brief, it represents the Messengers of God and is also a symbol of purity and tenderness. For centuries the lotus was associated with worship, and inspired deep, universal reverence. Its significance is rooted in the minds and hearts of the people of India through the epic poem of Mahabharata, in which the creator Brahma is described as having sprung from the lotus that grew out of Lord Vishnu's navel, when that deity lay absorbed in meditation. In Buddhism, the Buddhi Satwa Avalokiteswara is represented as being born from a lotus; he is usually depicted as standing or sitting on a lotus pedestal, and holding a lotus bloom in his hand. Buddhists glorify him in their prayers with the salutation, "*Om mani padme hum!*" ("Yea, O jewel in the lotus!"). Lord Buddha admonished his followers to model themselves after the lotus, which, although living in dirty water, still remains beautiful and undefiled by its surroundings. The loneliness and immaculacy of this flower, which sparkles everywhere like a star on the waters of India, have made it a symbol of spirituality and beauty in the mythology of all religions of that country. The dome of the Taj Mahal, in fact, is the bud of a lotus flower, and lotus symbols have adorned many Islamic, Christian, and Zoroastrian monuments. I thought perhaps lotus embodied the universal form of the universal faith of which Bahá'u'lláh speaks.

The realization of the Lotus Temple took about ten years, eight of which I spent in India to ensure it happened the way I wanted. During this period, I learned a lot about the country, its culture, its architecture, and its noble, ordinary people. Working with eight hundred laborers at a time—mostly unskilled workers speaking ten different languages, coming from different ethnic and religious backgrounds—taught me how to communicate and relate to them, how to motivate them, and how to make them appreciate and enjoy their work. By showing concern and respecting and appreciating the workers' way of life, I learned how to touch their hearts. The school that we created on-site to take care of their children became famous, and was visited often by dignitaries, including the American and Canadian ambassadors. The story of our relations of unity spread throughout the city, and remained in the minds of many who visited the temple, even during construction.

I think the way that a building is built, and the respect and reverence of the workers towards their work, have a lot to do with creating that story, which is needed for a sacred building. I recall when the temple was completed, and we were planning to open it to the public in a few days, one of our workers, who was a very knowledgeable man, came to me, insisting that we should not allow people to enter the temple with shoes, for in India, no one enters a sacred space with their shoes on. He was so emphatic and emotional that I realized how deeply he felt about the sacredness of the building.

An interesting aspect of the Lotus Temple is that it has incorporated a rich blend of the most sophisticated technology, complex geometry, and computer-aided engineering of its delicate, exposed concrete-shell structure with the highest-quality craftsmanship and hand-tool operations.

Workers engaged in the construction of the temple. Concrete was carried up the staging by women with 50-pound loads in a continuous 48-hour process

above: Fariborz Sahba, Terraces of the Shrine of the Báb (Hanging Gardens), Haifa, 1990, aerial view

above, right: Looking up the terraces on Mt. Carmel toward the Shrine of the Báb

This is a feature many of the followers of the Bahá'í Faith appear to cherish as the combination of science and religion, of science and the arts, and the employment of technology with aesthetic sensibility. Attention to proportion and beauty are among the central teachings of Bahá'u'lláh.

We started concreting every petal, which would take forty-eight hours of non-stop operation, by saying prayers and making *puja*, as it is called in India, so that the workers were aware of the significance of their work. I recall one midnight, as we were working on one of our forty-eight-hour shifts of non-stop concreting, one of our carpenters came to me. I asked if he wanted to tell me something. He replied, "Yes. My mother tells me: 'You are building a sacred building, but you work for money. You should be ashamed of yourself. This you should have done as *kar seva*'" (which means voluntary work). He said, "I told my mother that I get money because I have to provide food for my children, but I want you to know my contribution is that I work much harder."

The Lotus Temple uses the traditional Indian concept of wind towers and the desert architecture of Iran. This natural ventilation system is based on the fact that the building is designed to act like a chimney, drawing up warm air from within the hall and expelling it through the top of the dome. Thus, constant draughts of cool air pass over the pools and flow through the basement into the hall and out through the opening at the top.

The only decorative elements employed in the design of the Lotus Temple, to bring the peace and calm needed for the spiritual journey towards sacredness, are light and water. Geometry, rhythm, and continuity of space are used to enhance the space and to take a visitor from the busy, outside material world towards his or her own inner self and soul. To underline the spiritual principle of the Bahá'í Faith that we cannot worship the Creator without bowing our heads in respect of his creation, the concept of green and the protection of environment has been a main factor in the design of the Bahá'í house of worship. Referring to this principle in his book, *Earth in the Balance*, Al Gore writes:

> One of the newest of the great universalist religions, Bahá'í, founded in 1863 in Persia ..., warns us not only to properly regard the relationship between humankind and nature but also the one between civilization and the environment. Perhaps because its guiding visions were formed during the period of accelerating industrialism, Bahá'í seems to dwell on the spiritual implications of the great transformation to which it bore fresh witness: "We cannot segregate the human heart from the environment outside us and say that once one of these is reformed everything will be improved. Man is organic with the world. His inner life molds the environment and is itself deeply affected by it. The one acts upon the other and every abiding change in the life of man is the result of these mutual reactions."[2]

Since its inauguration in 1986, more than seventy million visitors, including many distinguished religious leaders of the world, have visited the Lotus Temple for prayer and meditation. According to a documentary made by CNN, with three and a half million visitors a year, it is one of the most-visited buildings in the world. Through the fact that every day one can see thousands of Hindus, Buddhists, Muslims, and Christians in meditation side by side, and hear holy verses from Hindu and Muslim scriptures, the Old

and New Testaments, and the holy scripts of the Zoroastrians and Bahá'ís recited with the utmost reverence and respect, it has now been established that sacredness does not need to be related only to commonly understood rituals. These rituals have, in fact, been causes of disunity and separation; one might even argue that such rituals are in conflict with the very essence of sacredness.

My second encounter with the design of sacred space was again commissioned by the same client: the Bahá'í World Center, this time on Mt. Carmel in Haifa, Israel. The project was to design the Terraces of the Shrine of the Báb, commonly known as the Hanging Gardens of Mount Carmel. This mountain has been at the crossroads of human history for as long as we have record. Cro-Magnon remains were found in the caves hollowed out of the limestone walls; Pythagoras stayed in these hills on his way to Egypt; the prophet Elijah made his home in two of Carmel's caves; Jesus' family is said to have paused here on their way back from Egypt; and the Crusaders made pilgrimage to this holy mountain in 1150 CE. Its name, which dates back to biblical times, is derived from the Hebrew word *karem*, which means vineyard.

Historical forces directed the footsteps of Bahá'u'lláh to the Holy Land. On one occasion he pointed out to his son and successor, Abdu'l-Bahá, the spot on Mt. Carmel where the remains of his martyred forerunner, the Báb, should be laid to rest. Many years later, what became the best-known landmark on Mt. Carmel was built in 1957, one of the most holy places of pilgrimage for the Bahá'ís of the world: the golden-domed Shrine of the Báb. Since that time, it had been the vision of the faithful that a majestic, monumental, sacred edifice provide an entrance to the shrine, to be

[2] Al Gore, *Earth in the Balance: Ecology and the Human Spirit* (New York: Houghton Mifflin, 1992), p. 262.

comprised of eighteen terraced gardens in memory of the first eighteen disciples of the Báb.

The terraces are a tribute to the Shrine of the Báb, a prelude, and approach to it. If the Shrine is considered a jewel, a diamond, then the terraces are supposed to provide a golden ring, which will bring the beauty of the diamond to the fore and provide a perfect setting for it. The gardens are a blend of the landscape of the East and West: they bring together all in one place the fragrance of the garden of Shiraz, where the Báb was born, with the geometry and order of the gardens of Kashmir, and the beauty of gardens of the West.

The architectural challenge was not to create a beautiful space, but a spiritual, sacred space. In my opinion, a beautiful space touches the hearts of the people, but a sacred space touches their souls. A beautiful space attracts one to it; a sacred space attracts one to the divine. In this case, passing through this heavenly approach, pilgrims coming from every corner of the world to visit the shrine of the martyred herald of their faith will be prepared for the spiritual encounter that is ahead of them.

The whole concept of the design is centered around light. Day and night provide two important facets of the design: at night, it is as if waves of light are emanating in concentric circles from the shrine, the center of illumination. During the day, the same impression is created by sunlight filtering through the lines of cypress trees and reflecting on the curved parallel surfaces of the emerald green lawns. The deliberate order and rhythm provide comfort and relaxation and contribute to the creation of a spiritual feeling—the lines appear to accompany the visitor, with no argument, no resistance, only continuity of space. When you are in the gardens, you feel you are in a different world. The environment enables you to become detached from mundane activities.

The prime minister of India, in a talk at the foundation stone ceremony for the construction of a spiritual garden next to the Lotus Temple, said that some people who have visited the Temple ask him, "Where is the deity in this temple?" He said: "I tell them, 'Sit and meditate; you will discover the deity inside your heart.'"

Canadian poet Roger White, in *Forever in Bloom*, a book published by Raghu Rai, famous photographer of India, gave an apt appreciation of the building with which I close:

Catching my first glimpse of the Temple, I thought it was an edifice transposed from a dreamscape, timeless and eternal, a form I had once either dreamed or envisioned on the inner screen of my mind, but only partially and tenuously and which was now suddenly manifested before my gaze, utterly right in every detail and more magnificent than I could have known how to visualize it, erected with meticulous, almost surgical precision, causing me to gasp with the light and recognition and creating in me a sense of having regained the irretrievable.[3]

Lotus Temple at dusk, showing the illumination of the thin concrete petals clad in panels of white marble

[3] Roger White and Raghu Rai, *Forever in Bloom: The Lotus of Bahapur* (New Delhi: Time Books International, 1992), p. 9.

THEISTIC—POLYTHEISTIC—NON-THEISTIC STEVEN HOLL
WITH DAVID VAN DER LEER

I recently listened to the Dalai Lama speak at Radio City Music Hall on his seventy essays on emptiness. It made me think of one of his quotes, from an interview with Fabien Ouaki, in the book, *Imagine All the People*. Ouaki and the Dalai Lama speak about emptiness, and how this Buddhist concept—*shunyata*—was misinterpreted as "nothingness" in the West during the nineteenth century. The Dalai Lama explains:

> It is not space *in itself*, but it acts as the space that allows all functions to arise. If absolute cohesiveness were present, then nothing could change, and all the laws of causality could not function. My hand could not move. But everything is moving, which indicates that there is some kind of empty space. In fact, it is the absence of independent existence—another term for emptiness—that allows things to function.[1]

I would like to take the words of the Dalai Lama, who explains emptiness as "a clear light as basis of all," as direction, to see if we can bring this collection of essays to the broader level of the non-theistic: to emptiness, space, and light.

[1] Tenzin Gyatso and Fabien Oauki, *Imagine All the People: A Conversation with the Dalai Lama on Money, Politics and Life as It Could Be* (Somerville, Mass.: Wisdom Publications, 1999), p. 136.

above: Steven Holl, Chapel of St. Ignatius, Seattle University, Seattle, Washington, 2007, view across the reflecting pool

above, right: Interior of chapel, looking up into a light vessel

THEISTIC

At the beginning of the selection process for the Chapel of St. Ignatius at the campus of Seattle University, the jury narrowed a group of thirty architects down to six. All six would be interviewed and all were asked to give a lecture at the university the following night. During the interview, I admitted that I had never done a chapel before and that I was not a Catholic and, in fact, if I were religious then maybe I would be a pagan. But I really wanted to contribute to the university in the form of a campus chapel that had this ideal stature, and I told them about my belief in the spirituality of architecture.

I gave the lecture, "Questions of Perception," which described the phenomenology of arch-itecture. It had just been published by *a+u*, and I drew a full house. After that presentation we were selected for the project, and I started reading about St. Ignatius. In one of his books, he returns to the metaphor of light, not being quite aware of where the light source is but knowing it's coming down from above. It gave me this thought of making the whole chapel a collection of light vessels. I called the key concept sketch, "Seven Bottles of Light in a Stone Box." These seven bottles would refer to the different aspects of the liturgical program: the Blessed Sacrament, the Choir, the Narthex, and the Procession. The second reading of the concept was the fact that sixty different nationalities attend Seattle University. By this gathering of different cultures, a global thought in that one specific place is created. These two concepts were vibrating inside the rectangle of the site, and we decided to divide the site into three quadrants: one to the west, a future one to the east, and a new square to the south, that would have a reflecting pond, a bell tower, and a stone for the Easter Vigil fire.

The campus ministry really appreciated the conceptual structure, just like they appreciated the tactile dimensions of my phenomenology lecture, which is, in a way, philosophically Jesuit. They saw parallels between our work and the spiritual exercises of St. Ignatius in teachings as well as in the openness to phenomenological thinking.

The Physical Planning Department wanted to make the building smaller, and they asked to get rid of a couple of those bottles of light. The ministry refused because, to them, the idea of the seven bottles of light as representation of the seven days was more important. We couldn't afford the stone. Together with the contractor, we decided that tilt-up concrete is also a kind of stone, especially if you stain it with an ochre-penetrating stain. So, the chapel became the largest figural tilt-up construction ever made on a university

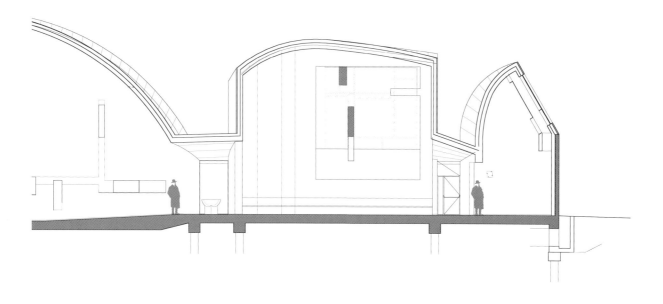

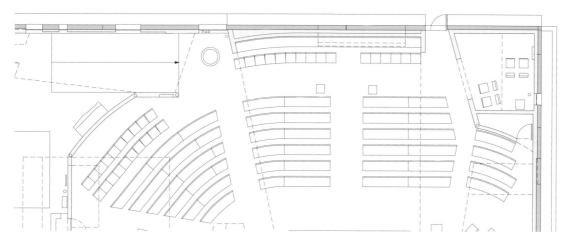

above: Section and plan

left: Raising of a concrete tilt

above: Chapel exterior, east façade

right: Chapel interior

opposite: Chapel entrance doors

campus, with some of the tilts being 30 feet tall and weighing 70,000 pounds.

I think there is a mythical quality to making a tilt-up building. There is no scaffolding. The whole thing is flat, but then, in one day, the entire structure is there! Students would be riding their bicycles on the campus and then they would stop, frozen, by this apparition that had unexpectedly appeared on the campus. When the chapel opened, it was a great celebration. There is a traditional consecratory ceremony of the space: the architect hands the drawings to the bishop and then there is a procession, and everyone goes into the space for a two-hour ceremony in which they take the sacred oils and make crosses, almost like graffiti, in the plaster. The building was no longer ours. It was theirs.

After that, the public embraced the building and, two years later, the University put an image of the chapel on the student I.D. card. Most touching was when I was there a few years later in a supermarket near Capitol Hill, buying something with my credit card. The lady at the checkout read "architect" on my card and said, "You're an architect? You'd better go up there over the hill, there on that campus, and look at that chapel. That's some building." To me, her enthusiasm was better than any architectural award.

POLYTHEISTIC

Ten years later, we were working on a polytheistic space for an eco-resort we were to design at the Akbuk Peninsula on the Turkish Aegean coast. Again, this project contains many aspects of my book, *Questions of Perception: Phenomenological Aspects of Architecture* (2006). The site is charged with history because it is within a 40-minute drive of the old ruins of Miletus, the greatest gridded city in the history of Western civilization. In Greek times this must have been one of the liveliest polytheistic cities on the horizon. When I was traveling the region, I somehow had the feeling that the many Greek gods had never died. The region is radiating history, and this became an inspiration for our new town development.

Overlooking the Aegean Sea, the site for the development has been untouched by construction for millions of years. Our basic strategy is to keep most land as a reserve, and to build in dense-pack urban "islands," which are strategically located within this eco-reserve, according to their critical relation to the site's topography. We aim to maximize natural landscape; minimize roads, surface parking, and infrastructure via the dense-pack strategy; and to maximize use of solar energy, grey and storm water recycling via ponds and cisterns, and the use of sustainable materials and natural materials free of toxins. This basic strategy organizes our specific site into three dense-pack constructions: A) under the ground … grass-roofed stone townhouses; B) in the ground … courtyard villas with pools; C) over the ground … dense-pack courtyard housing on a platform over a parking and cistern level below.

At the highest point of the site overlooking the main urban "island," floating over the ground, a polytheistic assembly space is topped by three "solstice spirals." The plan is to use it for any kind of gatherings, from holidays to poetry readings or concerts. Although this building was not part of the client's brief, we convinced them it would be important to create a space that everybody could connect to and understand. We thought about changes in season expressed in light coming from above, just the light, without any color. Three solstice spirals refer to the summer solstice, the two equinoxes, and the winter solstice. People can go there four times a year to find direct sunlight washing straight down through the shafts. During the rest of the year there are changing aspects of the play of light from above.

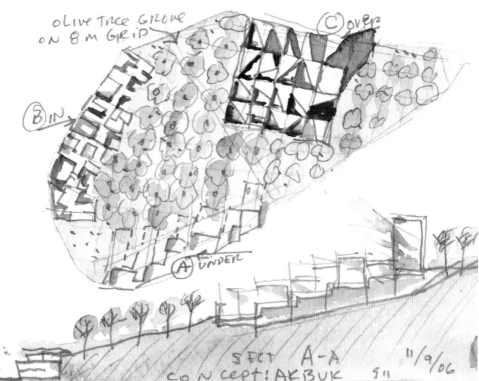

Steven Holl, eco-resort, Akbuk Penisula, Turkey, 2006, site sketches

OLIVE TREE GROVE
ON 8 M GRID

©over

B IN

A UNDER

SECT A-A
CONCEPT: AKBUK   511   11/9/06

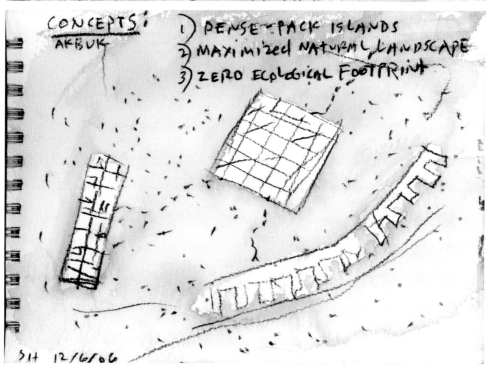

CONCEPTS:
AKBUK

1) DENSE-PACK ISLANDS
2) MAXIMIZED NATURAL LANDSCAPE
3) ZERO ECOLOGICAL FOOTPRINT

SH 12/6/06

NON-THEISTIC

Where *Questions of Perception* at first was the basis of the Chapel of St. Ignatius (a theistic building), the same themes have proven to be successful for many of our secular projects, which often have sacred spaces infused by light. For me, light is for space what sound is for music: the experience of architecture, overlapping perspectives, is the equivalent of spatial acoustics in light. If you have a piece of music you have the score, you have the rhythm, you have some kind of polyphony, you have some kind of a structure, then there is sound that executes and brings it all to life. The same applies to architecture. You have the spatial conception, the conceptual strategy, the integration of lenses in the landscape, the fusion of architecture and landscape and urbanism, but none of that is really alive until you infuse it with light.

In the Nelson-Atkins Museum of Art in Kansas City, we designed an architecture that is to be experienced from the inside-out. The dream of constructing in light reaches a comprehensive passion in this building. The interiors of overlapping perspectives in subtle, changing, natural light are constructed from an exterior architecture of translucent prisms emerging from the ground ... an architecture of sculpted bars of light and time. Here, one can really see that intensity in a billowing, cloud-like spatial energy above the gallery floor. This light changes by the hour, changes by the day, and by the season. It is as ephemeral as time. The spatial parallax experienced in moving through these galleries is also somehow related to time, whose passage is never in a straight line. Time is more mysterious, without a beginning, without an end, and without a final event. Likewise, these spaces turn and overlap with a cadence or rhythm, but, like time, without an absolutely defined direction. From the exterior, glass "lenses" luminously bracket the sculpture garden landscape, beginning to glow from within at dusk.

opposite top: Steven Holl, Nelson-Atkins Museum of Art, Kansas City, Missouri, showing original 1933 neoclassical building and 2007 addition, view from the southeast

opposite bottom: Museum exterior, line of galleries, "translucent prisms" descending along east side of Sculpture Park lawn

above: Museum interior, Bloch Building with path of stairs and ramps

right: Detail of Museum exterior showing "luminous lenses" stepped along eastern edge of the Museum's Sculpture Park

Also, a time relation is concretized, with the new building opening to the Neoclassical 1933 original museum architecture. Greek time was ideally aimed at cyclic return, and the perfections in art and architecture relate to repetitive cycles. To the Greeks, a notion of continuous progress, of a time always new, was unheard of. Aristotle placed his "present" on a point in the revolving circle of time "after" the Trojan War. His time circle continued to rotate. "After" would eventually bring again the Trojan War. Unlike Buddhist time, Aristotle's eternal recurrence was only of types or species—not of the individual. The Greek cosmological conception of time depended on a specific vision of the universe that was hierarchical and moving in a circle; it depended on the cyclical course of the stars. We play with the Buddhist ideas of being and non-being—a sort of non-theistic beginning and continuum based on the notion of the self—and set out to create continuous spaces in which compassion grows through light infusion.

With the open-ended geometry of the new architecture of the Nelson-Atkins Museum of Art, one experiences its spatial energy personally, from the viewpoint of one's eyes positioned in our moving bodies, as they glide through the new spaces. It isn't just the idea of this architecture being "of its time" that is at stake here; it is a proposal aimed at the experience of moving through these spaces as an individual act. We personally open ourselves to art as a phenomenon of central importance to the collective and to the individual. Opening up to potential knowledge, opening up to reflect on, and to become inspired by, something greater than just "of our time," the hope is that we experience, in a secular spirituality, that "we are our time."

The examples here move from Theistic to Polytheistic to Non-Theistic, while the sense of sacred space can be uniquely and individually experienced.

THE ARCHITECTURE OF MEMORY: SEEKING THE SACRED

MOSHE SAFDIE

I believe there are two equal, parallel, and entwined histories: the history of "building," and the history of "architecture."

"Building" is a term I do not use derogatorily. Consider this archetype's many implications. There is the building of shelter, as in nests in nature, and the building of urban fabric made up of houses, apartments, and workspace, for example. Its particular rules cause us to associate it with the notion of vernacular architecture. Comprehensively, we think of "building" as being governed by the economy of resources and by constraints—it is what Bernard Rudofsky called "architecture without architects."

"Architecture," on the other hand, comprises the sacred places of worship, culture, and government through which we aim for the sublime. In this history, the spiritual embraces the realms of iconography and symbol, ornamentation, and celebration. All resources are mastered in the service of these objectives. The rules seem very different. There is no holding back. We are in the realm of expressive art.

While I will focus here on the second history, that of "architecture," in regard to the challenges of seeking the sacred and manifesting the ineffable, I must begin by seeking the common denominator that governs everything we build in our environment.

As Karsten Harries invokes in his essay in this volume, the noted architecture critic Nikolaus Pevsner once observed, "A bicycle shed is a building; Lincoln Cathedral is architecture." In doing so, I believe Pevsner mistakenly polarized the two histories I have described. They are actually governed by similar laws or principles. Both emerge from the same syntax, the materiality of architecture: each must be rooted in place, site, and cultural setting. Both must deal with the issue of belonging. I believe there are common roots and sources for the iconographies each generates. This paradox, as to whether architecture emerges out of its material and constructive realities or is the result of more willful imagining, was the subject of debate with my friend, architect Nader Ardalan.

Many years ago, I visited with Nader the Friday Mosque in Esfahan, Iran, a building that has continually evolved since the late eighth century. We were standing under its magnificent brick dome and Ardalan said, "Isn't this wonderful how the dome was created to present a powerful expression of the Islamic vision of cosmic wholeness?" Taken aback, I asked him, "Isn't the dome's evolution really a result of the fact that here, in Iran's desert, there is no wood to make beams or trusses, only brick and stones to span? When you have no wood, you create arches, domes, and vaults."

To elaborate my point, I later expanded this discussion. Outside Esfahan are a series of pigeon houses, great brick silos that are really dung factories. I suspect those who built them thought that they were building utilitarian structures, not ones with high spiritual objectives. Yet, the contemporary observer cannot but look and experience these structures with wonder! Graceful vaults and domes reach upward, light streaming in, forming a space of extraordinary beauty and spirit. The pigeon houses resonate with the Friday Mosque's dome structure and the great celebration of light under it. In ways such

as this, "building" and "architecture" converge. I make the point because there is the tendency to think of the creation of sacred spiritual space as falling outside the traditional constraining frameworks of building.

In 1973, I was asked to design the public space, the square, in front of the Western Wall in Jerusalem, a remnant of the Second Temple built by Herod the Great around 19 BCE. The Temple Mount, or the Haram esh-Sharif as it is known in Arabic, is a place sacred to both Jews and Muslims. The only remaining segment of the original Herodian Second Temple construction, the Western Wall has evolved to become the most sacred site for Judaism today. After the unification of the city in 1967, the area in front of the wall was carved out as the result of a clearing of buildings to provide opportunity for the masses who wished to pray there, its final outline largely an accident of where the bulldozer stopped. This holiest of places for Jews thus seemed chaotic and haphazard.

The area in front of the Western Wall accommodates life at different times of the day and seasons in an endless sequence of diverse human events. At times it is a place of intimacy, accommodating but a few people praying and meditating; late at night, only two or three individuals might be standing by the wall. At other times, it is the destination of great pilgrimages, and tens of thousands of people fill the space from edge to edge. It is also a place for brides to be photographed, family celebrations, and bar mitzvahs, and the setting for secular and national events, such as the swearing-in ceremony of a military unit, or a gathering of youth visiting from abroad.

I wondered for a long time about how to create this space, this square, in light of this dichotomy: an intimate place for the few and a setting for the many, a place of both meditation and celebration. First, I naturally thought of creating a flat,

Interior of a pigeon house, Esfahan

left: View of Western Wall piazza

below: Moshe Safdie, Western Wall piazzas, Jerusalem, 1973, section showing site excavation

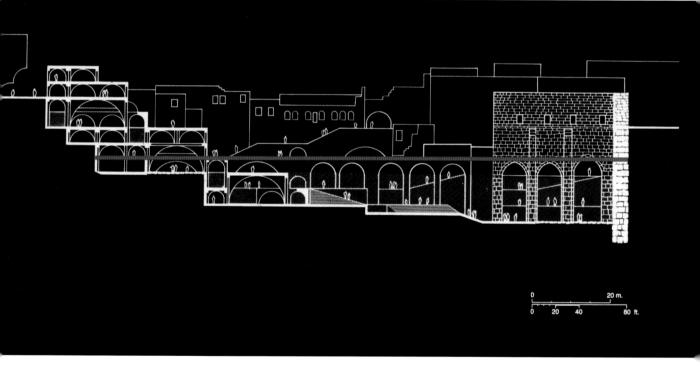

traditional piazza, a singular space extending from the wall to the surrounding building edges, but this type of space seemed overwhelming and did not satisfy the objective of intimacy for the few. I wondered also how one might recapture the awesome scale of the wall experienced in the past, when it was invisible until one was standing close to it. This led me to consider, "What would Herod have done?" I imagined that first he would expose the entire wall to its original height. Thirty feet of earth fill had gathered over the past two thousand years, burying half of the wall's height. My proposal was to excavate the space all the way down to the original Herodian street level, thus doubling its current height and presence in the piazza. As we excavated, it became clear that the wall was in perfect shape, crafted of beautifully cut Herodian stones. The street level at the bottom was, incredibly, intact, with paving in place and a functioning drainage system.

Still, I was not satisfied with attempting to create a large, flat piazza. Once again, I considered what Herod's considerations would have been. The natural topography rises rapidly from the Herodian street towards the west. Surely, Herod would not have excavated the rock; he would have allowed the piazza to step upward, following the bedrock towards the upper city. The resulting amphitheater of piazzas struck me as the obvious and perfect solution.

The lowest piazza abutting the wall fills up with thousands of people at times of festivities. As the piazzas step upward, they merge with the houses on the cliff, the edge of the Jewish Quarter facing the Western Wall. There is a gradual transformation of scale following the Fibonacci Series, from the palatial Western Wall to the smaller domestic scales of the Ottoman architecture. A network of paths leads you down towards the Herodian street, bypassing exposed archeological excavations preserved under the piazzas and linking the sacred past with the present.

––––––––––––––––

In 1976, the officials of Yad Vashem, Jerusalem's Holocaust Martyrs' and Heroes' Remembrance Authority, decided to build a memorial museum to the children who perished in the Holocaust, and I was asked to design it. I spent six months on and off in the Yad Vashem archives, viewing countless letters, dolls, clothing, and more. I felt that people coming to a historical museum would be completely saturated with information, distracting from the project's mission. So, I made a counterproposal, one in which there would be less reliance on artifacts to create a place in which one would be able to reflect and remember the children who perished.

One first descends through a natural cave within the site. Below ground is a room with photographs of the faces of children who died. One then moves to a large underground chamber. In its center is a candle surrounded by semi-transparent, semi-reflective glass walls. The floor, ceilings, and outer walls are all made of mirror. As you walk through the space on a bridge through the optical effects of glass walls and mirrors, the single candle reflects millions of times into infinity in all directions. A measured voice perpetually recites the names of the lost children, their places of birth, and their ages at death. Then one exits to the north, into light and life.

The Yad Vashem committee rejected my scheme. They said that people would misunderstand its intention and "think it was a discotheque." Ten years later, Abe Spiegel, a Holocaust survivor who had lost his two-year-old son in Auschwitz, came to Jerusalem and saw my model at Yad Vashem. He immediately understood and was moved by it. He wrote a check and the memorial was built in 1986.

Moshe Safdie, Yad Vashem Children's Memorial, Jerusalem, 1986, showing light reflected into infinity from a single candle

Some years later in 1997, I was in Jerusalem and had a call from the foreign ministry telling me that the Chief Minister of the state of Punjab had visited the memorial. He was very moved by it and wanted to meet its architect. When we met later that day, he said, very emotionally, "We Sikhs have suffered a great deal. We have lived in persecution, trying to maintain our identity as a minority in a large country. We want to build a place of national identity, a museum. I would like you to come and design it."

Two weeks later I was in Punjab. I was taken to the Golden Temple, the religious center of the Sikhs, and also to Anandpur, where Guru Gobind Singh, the last Guru of the Sikhs, died in his fort. The temple and fort were in the center of the small town. We headed in a vehicular convoy to the proposed site for the building, which turned out to be nine kilometers from the temple. En route,

I began to wonder how many of the pilgrims—hundreds of thousands arriving on foot and by car, bus, and train—would ever actually reach the museum. I suggested that we go back to town, leave the cars, and walk by foot. Whatever spot we could reach as pedestrians would be a potential site. We identified a pair of sand cliffs straddling a valley. I thought this was the perfect place, which was soon approved and the site purchased.

On my way home I began to sketch, thinking about how this building might rise out of the sand cliffs, be built from local sandstone, and somehow grow out of the land. I thought about Sikh temples, which always have water and gardens at their center. I came back with a preliminary model showing the historical museum on one side of the cliffs, and, on the other side abutting the town, an auditorium, library, and place for changing exhibitions. A pedestrian bridge linked the two with a series of water gardens in the valley, formed as a drainage basin from the Himalayan

above: Moshe Safdie, Khalsa Heritage
Memorial Complex, Punjab, 1997–present,
study sketch

opposite: View of Khalsa Heritage Memorial

Mountains beyond. The structure was to be concrete clad with sandstone, and would feature silver roofs of stainless steel to reflect light. Silver, not gold, was selected to imply secondary status in relation to the Golden Temple. From the north as visitors descended towards the site, they would see the silo-like stone walls rising from the cliffs.

When I came back a few months later, my little model had been made ten times bigger. Soon there was an amazing groundbreaking for this Khalsa Heritage Memorial, attended by half a million people. I emphasize this, because when I first arrived in Punjab, there was quite a controversy about the Chief Minister inviting a foreigner to design the national museum: "What will an Israeli-American know about Sikhism, and could he possibly come up with a scheme that would deliver a sense of identity and belonging for the Sikh community?" Apparently, the design was a success in these respects.

The building also elicits other provocative questions: "Is it a secular center or a religious center for the Sikh people? Do they think of themselves as a people, a nation, or a religion?" This is the same ambiguity the Jews experience, being both a people and a religion. The peasants have come to this place even before it is finished. They remove their shoes, wash their feet, and treat it as a religious destination. Our building seems to have captured that elusive sense of a Sikh identity, in a spiritual sense. The Chief Minister and the government, on the other hand, hope that this will be a national secular destination.

A few years later, Yad Vashem decided to completely rebuild its historic museum. Yad Vashem is set on the Mount of Remembrance, which also includes the national and military cemetery. The old museum, built in the 1950s, was to be replaced by a museum three to four times its size. By this time, the Holocaust Museum in Washington, D.C., had been built; in terms of content and completeness of information, it made Jerusalem's museum obsolete. Moreover, while the original museum was built for 300,000 visitors a year, the new museum at Yad Vashem was planned to accommodate three million visitors.

There was a three-stage international competition for the commission. We were invited to participate, and from the outset I had some very strong feelings about the project. The first was that I did not want to design a 60,000-square-foot building sitting atop the hill, totally dominating it. I also could not conceive of creating a building that was "business as usual," having galleries, doors, windows, and architectural details tell a story as horrific as that of the Holocaust.

Very early in the competition phase, I started thinking in terms of a building, not on top of the hill, but cutting through, under the hill. My plan

right: Moshe Safdie, Yad Vashem Holocaust Museum, Jerusalem, 2005, aerial view

below: Yad Vashem Holocaust Museum, reception building with light permeating through the skylights and trellis

was to cut through the mountain aggressively from the south, descending into the earth, and breaking out on the opposite side to the north. All of the galleries were to be below the earth, with light shafts penetrating upwards. Then, as one emerges to the north, the structure would burst into light overlooking the Jerusalem Forest. The narrative is imposed on you, as a story with a beginning and an end, through which you move. After several submissions, we won the competition.

As I noted previously, Jerusalem's bylaws demand that stone be used for a building's exterior. I felt that using local stone was "business as usual"; it was also much too pretty and golden in color for a museum with this subject matter. I asked for special dispensation to build the entire complex in concrete, based on the fact that Yad Vashem is technically and symbolically sacred, not municipal, ground. It is, unlike other Holocaust museums, a place where the ashes of victims are kept. I was granted permission.

The reception building that accommodates public services and the entrance is a very simple concrete structure. There, light permeates through skylights and a trellis, resulting in a striped shadow pattern. I realized in designing this space how symbolic associations provoked by architecture vary widely and personally. There was much reaction to the striped shadow patterns covering the walls and floor and visitors within the space. People would ask: "Did you mean this light, which creates stripes over the people who come in, to evoke the memory of the uniforms that the camp interns were compelled to wear?" I responded sincerely that I had meant nothing of the kind. I had created this system of skylights and trellises because I wanted to create a soft shadow pattern that would dematerialize everything in the space, creating a mood of ambiguity, and emotionally preparing the visitor for the next stop: entering the museum. Time and time again, people have also

Yad Vashem Holocaust Museum, exhibition space

above: Yad Vashem Holocaust
Museum, Hall of Names

right: Yad Vashem Holocaust
Museum, three-story-deep cut in the
bedrock in the Hall of Names

opposite: Yad Vashem Holocaust
Museum, terrace overlooking the city
of Jerusalem

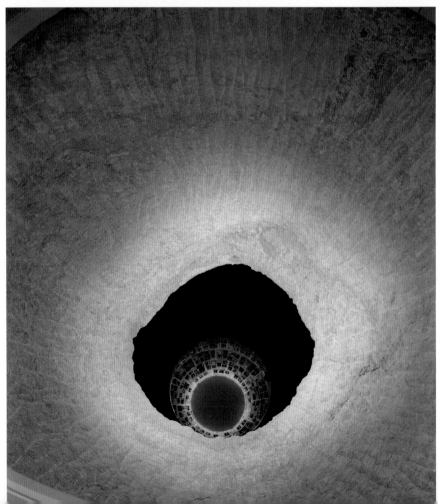

asked me about the form of the museum's terminus point, the two concrete walls that reach out over the mountain: "Is it the gesture of breaking out? Are they two arms stretched in prayer? Are these representing this or that?" Symbolic associations, I have discovered, are completely personal, not the subject of imposed narrative.

Leaving the reception building, you cross a bridge and enter a structure that seems to sustain the mountain above. Skylights high above make one aware of the depth of the earth. Cuts in the floor serve as barriers, bringing one to a halt, at which point you must move sideways into exhibit rooms. The exhibits and the building were designed at the same time, and the exhibit designer worked very closely with us. The rooms, the exhibits, the installations, and the position of each skylight were conceived in relation to each other.

The visitor is compelled, indeed forced, to go from chapter to chapter, culminating at the Hall of Names. Here are housed three million files of names and testimonies of victims. I proposed that the cylinder surrounding the space be the repository of those files. A cone suspended overhead in the center of the space contains photographs of the faces from the files and reaches to the light above. A three-story-deep cut into the bedrock reaches down to the water table, representing the names of those victims who will never be known. The water reflects the faces in the cone.

Curatorially, this space was to be the last chapter in the museum, the final destination. Yet, I felt a high level of discomfort with this. In a sense, here was the opportunity for architecture to have the last word. I proposed that the visitor should proceed to the mountain's edge, breaking into the light, an act of the reaffirmation of life. The dramatic view over the city of Jerusalem and the sense of renewal

one gets overlooking the forest below were living testimony that the objectives of the perpetrator of the Holocaust had failed. The walls of the concrete prism break out, cantilevering over the mountain and taking on a sense of total lightness. The caps over the post-tensioning cables imbedded in the walls allow the concrete to soar over the city, so that it can be seen from a great distance away.

The building committee was reluctant to accept this proposal at first. They asked whether such an exuberant gesture was appropriate. After considerable debate it was approved, and has proven to be one of the most memorable moments of the visitor's experience.

In the past, literal symbols were shared, evolved, and we all experienced them by direct association. A Gothic cathedral is a collective association, with a sense of "church and Christianity," for example. Today, I think this no longer holds true, yet there is still an attempt by many of us architects to define and prescribe symbolic narratives in our work. I've come to the conclusion that this is not possible or desirable. You cannot enforce a narrative of the symbolic, because it is deeply personal in nature. In a way, it is like trying to define "beauty." For me beauty has to do with the Darwinian notion of fitness, a sense of the greater order of nature. I have the sense of extraordinary beauty when I look at agricultural fields, thinking that it represents the overlaying of the human mind on the order of nature. Someone else's sense of beauty may differ entirely. This is the very reason why we must be so sensitive when we deal with the issue of interpreting symbols. Literal symbolism must be transcended; seeking beauty will yield the spiritual.

Yad Vashem Holocaust Museum, walls of the concrete prism breaking out, cantilevered over the mountain

IS THERE A RELIGIOUS SPACE IN
THE TWENTY-FIRST CENTURY?

PETER EISENMAN

My first question concerns the initial premise of this book: it answers a question with a question.

It is not necessarily the idea of "religious" that concerns us here. Rather, it is something more like the term "ineffable," or perhaps the term "sacred." There is an idea in French of *l'espace indicible*. Le Corbusier did a cover sketch for a book he was writing with that title, but never published. *Indicible* is difficult to translate, but probably has something to do with "unsayable." The idea of the unsayable refers to one of my mentors, Jacques Derrida, who talks about the problematic of orality, or speech, as opposed to writing. He might call writing ineffable, as opposed to that which is unspeakable. Taking it one step further, *indicible* also suggests the "undecidable," which is Derrida's term for the problematic of any dialectical resolution between such conditions as sacred and profane. In other words, can we today define what is meant by what is sacred or what is profane after Derrida's proscription of the possibility of a dialectical resolution?

When thinking about the term "sacred," I am reminded of my own office's entry into three design competitions for what might be considered sacred space. One was the Church of the Year 2000 in Rome, another the Memorial to the Murdered Jews of Europe, and the third was the City of Culture of Galicia in that great Christian pilgrimage town of Santiago de Compostela in Spain.

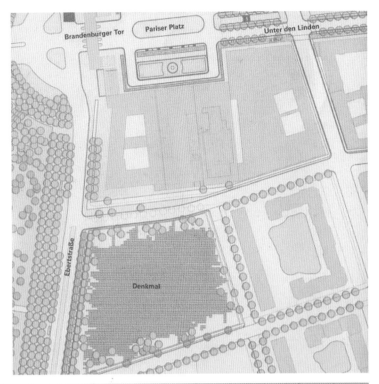

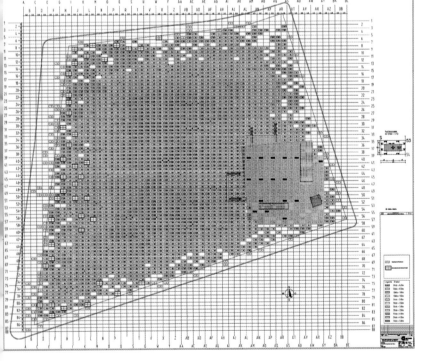

Initially, we were asked to participate in a competition for a Holocaust memorial in Berlin. The site in the center of Berlin is next to the Brandenburg Gate. It is also the site of Joseph Goebbels' home, and in fact Goebbels' bunker, where he murdered his own family, is under the site. When we were first asked to participate in the competition I rejected the idea, because I felt any memorial or monument would only trivialize the meaning of what had happened during the Holocaust.

From the beginning, the project attempted to refrain from banal references through symbolism or figuration, to stay in the realm of what one would call "the real," that is, without any representation of names, directions, or narrative references. As a place that was both different from the experience of the everyday but also had the possibility of the ordinary, the project could not want to replicate the experience of the camps, the actual sites of the Holocaust.

In that sense, the project was about something other, to make the experience of the present something that could not be easily resolved but would be part of an ongoing, impossible resolution. We sought to produce a condition similar to what Marcel Proust proposes in *Remembrance of Things Past*, when he writes about Swann on the Méséglise Way and the footsteps he heard on the stones, which reminded him of a moment in time when he was in Venice, walking on the stones of Piazza San Marco. In Proust there was this collapse of time from the past into a present, where the present became part of two times. Our project attempted to create a condition in space that could not necessarily be synthesized from past to present: the present would remain, as it were, in a future present of the past experience of being in this place.

There was a time in the 1960s when I was in an Iowa cornfield on a gray day. I had walked into that cornfield to pick some fresh sweet corn.

opposite, top: Peter Eisenman, Memorial to the
Murdered Jews of Europe (Holocaust Memorial),
Berlin, 1995, site map

opposite, bottom: Topographic diagram of pillars,
depths ranging from 1 to 5 meters

above: Study model of the two topographies

I walked 100 yards off the road because I did not want to be seen trespassing on this farmer's land. I took several ears of corn and then, for a moment, because of the grayness in the middle of the cornfield, I did not know which way to turn. I felt, as it were, lost in space. I remembered that moment because I wanted to see if it was possible to create an analogous situation in the memorial of being lost in space. Would it be possible, in the middle of a city, to create a moment in time of being lost in space?

The idea of being lost in space came from a woman who was brought to Auschwitz from Budapest in November of 1944. She had been sent to Auschwitz with her mother when she was eleven years old. When they stepped off the train they were confronted by Dr. Mengele, who grabbed her mother and sent her to one side and then pushed the daughter to another side. The daughter said, "No, no, I want to be with my mother." Mengele kicked her and said, "You'll have plenty of time to be with her." And she recalled that, at that moment

in space and time, she was speechless. She wanted to scream in horror, yet she could not utter a sound. This raised the question of the unspeakable, the impossibility of speech, the impossibility of sound, and the idea of silence. She said that at that moment she felt lost in space. The notion of the unspeakable, the impossibility of sound, silence, and of being lost in space were conditions that structured the thinking about this project.

At the time of the opening of the memorial in 1995, the Italian philosopher Giorgio Agamben said he thought that the project was the play between two kinds of memory. One was an archival memory, that is, things that needed to be remembered and could be recorded in physical time and space in a museum. The memorial has such a place underground, the Place of Remembrance, where the archival memory resides.

The second memory, he said, was contained in the field of pillars, which was the idea of the immemorable: that which is impossible to memorialize because of what was. For Agamben, the union between the archival memory and the immemorable resided in the memorial's illegibility. It has no direction, no center, no purpose, no names. It has, as it were, only silence.

Since the opening of the memorial, how it is thought of has slowly changed from the idea of a *Denkmal*, that is, a memorial, to a *Mahnmal*, which in German, loosely translated, means a warning, signifying the notion that memory becomes a warning about a possibility in the future of what happened in the past. In other words, rationality and abstraction can lead to something horrific: when reason becomes overbearing and excessive, it can also become irrational.

The project attempts to deny "the image," as for example, its absence of names. Even though there is a prohibition against imagery and representation

opposite: Study model

above: Men in field

left: The pillars with the Quadriga on the Brandenburg Gate and the dome of the Reichstag in the background

right: The pillars, which appear like the side aisle of a chapel
below: Close-up of rectilinear pillars

right: Interior of the
Place of Remembrance

overleaf: Landscape
of pillars

of God in Judaism, the Jewish community was against this project. They said it was not Jewish enough. When the American artist Barnett Newman was once asked to participate in a show of Jewish painters, he said: "There's no such thing as Jewish painting." Last year, I was asked to participate in a show about Jewish space and I suggested that there was no such thing as a Jewish space. The Holocaust memorial is about naming a condition in the present, whether it is Jewish or not. In fact, the Germans wanted a place that was built by Germans, paid for by Germans, and for the German people. The memory is for a third generation of Germans, which understands the issues of World War II differently from how the second and first post-war generations perceived them.

Many of the Germans I knew before the memorial was constructed thought it was too big. What they had in mind was something like Rodin's Burghers of Calais, seven weeping Jews under a tree somewhere, as quietly unobtrusive as the many German Jews who thought they were Germans back in 1939.

Yet, when one goes to the memorial, one sees children running out of school buses and playing tag in the field. Of course, when they go home and see their grandmothers and grandfathers, the children tell them, "We had a field trip to the Holocaust Memorial!" That idea has nothing to do with sacred space. It has to do with de-sacralizing the space, to make it more everyday, ordinary, so there would be no special and thus clumsy relationship between German and Jew. I have seen people take lunch there, I have seen people sunbathing there, I have seen people in love there—all of the things that make it part of the everyday, of the ordinary. This is why I bring up the notion of the undecidable, because if this is the sacred, if the sacred is also the everyday, then we truly are in the presence of the undecidable.

The project started as a marking of the ground, a surface that was part of the mythology of the Nazis: *Blut und Boden* (blood and soil). The ground was to be a Germanic ground and Jews were to be eradicated from it. We did not want people walking on that ground of Berlin, so we created an artificial topography out of the ground. A second, artificial landscape surface was created above the ground, and then the two surfaces were simply connected with the pillars, which are an index of the two topographies. The two surfaces cannot be seen at the same time. While one can walk on the ground, it is not possible see the tops of many of the pillars. Thus, the experience of the place and the conception of the place are two different things. They never come together as a single entity.

On the day of the opening a young Lubavitcher Rabbi came up to me and said, "Mr. Eisenman, what is the meaning in the number of pillars?"

And I said, "There's no meaning in the number of pillars."

He said, "Are you sure?"

And I said, "I'm absolutely sure. We had approximately 4,300 to begin with. Then Chancellor Kohl said there were too many, that we needed a few trees and sidewalks. So we cut the number down to 3,200. Then, the American embassy said they needed a few more meters of separation from the street, because they thought the field would be a great place for terrorists to shoot at the embassy. So we cut about 500 more pillars to accommodate the widened street. We counted the pillars at the end because we were paying for them individually, and found that we ended up with 2,711 pillars purely by accident."

The Lubavitcher Rabbi said, "Do you know what the number 2,711 is?"

I said, "No, I don't."

And he said, "It's the number of pages in the modern Talmud."

THE CONTEMPORARY MOSQUE   ZAHA HADID

I remember going as a child to see the Great Mosque in Córdoba, Granada. I was seven years old, and that was the most stunning space. Of course there are lots of other truly great spaces, but this mosque left a really tremendous impact on me. It is very dark inside, but then there is a white marble cathedral placed inside the space, and in this way it is like a modern hybrid project. Another sacred form that has impacted me is the spiraling Malwiya, the minaret of the ninth-century Great Mosque of Samarra in Iraq, built over a thousand years earlier than some of the modernist buildings that resemble it.

When I went to see the Umayyad Mosque in Damascus a few years ago, I was told that everything was covered in precious materials: the floor, the walls, the columns, the ceiling, and the great mosaic reliefs. Again, I thought, this connects us back to contemporary ideas of seamlessness—here everything is covered in the same material. Can you imagine over 1,200 years ago, someone walking into that space? It must have been heavenly!

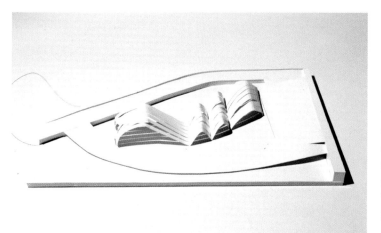

Our office's first mosque project was the comp- etition for the Grand Mosque in Strasbourg, France in 2000, which occurred in several stages beginning in March 1998. The initiative to construct this religious edifice came from two parties: the Muslim Institute of Europe presided over by Ali Bouamama and La Coordination des Associations Musulmanes de Strasbourg (CAMS). Despite efforts to mediate the two proposals from the respective groups, the mayor of Strasbourg, Roland Ries, finally decided to take up the CAMS proposal and sign a civil partnership with the Société Civile Immobilière (a non-commercial real-estate company) Grande Mosquée de Strasbourg. In July 2000, Catherine Trautman, a member of the European Parliament for Eastern France and a former mayor of Strasbourg (elected in 1989 and 1995) as well as former Minister of Culture of France, launched an architectural contest for the design of the mosque. The principal competitors involved were the architecture firms of Valente et Pfister, Jean-Marie Wilmotte, Mario Botta, Benjelloun et Rochd, Paolo Portoghesi, and our office. The winner, Paolo Portoghesi, was chosen in November 2000 by two jury sessions open to the public under the leadership of Abdallah Boussouf from the Palais du Rhin. The mosque opened in 2009.

Although our scheme was not the selected project, it proved to hold many design and organizational concepts that we are using for three mosques currently in design. For example,

the project for the Grand Mosque in Strasbourg is organized as a matrix set up by the axis for prayer, or *qiblah*, in one direction, and the curvature of the river in the other. Where the two directions intersect, they fractalize and generate volume. The focus or the apex of this directional field is the mosque itself. Its spatial significance is seen, therefore, above and beyond the individual elements that comprise the building.

The main secular spaces are at the street entry level, including the hall, auditorium, dining areas, and exhibition spaces. The mosque and courtyard are lifted above the ground, removing the building from its urban context and enabling it to form a floating sacred space above the city. The courtyard is a private internal space reached from the lower secular parts of the building below and is used almost exclusively as the entry to the mosque. It is both a contemplative space and an area of transition between the outside world and the inner space of the mosque. The courtyard also constitutes a sheltered space formed by the walls of the auditorium, the library, and the kindergarten. While this spatial composition has its origins in the historic four-walled mosques, or four *iwans* (three-walled domes with one open wall) it also provides additional outdoor space for prayer when the mosque is full on *Eid* or *Jumma*.

Following the design principles of traditional Islamic architecture, a series of transitional spaces plays an essential role in the unfolding of the entry passage. The prayer hall, being the focal point of arrival, is placed on a separate level entirely dedicated to an embracing and serene enclosure, while remaining connected to the rest of the building below.

The distinct seclusion of the main prayer halls—the focus of the project—creates a distinguished space removed from the clamor of public interaction. The use of the courtyard space, on the other hand, articulates the visual separation

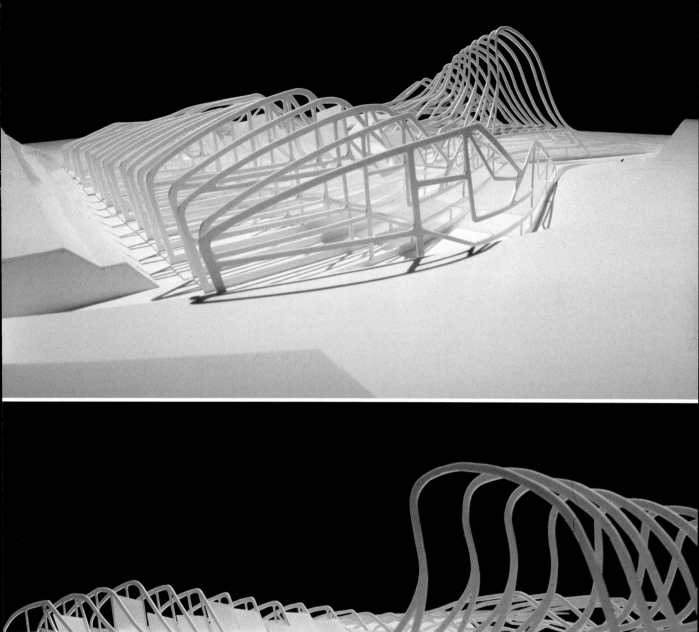
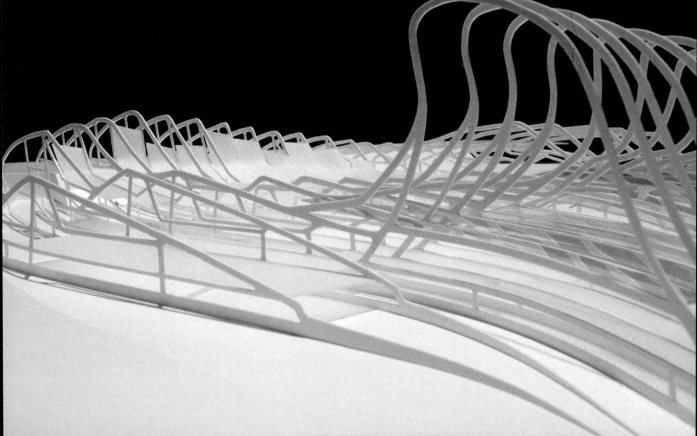

right: Zaha Hadid, Avenues Mall
Mosque, Kuwait, 2009–present,
image of exterior

below: Avenues Mall Mosque,
rendering of interior

enhancing the privacy between the men's and women's prayer spaces, while providing for additional prayer space if required. The delineation of the *qiblah* wall, located along the longer side of the prayer hall, accommodates the "prayer rows" in the favorable orientation towards Mecca. In our design, the women's prayer area is a separate hall, rather than a more traditional, mere secondary gallery space. This separate hall enriches the innovative approach of the scheme, while acknowledging the contribution of women's spiritual and material culture in Islamic society in particular, a role they have maintained since early Islam.

The metaphor of Islamic calligraphy is apparent in the flowing lines of the structure and the sections of the building. The elegant, classical Jali Thuluth script, in particular, has been contemplated in our work. The design called for Qur'anic verses to be selected and executed by hand by a traditional master calligrapher.

The journey, or ascent to the mosque, is organized by the narrative of light and sound. The base of the building slopes down to meet the river and the ground-level entry area. Slits on the floor of the raised mosque enable light and sound to fill the area below, thus dematerializing the volume above. The secular program, in contrast, is seen as semiautonomous pieces. These act as a collection of fragments with their own light and aural textures, similar to the pavilion arrangement of a citadel. The daylight of the raised courtyard, for example, is framed by the austere or blank canvases of the adjoining buildings. These buildings, including the auditorium at the back, provide an acoustic or sound barrier between the railway lines, the road, and the mosque.

The idea of Islamic geometry was used to generate a fractal space. The fractal informs the reinforced concrete arches as primary structure. This, in turn, supports a secondary layer of interspersed concrete paneling, glass, and ceramics.

The effect is intended to generate a mosaic or fragmented skin, which provides an unexpected composition of light and sound. Black-and-white pigmented concrete, hints of turquoise ceramics, and translucent glazing elements provide color.

In a more current project, the Avenues Mall Mosque in Kuwait, the site for the proposed mosque is at the intersection of major commercial shopping spaces and a retail center. The organic volume, which includes one larger dome and a sequence of ovoid and circular domes with smaller side spaces, creates sacred and community spaces. Since it is sited in a commercial area as part of the master plan, and developed privately, the focus is more on community life as a gathering place, rather than only as a place of prayer. Taking the lines of circulation of the site, the sculpted form flows from space to space to the external environment. The 700-square-meter hall is housed under lacy concrete roofs comprised of geometric patterns that flow over an armadillo-like plan figure.

The desire of people is to make heaven on earth: literally, heavenly space, great space. People always aspire to invent such spaces. Like my childhood experience of going into the Great Mosque of Córdoba, being within them is uplifting and that is why people have invested so much time to create and make them possible over the centuries. Yet it is very, very difficult to invent these heavenly spaces—spaces that can nevertheless offer so much to visitors.

EPILOGUE: ON THE RELEVANCE OF
SACRED ARCHITECTURE TODAY

PAUL GOLDBERGER

In one way or another, every one of the essays in this book brings to mind that wonderful word that Le Corbusier famously used in describing his great chapel at Ronchamp: "ineffable," the un-utterable. This is no mere semantic point. I think it brings to the fore a paradox that gets to the heart of the making of sacred architecture, which is the fact that in the realm of the sacred, architecture—the discipline most dependent on materiality, indeed the ultimate expression of materiality—must try to express what is not material, what cannot ever be material. In the quest to create sacred space, then, architecture is in a way working against itself, working against its nature, we might say, since it must struggle to use the material to express what transcends the material. In the making of sacred architecture, we must use the physical to express the transcendent.

It should be no surprise, then, that we inevitably start, as the title of this book does, with the idea of space, not structure. Space is intuitively less rational, and it is obviously less material. No one ever talks of sacred structure. We may study Gothic cathedrals as works of structure, but when we talk of them in sacred terms, we talk about things far less tangible—we talk of space, and light. Even though, as Kurt Forster remarked at a symposium on writing about architecture, the word "space" was not part of the standard architectural parlance until the nineteenth century, what we now use that term to connote has been there throughout the history of architecture. The creation of sacred architecture was very much the creation of sacred space. But the fact that the term was not in common use until relatively recent times is of more than passing significance, because it reminds us that the creators of much of the space we hold most sacred were not thinking of themselves as makers of space, at least not primarily. For much of history, that concept was too abstract. As Vincent Scully has shown us in looking at sacred space made by the Native Americans and the ancient Greeks, space was the product of a design process that had its basis in ritual and metaphor—a point that is consistent with the building of Christian cathedrals and churches, as Thomas Beeby reminds us in his remarkable essay on the connection between Rudolf Schwarz's treatise on sacred architecture and the work of Mies at the Illinois Institute of Technology (IIT).

The second part of the paradox is that architecture, as well as being material, is also by nature and expectation rational—structure must have logic or it cannot stand. But the sacred is otherwise. It not only does not demand logic, it defies it. Logic, the thing that is utterly essential in the creation of structure, is quite beside the point when it comes to the sacred. But we need it to get there. If the goal is to make sacred architecture,

there is a contradiction between the means and the end: the means must be rational, even as the end cannot be.

Another way to get at this might be to say that you can contemplate the idea of God, but you cannot engineer the physical reality of God. Or can you? When Richard Meier writes about the machine that was invented to create the shell-like vaults of his church in Rome, I began to think otherwise. The architects of the Gothic cathedrals, of course, were engineers who used structural systems to create otherworldly, far-from-rational effects. The physical structure of any Gothic cathedral is measurable, describable, capable of being analyzed down to the last stone. Yet as every one of us knows, it evokes feelings beyond the measurable, beyond the rational. The structure exists to bring us to a place that, for all intents and purposes, defies the very essence of structure.

I would be tempted to say that this is in fact a good definition of sacred space—the use of material forms to evoke feelings that go beyond the material, and which cannot be measured. I think that is basically right, and it surely describes the spaces described in this book, whether they are the Greek temples Vincent Scully has once again written of so movingly, or the buildings of Ando or Holl or Moneo or Meier. I think that definition may also describe a kind of space not much mentioned in these essays—sacred spaces like simple Quaker meeting houses, which are not complex and that seem, at least superficially, not at all "ineffable." They are often symmetrical and relatively unadorned, and seem very easy to understand. Yet somehow they evoke profound thought and transcendent feeling, as does too a Japanese temple or a Zen garden—outwardly simple and by all appearances rational in a way that, say, Ronchamp is not. Yet they are capable of evoking feelings of equivalent mystery. In a way the Quaker meeting house is the most amazing

Friends Meeting House, Plymouth
Meeting, Montgomery County,
Pennsylvania, 1708 (with 1780 addition)

of all, because we cannot even see that something startling and otherworldly is going on. It is like the magician who doesn't use smoke and mirrors or flashy costumes, who just stands there and makes you think nothing is happening and then suddenly you notice that your watch has disappeared. Scully suggests that the power of such spaces—and he includes Wright's Unity Temple among them—comes from the centrality of the preacher, upon whom all focus, since there is no elaborate altar or stained glass or decorative detail to distract. While it is true that a centrifugal space has a wholeness and completeness to it that is different from an axial one—since you always feel that the axis could keep extending itself, as if the façade and front door were just arbitrary—I think the intensity of the meeting house, like that of Shaker objects, comes also from its purity, from a sense that this is not plainness, but simplicity pared down to its powerful essence.

Early in this collection, Karsten Harries raises the possibility that architecture itself does not create the sacred, but that the users of a building and their activities do. In other words, do we confer the quality of sanctity upon spaces, or do certain spaces confer sanctity upon us? That is not precisely what Harries asked, but his words stimulate that question in my mind, and it is also implicit in what Peter Eisenman, Mark Taylor, and Stanley Tigerman have written. Perhaps what is sacred is

Jože Plečnik, Church
of the Sacred Heart,
Prague, 1928–32

simply what we choose to sanctify. I think of small Protestant and Jewish congregations in many cities whose synagogues are essentially storefronts or leftover urban spaces; or of similarly improvised Islamic places of worship in Western cities; or of rural churches like the ones Emilie Townes describes so compellingly that are roadside boxes; or even of those new mega-churches that plenty of people, myself included, have derided as looking like shopping centers. Yet those churches obviously perform a sacred function for many people, and inspire in them feelings of transcendence, even while looking more like big-box warehouses.

In the Ethical Culture Society in New York, the words "The Place Where People Meet to Seek the Highest Is Holy Ground" are inscribed over the proscenium arch, and that, for many people, is so. It may be no accident that Ethical Culture emerged in large part out of Judaism's Reform movement, since the Jewish tradition has never been particularly architecturally centered (although compared to the mega-churches of the Christian Evangelical movement, it would seem deeply committed to architecture). There have been many elaborate and beautiful synagogues built over time, but they have almost always tended to follow the local vernacular, and however elaborate they may be, they share the desire to express the idea of the book, in the form of the Torah scrolls, as the primary sacred element. Whatever form space takes in a synagogue, it is never supposed to overshadow the sanctity of the word. I think this notion—that however elaborate the building, it should do nothing to suggest that physical structure takes precedence over the importance of the written word—would even have been true in what may be the greatest unbuilt synagogue of modern times, Kahn's Hurva Synagogue, intended for Jerusalem, to which Scully refers.

Recently I was in Prague, where I visited Jože Plečnik's Church of the Sacred Heart, which

I must say is one of the most amazing buildings I have ever seen in my life, but whose sanctuary could not be described as ineffable space. The interior of this church, though hardly simple, has little mystery about it. It was intended by Plečnik to be flexible; it is based on a grid, and his concept was to have multiple altars and not have the space be exclusively frontal in its orientation and use. In this sense, it is not entirely dissimilar to the "way form" space described by Rudolf Schwarz that, as Tom Beeby shows us, provided a spiritual basis for Mies at IIT (though, given the fact that this church is Catholic and not Protestant, and that Plečnik ornamented his building richly, I would be wary of carrying that analogy to a deeper level).

I mention Plečnik's Church of the Sacred Heart, however, to make another point, which is that I felt a certain disconnect there between those who worshiped in it—and by chance, I visited during mass—and those who came to see its architecture. I sensed that these two groups of people experienced the building in quite different ways, and were moved by different things. I would almost be tempted to say that the worshipers were moved in spite of the architecture, and the architectural pilgrims because of it. To the former group, this staggering and stunning work was largely a container, made potent not by its form so much as by the rituals that go on within it, as well as by certain iconic objects contained inside it: statues and paintings that were not designed by the architect and in some cases were even put there over his objection, rather like the traditional cross that was installed in Richard Meier's Jubilee Church. The point is that, unlike the exterior of this building, much of the interior was not finished as the architect specified. Now to the other group, not the worshipers but the seekers of architectural experience, the rituals mattered even less, probably, than the architecture mattered to the worshipers. It is Plečnik's astonishing form, his slab of a bell tower, his merger of classicism and modernism into something at once rich and bombastic, that give this church its aura, its magnetic allure. So what makes a space sacred can differ hugely depending on who is doing the experiencing.

This is true in plenty of cases—who has not felt in Sant'Ivo or San Carlino a similar disconnect between those who come to worship Borromini and those who come to worship God (even though, most of the time, the former group seems clearly to outnumber the latter)? At Ronchamp or Unity Temple or Kahn's Unitarian Church, it is even more the case—architectural pilgrims seem to dominate. There is nothing wrong with this, and obviously there are plenty of people who belong to both groups and have both deep architectural and deep religious experiences when they visit great sacred space. Not all who are attracted by architecture do so solely because they—or the architect—have substituted aesthetic appeal for the aura of the sacred, to quote Karsten Harries yet again. It is not wholly a zero-sum game.

My point, though, is only to note that even when these experiences, the aesthetic and the sacred, co-exist, we as architects tend to assume that the power of the experience comes wholly or largely from the architecture. I think this is architectural hubris. While great architecture surely can and often does enhance religious experience, it is not particularly likely to create it. The qualities that most architecturally aware people respond to, the qualities that we might feel confer sanctity, are not always the ones that make space sacred for the people for whom it was, at least ostensibly, created. It is transcendent for them because of what they bring to it at least as much as because of what the architect has done with it.

This is not to minimize the potential of architecture, even in our time, to create a sense of awe, and the aura of the sacred. That we continue to aspire to the sacred is itself significant—since, as Rudolf Schwarz would remind us, the quest for the sacred is itself sacred. And, often, the quest is successful. Ando's work surely achieves a level of the sublime, its qualities emerging, as Kenneth Frampton explains, in part from his view that nature is not static but active, that we can often come closest to nature by being the most man-made, not by deferring to nature but by actively re-interpreting and almost controlling it, by abstracting it. One might contrast Ando's Church of the Light with, say, Fay Jones' Thorncrown Chapel to underscore the point. In Ando nature is almost hidden, mysterious, and awesomely powerful. The concrete structure seems, when you first see it, to suggest no sympathy with nature at all, and no mystery, yet it brings forth the most profound connection to nature and the greatest mystery, as daylight glows through the cross cut into the concrete wall and between the two concrete planes of the entry wall. The Fay Jones chapel is superficially far more spectacular as a structure, and seems, with all that glass and all those ribs and vaults, to be celebrating nature and revealing it, showing us both the glories of nature and the bedazzling abilities of man to a far greater extent than Ando's closed concrete structure. Yet what Ando reveals, of course, is vastly subtler, and infinitely more powerful.

The ability of architecture to create the sacred, and not merely to enclose it, so to speak—that is to say, the ability of architecture to create a sense of awe, regardless of whether one comes to it with the rituals of religious practice in mind–is borne out, paradoxically, by non-religious buildings, since they are places to which no one brings an expectation of ritual or a predisposition to religious experience. Where in the realm of sacred space are we to place, say, Jefferson's Lawn at the University of Virginia, or Sir John Soane's Breakfast Room, or the Farnsworth House? There, architecture is transcendent, as surely as in the chapels of Tadao Ando. And what are we to make of the fact that while Unity Temple's extraordinary space surely possesses a sacred aura, so, too, does Fallingwater, perhaps just as much of it? We might say the same of Kahn's Unitarian Church and his Kimbell Art Museum, or his Center for British Art in New Haven, Connecticut. In these cases, and they stand for many others, is it merely that the aesthetic has reached such intensity and risen to such heights that it becomes indistinguishable from the sacred?

It is easy to think so, particularly when one considers the common observation that the art museum seems to have replaced the cathedral in our culture, a point reiterated by Kenneth Frampton. We have no sense of commonality of faith as motivated the cultures that built the great sacred spaces of earlier eras, and it is no accident that we have made the art museum the most intense arena of architectural expression today. For all that commercial skyscrapers have come to represent as cultural symbols in one sense, we now use art museums as emblems of our aspirations with far more conviction. Steven Holl perhaps intentionally underscores this point when he chooses to present his remarkable Nelson-Atkins Museum as a kind of coda to his presentation of St. Ignatius Chapel, with the clear implication that if we observed certain similarities between the chapel and the museum, the architect would not object.

Still, I'm not entirely sure that Karsten Harries' fear has been borne out, that we have simply substituted the aesthetic for the sacred—or, to use Fariborz Sahba's formulation, that we have chosen to be attracted to the beautiful rather than to the divine, and therefore to have our hearts (or our eyes) satisfied instead of our souls. I am not sure it is so simple, in part because the connections between art and religion, between art and the soul, are far deeper and more interdependent, not to say ambiguous, than these formulations would suggest. I would hope that our failings are not quite so clear-cut as merely the elevation of the aesthetic over the sacred.

We also need to keep in mind that our time is altogether different from any other in terms of what architecture can do to create the aura of the sacred. Ronchamp was a radical building, an extraordinary work of sculpted space and directed light. The very strangeness of its shape seemed appropriate as a way to pull away from the rational and to suggest an unseen, spiritual power. Though the space within Ronchamp is as beautiful and as moving as ever, to the visitor today it is surely no longer as strange. Technology now brings within the reach of every architect shapes and forms that could barely be imagined before. If you have a computer, you can be Frederick Kiesler now, a creator of endless space that can turn in on itself. Technology has made the ineffable migrate from the spiritual to the secular sphere. Fifty years ago, when Ronchamp was new, unusual space, complex space—mysterious space—it was in and of itself a signifier of the sacred. Today, that is much less so, and not only because of our culture's secular and aesthetic leanings; it is also because technology has debased the currency of ineffable space.

This has been happening gradually for a while—some time after Kiesler did his most interesting work there was Saarinen, who was a shaper of space that had many of the qualities we associate with the ineffable, even though his most potent spaces were not his religious ones, but places like the TWA Terminal, striking in its time and now looking rather tame. But today, thanks to technology, we can and often do make spaces like TWA, and many of them are far richer and more complex. It would seem inevitable, given the technology that is available to us, that what constitutes our sense of truly ineffable space would have to change in an age in which every airport aspires to being Ronchamp.

Fay Jones, Thorncrown
Chapel, Eureka Springs,
Arkansas, 1980

The challenge, surely, is to maintain a sense of mystery, which in an age of technology enabling all, or seeming to enable all, is not easy. It is mystery, after all, that distinguishes, say, Nicholas Hawksmoor from Sir Christopher Wren, the irrational from the rational. Brilliant and magnificent as Wren is, we can analyze and understand it—Wren's St. Stephen Walbrook is logic raised to its highest, most glorious potential. Go next door to Hawksmoor's St. Mary Woolnoth, or a short distance away to his Christ Church Spitalfields, and you experience something else, something startling, perhaps a bit terrifying, and compelling in a whole different way. One is the earth, perfected, and it holds forth the promise of enlightenment. The other is also ordered, but its order calls up in us a sense that there is something we will never fully understand, that we will never entirely grasp—that we can never truly know. That is the ineffable; that is the sacred. It is the moment where architecture reaches its highest, where material form takes us to a non-material realm. In the profound joining of the rational and the unexplainable, Hawksmoor—or Borromini or Kahn or Ando—unite the aesthetic and the sacred, and make of them not separate realms but one inseparable thing.

There will always be those to whom the aesthetic is the sacred, and there will always be those to whom the sacred has no need for the aesthetic. But I would like to believe that part of the reason for the assembly of this collection of essays is the hope that it can be otherwise, and that the very idea of the transcendent can in itself become a kind of common language that joins architectural and religious experience, seeing them not as the same, but each of them as something that can enrich the other, and that can bring the transcendent to a new level of meaning.

Nicholas Hawksmoor, Christ Church Spitalfields,
London,1729

CONTRIBUTORS

THOMAS H. BEEBY was dean of the Yale School of Architecture from 1985 until 1992, where he continues to teach design. He was director of the School of Architecture at the University of Illinois at Chicago from 1980 to 1985. As a principal of the Chicago-based firm, HBRA Architects, he has designed Chicago's Harold Washington Library and the Hole-in-the-Wall-Gang Camp in Connecticut.

KARLA CAVARRA BRITTON teaches the history of architecture and urbanism at the Yale School of Architecture. Before coming to Yale in the fall of 2003, she taught at Columbia University and served as director of its architecture program in Paris. She received her Ph.D. in Architecture History and Theory from Harvard University. Her publications include the monograph *Auguste Perret*, published by Phaidon in both English and French editions, and with Dean Sakamoto, she edited *Hawaiian Modern: the Architecture of Vladimir Ossipoff*. She was a co-convenor of the Yale symposium, "Constructing the Ineffable," in fall 2007.

DIANA ECK is Professor of Comparative Religion and Indian Studies and Frederic Wertham Professor of Law and Psychiatry in Society at Harvard University. Her books include *Banaras, City of Light* and *Darsan: Seeing the Divine Image in India*. With Devaki Jain she edited *Speaking of Faith: Global Perspectives on Women, Religion, and Social Change*. With Françoise Mallison, she edited *Devotion Divine: Bhakti Traditions from the Regions of India*. Her book, *Encountering God: A Spiritual Journey from Bozeman to Banaras*, studies

the question of religious difference in the context of Christian theology and the comparative study of religion.

PETER EISENMAN is the Charles Gwathmey Professor in Practice at the Yale School of Architecture. His projects include the Memorial to the Murdered Jews of Europe in Berlin, the Wexner Center for the Arts and Fine Arts Library at Ohio State University in Columbus, and the Aronoff Center for Design and Art at the University of Cincinnati. Eisenman Architects' current projects include a one-million-square-foot cultural complex, the City of Culture of Galicia in Santiago de Compostela, Spain; two railroad stations in Pompeii; and housing in Tenerife. The firm's stadium for the NFL Arizona Cardinals opened in August 2006. In 2007, Yale University Press published Mr. Eisenman's *Written Into the Void: Selected Writings, 1990–2004*.

KENNETH FRAMPTON is the Ware Professor of Architecture at Columbia University's Graduate School of Architecture, Planning, and Preservation. He has taught on the faculty at Columbia since 1972. He is an architect and architectural historian and was technical editor of the magazine *Architectural Design*. His books include *Modern Architecture: A Critical History* and *Studies in Tectonic Culture: The Poetics of Construction in Nineteenth and Twentieth Century Architecture* and *Labour, Work, and Architecture*.

PAUL GOLDBERGER is the architecture critic for *The New Yorker*, where since 1997 he has written the magazine's "Sky Line" column. He holds the Joseph Urban Chair in Design and Architecture at The New School in New York City. He was formerly Dean of Parsons School of Design, a division of The New School. He began his career at *The New York Times*, where in 1984 his architecture criticism was awarded the Pulitzer Prize for Distinguished Criticism. He is the author of several books, including his chronicle of the process of rebuilding Ground Zero, titled *UP FROM ZERO: Politics, Architecture, and the Rebuilding of New York*, which was named one of *The New York Times*' Notable Books for 2004.

ZAHA HADID is the first woman to be named Laureate of the Pritzker Architecture Prize and she received an Honorary Doctorate from Yale University in 2006. In addition to the mosque projects she is currently designing, she also tested the boundaries of traditional mosque design with her competition entry for the Mosque in Strasbourg. Hadid is currently Professor at the University of Applied Arts, Vienna. She has held the Kenzo Tange Chair at the Graduate School of Design, Harvard University, the Sullivan Chair at the University of Chicago School of Architecture, and guest professorships at the Hochschule für bildende Künste in Hamburg, the Austin E. Knowlton School of Architecture at Ohio State University, and at Columbia University Graduate School of Architecture, Planning, and Preservation. She is also a frequent Visiting Professor at the Yale School of Architecture.

KARSTEN HARRIES is the Brooks and Suzanne Ragen Professor of Philosophy at Yale University and director of graduate studies in philosophy. He has published and lectured widely on Heidegger, early modern philosophy, and the philosophy of art and architecture. He is the author of countless articles and books, including *The Meaning of*

Modern Art, *The Bavarian Rococo Church: Between Faith and Aestheticism*, and *The Ethical Function of Architecture*, which won the 8th Annual International Architecture Book Award for Criticism.

STEVEN HOLL is Professor of Architecture at the Graduate School of Architecture, Planning, and Preservation at Columbia University. He is best known for his Kiasma Contemporary Art Museum in Helsinki, Finland, and Simmons Hall at MIT in Cambridge, Massachusetts. He recently completed the addition to the Nelson-Atkins Museum of Art in Kansas City, Missouri. His other major works include the chapel of Saint Ignatius in Seattle, Washington.

JAIME LARA is Visiting Professor of Theology and Art History at the University of Notre Dame, and was recently a Guggenheim Fellow and a Kress Fellow at the National Gallery of Art, Washington, D.C. He has taught at Yale University and California State University at Los Angeles. He was a co-convenor of the 2007 symposium, *Constructing the Ineffable*, organizing in particular the Yale Institute of Sacred Music portion of the conference, "Sacred Space: Architecture for Worship in the Twenty-first Century." He teaches and writes on Christian art, liturgy, and architecture, focusing on the praxis of the Spanish New World. His written work includes the books *City, Temple, Stage: Eschatological Architecture and Liturgical Theatrics in New Spain*; *Christian Texts for Aztecs: Art and Liturgy in Colonial Mexico*; and *The Flowering Cross: Holy Week in an Andean Village*. He is currently finishing a book on solar orientation in the colonial churches of Peru.

RICHARD MEIER has taught at Cooper Union, Princeton University, Pratt Institute, Harvard University, Yale University, and UCLA. He has been awarded major commissions in the United

States and Europe, including courthouses, city halls, museums, corporate headquarters, public housing and private residences. He is the architect of major works, including the Ara Pacis Museum in Rome, Italy; the ECM Tower in Prague; the City Hall in San Jose, California; and the Jubilee Church in Rome, Italy. Some of his other major projects include The Getty Center in Los Angeles, the High Museum in Atlanta, and the Frankfurt Museum of Decorative Arts in Germany.

RAFAEL MONEO teaches design at Harvard University where he was chair of the Graduate School of Design from 1985 to 1990. Some of his major works include the headquarters of Bankinter in Madrid; the National Museum of Roman Art in Mérida; the Davis Art Museum at Wellesley College; the Museums of Modern Art and Architecture in Stockholm; an expansion of the Museum of Fine Arts in Houston (the Audrey Jones Beck Building); and the Cathedral of Our Lady of the Angels in Los Angeles, California. His most recent work includes the enlargement of the Prado Museum in Spain.

MOSHE SAFDIE is Director of the Urban Design Program and the Ian Woodner Professor of Architecture and Urban Design at the Harvard Graduate School of Design. He was responsible for major segments of the restoration of the Old City of Jerusalem and the reconstruction of the new center and has worked in Senegal, Iran, Singapore, and in the northern Canadian Arctic. In the last decade, he has focused on a number of major commissions, including the Telfair Museum of Art in Savannah, Georgia; the Yad Vashem Museum in Jerusalem; the Lester B. Pearson International Airport; the Ben Gurion International Airport; the Salt Lake City Main Public Library; and the Peabody Essex Museum.

FARIBORZ SAHBA is an Iranian architect now living in Canada. He is the architect for the Bahá'i House of Worship, known as the Lotus Temple, in Delhi, India, and the Terraces at the Shrine of the Báb, in Haifa, Israel. In Iran, he was involved in the design of a wide range of prestigious buildings such as the Centre of Handicraft Production and Arts Workshops, Tehran; the New Town of Mahshahr; and the Pahlavi Cultural Centre and School of Art in Sanandaj.

VINCENT SCULLY is Sterling Professor Emeritus of the History of Art at Yale University. He is author of numerous books on art and architecture including *The Earth, the Temple, and the Gods: Greek Sacred Architecture* and *Architecture: The Natural and the Manmade*. In 2004 he received the National Medal of Arts, the United States' highest honor for artistic excellence.

MARK C. TAYLOR is the Chair of the Department of Religion at Columbia University. Both a philosopher of religion and cultural critic, he is a leading figure in debates about postmodernism, and has written on topics ranging from philosophy, religion, literature, art, and architecture to education, media, science, technology, and economics. His many books include *Erring: A Postmodern A/Theology* (one of the first attempts to study religion from the viewpoint of poststructuralist thought); *Disfiguring: Art, Architecture, Religion; About Religion: Economies of Faith in Virtual Culture*; and *After God*.

STANLEY TIGERMAN is the architect for the Illinois Holocaust Museum & Education Center in Skokie, Illinois. He has directed the School of Architecture at the University of Illinois at Chicago, and is the author of a number of works on architecture, including *The Architecture of Exile*. His projects include the Five Polytechnic Institutes in Bangladesh; the Illinois Regional

Library for the Blind and Physically Handicapped in Chicago; and the POWERHOUSE Energy Museum in Zion, Illinois. He has completed housing projects throughout the United States, as well as in Germany and Japan, and he has designed exhibition installations for museums in the United States, Portugal, and Puerto Rico.

EMILIE M. TOWNES is the Andrew W. Mellon Professor of African American Religion and Theology at Yale Divinity School. She is editor of two collections of essays, *A Troubling in My Soul: Womanist Perspectives on Evil and Suffering* and *Embracing the Spirit: Womanist Perspectives on Hope, Salvation, and Transformation*. She has also authored *Womanist Ethics and the Cultural Production of Evil*; *Womanist Justice, Womanist Hope*; *In a Blaze of Glory: Womanist Spirituality as Social Witness*; and *Breaking the Fine Rain of Death: African American Health Care and a Womanist Ethic of Care*.

MIROSLAV VOLF is Director of the Yale Center for Faith and Culture, and Henry B. Wright Professor of Systematic Theology at Yale Divinity School. He received his doctorate at the University of Tübingen, where he studied under Jürgen Moltmann. Based on his early experiences of growing up in a part of the world fraught with cultural and social turmoil, Volf has explored deeply the issues of cultural identity, violence, and reconciliation in such works as *Exclusion and Embrace: A Theological Exploration of Identity, Otherness, and Reconciliation*, and most recently *The End of Memory: Remembering Rightly in a Violent World*.

ACKNOWLEDGMENTS

I would like to express my appreciation for the interest and support of numerous colleagues and students who were critical to the inauguration and completion of this project. First my thanks go to all those who were participants in the original symposium and who became contributors—indeed, collaborators—in the production of this book. My thanks also go to Robert A.M. Stern, Dean of the Yale School of Architecture, who initiated the original symposium and encouraged my engagement with the topic. Without the generous support and continuous involvement of Harold Attridge, Dean of Yale Divinity School; Martin Jean, Director of the Yale Institute of Sacred Music; and Barbara Shailor, Deputy Provost for the Arts at Yale, this project would never have come to fruition. From the start, Jaime Lara served as a close collaborator and creative partner in organizing the symposium, including the companion Institute of Sacred Music (ISM) conference on sacred space and worship. John W. Cook, with whom I co-taught a course on the topic of sacred architecture, provided constant encouragement. I am also grateful to Kenneth Frampton, to whom I continue to owe a great personal and intellectual debt, for his critical insights. Among those more indirectly involved in the project, I want to thank Alexander Tzonis, Alexandros Tombazis, Sallama Shaker, Brigitte Shim, Geetanjali Chanda and the Yale Women, Religion and Globalization initiative for having provided opportunities for deepening discussions of the topic's timely importance. The Yale University Press provided a particularly helpful set of reviewers' comments, which helped significantly in shaping the final manuscript.

In addition, I have recently been fortunate to work with a number of talented graduate and undergraduate students at Yale, each of whom has contributed to a deeper appreciation of sacred architecture's symbolic power in architectural, socio-political, and urban discussions. In particular, I want to express appreciation to Yale School of Architecture students Gary Ku, Gregory Melitonov, Taekyoung Lee, and Courtney Crosson; the ISM students Gilbert Sunghera, S.J. and Roman Hurko; and Yale College students Erene Morcos, Christopher Palencia, Garrett Wong, and Russell LeStourgeon.

No project such as this coalesces without the combined efforts of an editorial team: my gratitude goes to Nina Rappaport, Director of Publications at the Yale School of Architecture; assisting editor Ann Holcomb; image and permissions editors Victoria Koppel and especially Heather Kilmer; and graphic designer John Clifford of Think Studio. Their dedication and professionalism were decisive at every turn. Above all, I thank my son, Nico, for his enthusiasm while visiting many sites mentioned in this book; and my husband Joseph Britton for his unwavering confidence in the project—indeed, my gratitude to him may be rightly said to be inexpressible.

Karla Cavarra Britton

INDEX

Numbers in *italics* indicate images.

A

Aalto, Alvar, 23, 149
Abbey Church of Ste. Marie Madeleine
    (Vézelay), 35
Abdu'l-Bahá, 179
Abelard, 35–36
Abraham (Feiler), 146
Acropolis, *32*, 33
action, framework for, four components of, 65
actualization, 137
Adorno, Theodor W., 71
aesthetic emotion, 13
African Zion Baptist Church (Malden, WV), *77*
Agamben, Giorgio, 210
Aldrin, Buzz, 128n34
Amiens, 36
Anabaptists, 86
Anandpur (Punjab), 197
Ando, Tadao, 23, 81, 97, 152, 119, 224, 228, 230
    architecture of, nature playing fundamental
        role in ontology of, 98
    commercial commissions of, displaying
        secular spirituality, 109
    creating a "dialogue with geometry," 109
    employing water as embodiment of the
        spirit, 105
    evoking Christian iconography and its
        Japanese other, 99
    on light and darkness, 99
    museum designs of, 106–8
    orchestrating landscape to evoke the
        spiritual, 106, 108
    political intent in works of, 108
    role of natural phenomena in architecture of,
        98, 105, 106
    self-enclosed architecture of, 98–99
    on *shintai*, 98
    spiritual presence in work of, 99
Apollo, temple of (Corinth), 32
Apollo, temple of (Delphi), *31*
Aquinas, Thomas. *See* Thomas Aquinas
archetypes, theory of, 19
architects
    consciousness of, 23

    work of, as utopian, 53
    charged with being futurists and visionaries, 81
    communicating meaning in new
        circumstances, 81
    as high priests of futurism and progress, 121
    offering own versions of sacred space, 76,
        159
    relations with workers, 133, 177
    working reality of, 133
architecture
    aesthetic approach to, 53
    bound with religion, 50
    building a home for the soul, 56
    as decorated sheds, 56, 58, 61, 62
    dependent on materiality, 223
    distinct from functional buildings, 50–53
    experiencing, as sacred, 53
    framing function of, 113
    governed by same laws as building, 194
    history of, related to history of building, 193
    intrinsically abstract nature of, 145
    modern, distancing itself from the sacred, 49
    needing the sacred, 49, 50–54, 59, 61–62
    as passionate pursuit, 135
    phenomenology of, 184
    prompting symbolic associations, 201–4
    pseudo-sacred, 64
    rational nature of, 224
    reduced meaning in achievements of, 62–64
    representation at heart of, 71
    representing the center, 79
    as revelatory art, 113
    sacredness of, 44
    as self-sufficient aesthetic whole, 53
    separating engineer from architect-artist, 56
    as site of sacred memory, 64
    social art of, 7
    spirituality of, 184
    transcendent, 228–29
Ardalan, Nader, 194
Aristotle, 191
Armstrong, Neil, 127
art, losing sense of aura, 53
art museums, 229. *See also* museums
Artless Word, The (Neumeyer), 80
ascetic communities, isolation in, 88–89

asceticism, 86
Asterius of Amasia, 59
Athena, temple of, 31–32
Athens, organization of, 33
Augustine, 50, 95
aura
    experience of, incompatible with spirit of the
        modern world, 57
    loss of, 53, 55
avatara (Hindu: descent), 115
Avenues Mall Mosque (Kuwait; Hadid), *220*, 221
Awaji Yumebutai development (Tsuna-gun;
    Ando), 108

B

Báb, the, 179
Bahá'í Faith, 171, 172, 175, 179
    definition of "love" for, 176
    Houses of Worship, 171
Bahá'í World Center (Haifa; Sahba), 179–80
Bahá'u'lláh, 171, 172–74, 178, 179
Banaras (India), 81, 114
Banaras waterfront, *114*
Barragán, Luis, 105
Bartning, Otto, 23
basilica, form of, 34, 35
Basilica of Our Lady of Peace (Yamoussoukro),
    21
Bataille, Georges, 70
Baths of Caracalla, vaults of, 33
Baudot, Anatole de, 16
Becket, Welton, 123–15
Beeby, Thomas, 80, 224, 227
Behnisch, Günter, 152
belonging, 194
Benjamin, Walter, 53, 57
Benjelloun et Rochd, 218
Berlage, Hendrik Petrus, 16
Bernini, Gian Lorenzo, 37, 149
Black Circle (Malevich), *69*
Blanshard, Brand, 54
body, sacredness of, 40–42
Bohm, Dominkus, 23
Book of Remembrance (Holocaust Museum
    & Education Center [Skokie]; Tigerman),
    140, *141*

Borromini, Francesco, 149, 230

Boston (MA), first purpose-built Hindu temple in, 118

Botta, Mario, 20, 218

Bouamama, Ali, 218

Boullée, Étienne-Louis, 122

Boussouf, Abdallah, 218

Bramante, Donato, 37, 149

Breuer, Marcel, 81, 124, 127

Brunelleschi, Filippo, 36

Bryggman, Erik, 23

Buddhi Satwa Avalokiteswara, 176

building

as azimuth, in Ando's architecture, 98–99

governed by same laws as architecture, 194

history of, related to history of architecture, 193

modern, inviting cloning, 53

Burgee, John, 55

Burghers of Calais (Rodin), 213

C

Calabasa, Hindu temple in, (Malibu [CA]), 118

Calatrava, Santiago, 53, 152, 160

Candela, Felix, 23, 81, 124, 127

Cangrande, statue of (Castelvecchio Museum, Verona), 168

Capitol Records building (Los Angeles; Becket), 123

Carceri d'invenzione ("The Smoking Fire"; Piranesi), 122

Cathedral of All Times, The (Schwarz), 84, 91–92, 95

Cathedral of Our Lady of the Angels (Los Angeles; Moneo), 159–69

Cathedral of Santa Vibiana (Los Angeles), 160

Catholic Reform movement, 110

census, fear of, 136–37

center, the, 74–79

Center for British Art (New Haven; Kahn), 229

Chapel of the Resurrection (near Stockholm; Lewerentz), 16

Chapel of St. Ignatius (Seattle; Holl), 184–88, 190

Chauvet, cave of, 40

Chicago, grid of, 88, 89

Chikatsu-Asuka Historical Museum (Osaka; Ando), 106–8

Children's Museum (Himeji; Ando), 106

China, house-church movement in, 62

Christ Church Spitalfields (London; Hawksmoor), 230, 231

Christianity, first centuries of, devoid of sacred architecture, 61

church building, as a work in its own right, 76

Church of Christ the Worker (Atlándia; Dieste), 23

churches, modern, evoking primitive states of feeling, 40

Churches (Dupré), 55

Church of the Holy Trinity (Fátima; Tombazis), 21

Church Incarnate, The (Schwarz), 75–76, 80, 84, 87

Church of the Light (Ibaraki; Ando), 98, 99, 119, 228

Church of the Sacred Heart (Prague; Plečnik), 226, 227–28

Church of Santa Maria (Marco de Canavezes; Siza), 81

Church of St. Joseph (Le Havre; Perret), 22

Church of St. Pierre (Firminy-Vert; Le Corbusier), 14, 18

Church of the Three Crosses (Imatra; Aalto), 23, 149

Church on the Water (Tomamu; Ando), 100–105, 119

Church of the Year 2000 competition (Rome), 207

Cinq semaines en ballon (Five Weeks in a Balloon; Verne), 122

City of Culture of Galicia competition (Santiago de Compostela, Spain), 207

clients, for sacred architecture, dialogical relationship with, 133

Collective Memory, The (Halbwachs), 64

Colonna, Francesco, 122

"Colony on the Moon" (Scarfo), 126

concrete, new use of, 15–16

Constantine, church architecture changing after conversion of, 85

"Constructing the Ineffable: Contemporary Sacred Architecture," 7

construction, role of, in defining a building's character, 167

constructional materials, revealing, 145

consumerism, 81, 108

consumption, gratuitousness of, 70

Corpus Christi Church (Aachen; Schwarz), 18, 84

Couturier, Marie-Alain, 18, 19

Crete, 30–31

cross, the (Schwarz), 87–88

Crown Hall (Illinois Institute of Technology; Mies van der Rohe), 90, 91–92, 94–95

Crystal Cathedral (Garden Grove; Johnson), 47, 55, 56, 57, 124, 149

Crystal Palace (London), 55

Cubism, 13

cubits, 143–45

Curtis, William, 108

cyclic return, 191

D

Dalai Lama, 183

darshan (Hindu: seeing), 114–15, 116

Das Heilege (Otto), 68–70

Davies, J. G., 19

death drive, 70

decorated shed, 55–56, 58, 61, 62

decoration, urge for, 55–56

Delbanco, Andrew, 62

democracy, rise of, 86

denial, as biblical theme, 137

dense-pack construction, 188

Derrida, Jacques, 207

Der Wanderer über dem Nebelmeer (The Wanderer above the Sea of Fog; Friedrich), 95

Descartes, René, 53

Dieste, Eladio, 23

Doman, Emeric, 127

Doman Moon Chapel (Mills), 126, 127, 128, 129, 130

domes, building of, related to materials available, 194

dualism, of sacred and profane, 19

Dupré, Judith, 55

Dyckhoff, Tom, 124n16

E

Earth in the Balance (Gore), 179

Eastern orientation, 137, 140–42

East Rock (New Haven, CT), 29

Eck, Diana, 81

eco-resort (Ahkbuk Peninsula; Holl), 188, 189

Eisenhower, Dwight, 123

Eisenman, Peter, 25, 70, 71, 152, 226

Eliade, Mircea, 70, 74–75, 76

on experience of sites as hierophanous, 18–19

on necessity of sacred space, 19

shifting away from law and ritual, 19–20

El-Wakil, Abdel Wahed, 44

Empire State Building, 30

emptiness, 133, 183

environmental considerations, in building the Lotus Temple, 179

Ethical Culture Society, 227

Exodus, memory of, 64–65

F

Fallingwater (Mill Run; Wright), 229
Falwell, Jerry, 47
Farnsworth House (Plano [IL]; Mies van der Rohe), 228–29
Federal District of Brasilia (Brazil; Niemeyer), 123–24
Feiler, Bruce, 146
Festival building (Naha City; Ando), 109
fifth dimension, 176
First Christian Church (Columbus [IN]; Saarinen), 23
First Church of Christ, Scientist (Berkeley; Maybeck), 23
First Church of Christ, Scientist (The Hague; Berlage), 16
First Unitarian Church (Rochester [NY]; Kahn), 22, 42–43, 229
Forest of Tombs Museum (Kumamoto; Ando), 106
Forever in Bloom (Rai), 180
Forster, Kurt, 224
fourth dimension, search for, 13
Frampton, Kenneth, 23, 81, 228, 229
Freud, Sigmund, 70
Friday Mosque (Esfahan, Iran), 194
Friedrich, Caspar David, 92, 95
From the Earth to the Moon (De La Terre à la Lune; Verne), 121, 122, *123*
Fuller, Buckminster, 43, 124, 127
fundamentalism, 27
Fushimi Inari shrine (Kyoto), 99
future, remembering, 64–65
futurism, 123

G

Gallup, George, Jr., 54
Gangotri (Himalayas), 115
Ganz Andere, 68, 70
Gaudí, Antonio, 22, 40
Gebetsscheune (prayer barn), 50
Gehry, Frank O., *28*, 152, 160
generic city, 20
German Pavilion, 1967 World's Fair (Montreal; Otto), 124n20
German Romanticism, 92
Giedion, Sigfried, 21–22
Gizeh, 30
God
    as denegation of the sacred, 68
    memory of, 65
    transcendence of, shifting concern from the material to the spiritual, 87

Goebbels, Joseph, 208
Golden Temple (Punjab), 197
good, vision of, narrowed scope of, 62
Gore, Al, 179
Gothic architecture, 35–36
Gothic cathedrals, 204, 224
Graham, John, 123n15
Graham, Robert, 167
Grand Mosque project (Strasbourg; Hadid), 218–21
Great Mosque (Córdoba), 217, 221
Great Mosque of Samarra (Iraq), 217
Greeks, art and architecture of, related to repetitive cycles, 191
Gropius, Walter, 42
Guardini, Romano, 17–18, 80, 81, 84, 110
Guggenheim Museum (Bilbao; Gehry), 28

H

Habermas, Jürgen, 9
Hagia Sophia, at Église du Saint-Espirit (Tournon), 22, 34
Halbwachs, Maurice, 64
Hall of Reflection (Holocaust Museum & Education Center [Skokie]; Tigerman), *143, 147*
Hall of Remembrance (Holocaust Museum & Education Center [Skokie]; Tigerman), *142*
Hanging Gardens of Mount Carmel (Haifa; Sahba), *178*, 179–80
Harries, Karsten, 25, 61, 62, 115, 194, 226, 228, 229
Hasaw Chan K'awil, tomb of (Guatemala), 29–30
Hawksmoor, Nicholas, 230
Hegel, G.W.F., 50
Hejduk, John, 135
Hera, temples of (Paestum), 31
hero-architect, myth of, 36
Hervé, Lucien, 18
hierophanous space, 20
Hindu temples
    architects for, 172
    consecration of, 118–19
    embodying the Divine, 116–18
    in the United States, 118–19
Hockney, David, 168
Holl, Steven, 224, 229
holocaust, manifesting the sacred, 70–71
Holocaust memorials and museums, 70–71.
    See also Memorial to the Murdered Jews of Europe; Yad Vashem *listings*
Holocaust Museum (Washington, D.C.), 198

Holocaust Museum & Education Center (Skokie; Tigerman), 135–47
holy, as numinous, 18
Hompukuji Temple (Awaji Island), 105
Honshu-Shikoku bridge, 109
hope, linked with memory, 64
Horns of the Phaedriades, 32
horror religiosus, 70
house, cult of, 37
house-church movement, 62
human form, fitting into the square and the circle, 34
human will, as reality, 35
Hurva Synagogue (Jerusalem; Kahn), 22, 44, 45, 227
Hymettos, 33
Hypnerotomachia Poliphili (Colonna), 122

I

Idea of the Holy, The (Otto), 68–70
Ignatius, Saint, 184
Il Gesù (Rome; Maderna), 38
Illinois Institute of Technology (Chicago; Mies van der Rohe), 80, 88–95
Il Redentore (Venice; Palladio), 37–38
Imagine All the People (Gyatso and Oauki), 183
immaterial, constructing, 74–75, 78
India
    architecture in, 116–18
    guides in, for historical sights, 175–76
    sacred space in, meanings of, 114
indicible, 207
industrialization, 87, 145
ineffable
    architecture's attempt to express, 223
    ecumenical sensibility of, 119
    expressing, through the non-verbal, 16
    multiple meanings of, 17
    as product, 20
    speaking of, paradox of, 16–17
    tracing the limit of, 68
ineffable space, 13–15
inertia, presenting an impasse to building, 137
Innocenti, loggia of (Florence; Brunelleschi), 36
Institute for Lightweight Structures, 124
Interieur van de Nieuwe Kerk te Haarlem (Saenredam), *38*
introversion, 59
Iran, desert architecture of, 178
Islamic architecture, 218–21
Islamic calligraphy, 221
Islamic geometry, 221

J

Japan, consumerist society of, 81
John Paul II, 150–52
Johnson, Philip, 47, 55, 124, 149
Jones, Fay, 228
Jubilee Church (Rome; Meier), 119, *150–52,*
    153–57, 227
Jubilee Year, 150–52
Julius II, 37
junkspace, 20
jyotirlinga (Hindu: manifestation of light), 114,
    115–16

K

Kahn, Louis I., 22–23, 42–44, 230
Kedarnath (India), 114
Khajuraho (India), 116
Khalsa Heritage Memorial Complex (Punjab;
    Safdie), 197–98, *199*
Khrushchev, Nikita, 123
Kierkegaard, Søren, 59
Kiesler, Frederick, 229
Kimbell Art Museum (Fort Worth; Kahn), 229
King Saud Mosque (Jeddah; El-Wakil), *46*
Koselleck, Reinhart, 65
Kundera, Milan, 64
Kursaal Congress Hall (San Sebastian; Moneo), 167

L

La Coordination des Associations Musulmanes
    de Strasbourg (CAMS), 218
Lactantius, 50
Langenheim, James, 123n15
Lara, Jaime, 81
Larkin Building (Buffalo; Wright), 15
L'Art Sacré, 18, *19*
La Sainte-Baume (near Aix-en-Provence; Le
    Corbusier), 14
Latter Day Saints (Mormons), 127–28
lattice (Schwarz), 88
Learning from Las Vegas (Venturi, Brown, and
    Izenour), 55
Le Corbusier, *15, 19,* 22, 40, 44, 127, 149, 207
    on the Acropolis, 33, 47
    association of, with Couturier, 18
    concerned with metaphysical and religious
        themes, 14
    evoking sacredness of the body, 40–42
    on ineffable space, 13–15
    on Notre Dame du Raincy, 16
    sense of sacredness in work of, 42
Ledoux, Claude-Nicolas, 122n7
l'espace indicible, 207

Lefaivre, Liane, 53
Léger, Fernand, 21–22
Leonardo da Vinci, 34, 36, 122
Lequeu, Jean-Jacques, 122n7
Les Pierres sauvages (Pouillon), 18
Les Voyages Extraordinaires (Verne), 122
Le Thoronet (Provence), 18
Letters from Lake Como (Guardini), 110
Lewerentz, Sigurd, 16
Life of David, The (Pinsky), 136
light
    bringing life to architecture, 190
    divine, manifestations of, 114–15
    as effective media for exploring the sacred,
        133
    hierophany of, 149
    as icon, 116, 119, 157
    as one of two decorative elements in Lotus
        Temple, 178–79
    relation of, to Hindu temples and India's
        landscapes, 81
    source of, 184
    symbolism of, progressive secularization of,
        55
    theological implications of, 119
Lin, Maya, 40, *63*
Lincoln Cathedral, 50, *51,* 56–58
Liturgical Arts, 124–27, 128
Lombard basilicas, 35
lost in space, 210
lotus, concept of, 176
Lotus Temple (Delhi; Sahba), *173–75,* 177–79,
    180, *181*
Luther, Martin, 85–86
Lutyens, Edwin, 22, 40

M

machine, metamorphosis of, 122
Mahabharata, 176
Mahony, Roger, 160–62, 168
Maki, Fumihiko, 109
Malevich, Kasimir, 69
Malwiya (Iraq), 217
Mangan, Terence, 127
mankind, image of, introduced into natural
    spaces, 31
Martin, Agnes, 168
Masjid Negara National Mosque (Kuala
    Lumpur), 21
mass tourism, consumption of, 108
materiality, architecture's dependence on, 223
Maya, temples of, 29–30
Maybeck, Bernard, 23

Mayne, Thom, 160
McDermott, Gerald, 54
measurement, 136–37
meetinghouses, 50, 224–26
mega-churches, 227
Meier, Richard, 119, 152, 224, 227
Memorial to the Murdered Jews of Europe
    (Holocaust Memorial, Berlin; Eisenman),
    207–15
memorials, as sacred architecture, 65
memory
    communal, 64
    linked with hope, 64
    sacred and ordinary, 64–65
Mengele, Josef, 210
Mesopotamia, ziggurats of, 30
Methodists, tent-meeting revivals of, 127
Metropolitan Cathedral (Brasilia; Niemeyer), 81,
    123–24, *125,* 127, 128
Metropolitan Cathedral of Christ the King
    (Liverpool; Lutyens), 22
Michelangelo, 37, 149
Mies van der Rohe, Ludwig, 17, 42, 80, 81, 83,
    93, 127
    foreword to *The Church Incarnate,* 84, 91
    relationship with Catholic Reform movement,
        110
    Schwarz's influence on, for Illinois Institute of
        Technology design, 88–95
Mikveh Israel Synagogue (Philadelphia; Kahn),
    21, 22, 44
Miletus (Turkey), 188
Mills, Mark, 127, 128
Minos, palace of, 30–31
mobility, 53
modernism
    exploring alternative forms of expression, 14
    influenced by transcendent ideals, 25
    institutionalizing the industrial look, 145
    problem of, 28
modernity
    presumed separate from the secular, 68
    relationship of, with secularity, 25
Modulor philosophy, 15
Monastery of Notre Dame de la Tourette
    (Eveux; Le Corbusier), 14, *18,* 42
monastic orders, 85
Moneo, Rafael, 76–78, 224
money, as god, 64
monumentality, 21–23
monuments, as sacred building, 25
moon base, as form of contemporary
    monasticism, 127

Moretti, Luigi, 150
Morgan, David, 20
Moser, Karl, 16
Moses (Michelangelo), 149
Mount Rokko Chapel (Kobe; Ando), 99–100
mountains, sacred nature of, 30–31
Museum of Literature (Himeji; Ando), 106
museums, 229
    as sacred buildings, 25, 28
    as surrogate religious institutions, 106
Muslim Institute of Europe, 218
mysterium tremendum, 68
mystery, maintaining a sense of, 230

N
narcissism, 54
natural forms, worship of, 30–31
nature
    as reality, 35
    reinterpretation and control of, 228
Nelson-Atkins Museum of Art (Kansas City;
    Holl), 190–91, 229
neo-Gothic churches, Schopenhauer's rejection
    of, 58
Neumeyer, Fritz, 80, 110
New England meetinghouse, 38
New Haven (Connecticut), constructed as
    sacred city, 28
Newman, Barnett, 213
New World of Space (Le Corbusier), 13
Niemeyer, Oscar, 81, 123–24, 127, 128
Nietzsche, Friedrich, 49, 56–57, 64
"Nine Points on Monumentality" (Sert, Léger,
    and Giedion), 21, 22, 23
non-theistic space, 190–91
Notre Dame Cathedral (Laon), 28
Notre Dame du Haut (Ronchamp; Le Corbusier),
    11, 14, 18, *19*, *22*, 40, *41*, 149, 229
Notre Dame du Raincy (Le Raincy; Perret),
    15–16, *17*

O
oku, 109
Olympia, 32–33
orality, problematic of, 207
orientation, as biblical theme, 137
ornament, fresh interpretation of, 16
orthogenetic city, 81
otherness, as location of one's object of desire,
    140
Otto, Frei, 124
Otto, Rudolf, 18, 68–70
Ottonian basilicas, 35

Ouaki, Fabien, 183
Outline of European Architecture, An (Pevsner), 50
Oyamazaki Villa Museum (Kyoto; Ando), 108
P
Palladio, Andrea, 37–38
Panofsky, Erwin, 159
Pantheon (Rome), 33–34, 90, 149
Parthenon (Athens), 33
Passion, memory of, 64–65
Pelli, Cesar, *52*, 53
permanence, 22
Perret, Auguste, 15–16, 22
Petén, 29–30
Petronas Towers (Kuala Lumpur; Pelli), *52*, 53,
    58, 64
Pevsner, Nikolaus, 50–53, 56, 194
Philips Pavilion (Brussels World Exhibition;
    Le Corbusier), 14
pigeon houses, 194
Pindar, 32, 33
Pinsky, Robert, 136
Piranesi, Giovanni Battista, 122
place, tyranny of, freedom from, 53
Plečnik, Jože, 16, 227–28
political intentions, in Ando's architecture, 81
polytheistic space, 188
Portoghesi, Paolo, 218
post-secular age, 9
Pouillon, Fernand, 18
production, utility of, 70
Promey, Sally, 20
Propylaia (Athens), 33
Protestantism, bringing about the modern
    world, 86–87
Protestant Reformation, 85–87
Proust, Marcel, 208
puja (Hindu: worship), 114, 178
Puritans, 86
"Purusha Sukta," 116
Puryear, Martin, 168

Q
Quaker meeting houses, 224–26
*Questions of Perception: Phenomenological
    Aspects of Architecture* (Holl), 188, 190
Quetzalcoatl, temple of (Mexico), 29

R
Rai, Raghu, 180
Real American Dream, The (Delbanco), 62
realities, Greek recognition of, 35
reality, modern understanding of, 53
Reims, cathedral of, 36

religion
    biblical, shadowed by iconoclasm, 59
    bound with architecture, 50
    defining, 68
    misunderstanding of, 68
    narcissism and, 54
    reasserting the role of, 9
    requiring introversion, 59
    strengthening of, 54
Religion after Religion (Wasserstrom), 19
religions, complementary and progressive
    nature of, 175
religiosity, in the United States, 54–55
religious
    distinguishing, from the sacred, 68–70
    return of, as post-modern phenomenon, 68
religious buildings. *See also* sacred buildings
    alluding to spiritual dimensions of human life
    in community, 23
    communal expectations for, 21–22
    discussing, in a non-modernist context, 20
    as foundations for new architecture, 15
    innovations of, 15
    as locus for innovation, 7
    perception of, in modern architecture, 15
    reflecting history of architecture, 15
    relationship to, of material things, 20
religious experience, architecture unlikely to
    create, 228
religious rites, emphasizing, within architectural
    context, 164
Remembrance of Things Past (Proust), 208
Renaissance, changed role of religion after, 159
Renaissance architecture, 36–37
repetition compulsion, 70
representation
    failure of, 71
    issue of, at heart of architecture and
    philosophy, 71
re-presentational function, 57–58
reproduction, tearing artwork from its historical
    context, 53
Resurrection Chapel (near Stockholm;
    Bryggman), 23
Ries, Roland, 218
Riley, Terence, 131
ritual expression, 10–11
River Ganga, 115
Rodin, Auguste, 213
Roman Catholic Church
    guide of, for architects and designers, 131
    ornate edifices of, 85
Rome, 33–38

displaying relationships between form and light, 149
New Evangelization in, 150
overtaken by dense apartment complexes, 149
Ronchamp. *See* Notre Dame du Haut
Rossi, Aldo, 44
Rothenberg, Susan, 168
Rothko Chapel (Houston), 159
Rudofsky, Bernard, 193
Ruini, Camillo, 150, 152

S
Saarinen, Eero, 123n15, 124n18, 229
Saarinen, Eliel, 23
sacred
construction of, in a new place, 119
defining, within a material object, 55
as denegation of God, 68
dependent on history and memory, 53
descending into the visible, 115
distinguishing, from the religious, 68–70
emerging from what people choose to sanctify, 226–27
encountering concept and realization, 10
experience of, 53
experiencing architecture as, 53
manifest in holocausts, 70–71
needing architecture, 49–50, 59, 61–62
non-producible by human effort, 62
relation of, to architectural form, 10
violent destructiveness associated with, 70
as the wholly other, 70
sacred architecture
as home for sacred memories, 65
reaction to, 227–28
relation of, to natural forms, 29
writing about, context for, 27
sacred buildings. *See also* religious buildings
architects' responsibility toward, 23
emphasizing different aspects of the structure and interior, 36–40
inserting a figure of utopia, 58
reference to, as aesthetic gesture, 58
variety of structures considered, 133
vernacular expressions of, 25
sacred memory, 64–65
Sacred Parting, 86
sacred places
contributing to cultural and urban fabric, 10
taking many forms, 10
sacred space, 19, 224
communal expectations for, 21–22
construction of, asserting meaning within, 23

distinguished from beautiful space, 180
in non-religious places, 228–29
need for, 19, 20
Roman impression of, 33
Sahba's definition, 172, 175–76
"Sacred Journey," 87
Sacred and the Profane, The (Eliade), 70
sacrifice, 70
Saenredam, Pieter, 38
Safdie, Moshe, 25, 70
Sagrada Familia (Barcelona; Gaudi), 22, 40
Sahba, Fariborz, 229
Said, Edward, 133
Saint-Denis, basilica of (Saint-Denis), 35–36
Sainte Baume (Troume), 40
Sainte-Chapelle (Paris), 55
Sainte-Jeanne d'Arc (Paris; Perret), 22
Sainte-Marie de La Tourette (Eveux; Le Corbusier), 14
Saint-Jean-de-Montmartre (Paris; Baudot), 16
Saint Savior Chapel (Illinois Institute of Technology; Rohe), *94*
San Vitale (Ravenna), 34
Santa Maria della Consolazione (Todi; Bramante [?]), 36–37
Santa Maria Rotunda (Rome), 128
Sant'Elia, Antonio, 123–24
"satisfied self," as biggest hope, 62
satisfaction, experience of, 62
Scarfo, Roy, *126*, 128n30
Schopenhauer, Arthur, 58
Schuller, Robert, 47, 55
Schwarz, Rudolf, 17–18, 55, 75–76, 80, 81, 84, 110, 224, 227, 228
on bridging the gap between world and other world, 92–94
describing development of the church as the Sacred Journey, 87
interest of, in architectural interpretation of Catholic liturgy, 84
on the relation of man to the land, 92
tracing development of forms of Christianity, 84–85
Scully, Vincent, 7, 25, 224, 226
Seattle University, 184
secular, presumed separate from increasing modernization, 68
secularism, misunderstanding of, 68
secularity
as religious phenomenon, 68
relationship of, with modernity, 25
secularization, resulting from the Reformation, 86

secularization hypothesis, 9
secular spirituality, 23, 81, 97
in Ando's work, 110
of Mies van der Rohe, 110
self-transcendence, 59
September 11, 2001, impromptu memorial following, 20
Serra, Junipero, 168
Sert, José Luis, 21–22
Shapiro, Joel, 168
Sharika Devi (Kashmir), 115
shed, decorated, 55–56
shelter, 193
shikara (Hindu: mountain peak), 118
Shikara temple (Khajuraho), *117*
shintai (Japanese: body) 81, 98
Shiva
presence of, 115–16
theological understanding of, 116
Shrine of the Báb (Haifa), 179–80
shunyata (Sanskrit: emptiness), 183
signification, absence and presence of, 140
Sikh temples, 197
silence, 84, 133
Singh, Gobind, 197
Siza, Álvaro, 15, 81
slippage, 140, 145
Sloterdijk, Peter, 64
Soane, John, Breakfast Room of, 228–29
Societé Civile Immobilière Grande Mosquée de Strasbourg, 218
Soleri, Paolo, 127
Somme, Memorial (Thiepval; Lutyens), 40
Sophocles, 31
soul, building a home for, 56
space. *See also* hierophanous space; ineffable space; junkspace; sacred space
controlling, 13
creation of, 224
experience of, 20
hierarchical visualization of, 20
hierarchy of, 18–19
Roman worship of, 33
Space Needle, World's Fair (Seattle; Steinbruck and Graham), 123
Spaceship Earth (Fuller), 124
Spiegel, Abe, 196
St. Anthony's (Basel; Moser), 16
St. Ignatius Chapel (Seattle; Holl), 229
St. John's Abbey (Collegeville; Breuer), 81, 124
St. Leopold am Steinhof (Vienna; Wagner), 16
St. Mary Woolnoth (London; Hawksmoor), 230

St. Mary's Cathedral (Lincoln). *See* Lincoln
    Cathedral
St. Peter's Basilica, new central plan for (Rome;
    Michelangelo), 37
St. Stephen Walbrook (London; Wren), 230
Steinbruck, Victor, 123n15
STEP (Takamatsu; Ando), 109
storefront churches, 74, 227
Suger, Abbot, 35–36
symbolic associations, 201–4
symbolism, importance of, in religious
    buildings, 172
synagogues, Jewish, following the local
    vernacular, 227

T
Tabernacle (Salt Lake City), 127–28
Taj Mahal (India), 175–77
Taylor, Mark, 25, 226
Teatro del Mondo (Venice; Rossi), 44
Temple I, Tikal (Guatemala), 29–30
Temple orientation, 140–42
temples
    as physical bodies of a divinity, 31
    rising as sacred monuments, 29–31
10-pew churches, 74
Tennyson, Alfred Lord, 172
tents, 127–28
Teotihuacán (Mexico), 29
Terraces of the Shrine of the Báb (Haifa; Sahba),
    178, 179–80
Tezukayama House (Osaka; Ando), 98–99
Theme Building, Los Angeles International
    Airport (Langenheim), 123
Theory of Religion (Bataille), 70
Thomas Aquinas, 50, 122
Thomas Road Baptist Church (Lynchburg), 47
Thorncrown Chapel (Eureka Springs [AR];
    Jones), *228*, *230*
Tigerman, Stanley, 25, 70, 226
tilt-up construction, 184–88
time
    collapse of, 208–10
    Greek cosmological principle of, 191
timelessness, 22
"Time's" shops (Kyoto; Ando), 109–11
tirtha (Hindu: ford), 114–15, *116*, 118, 119
Todd, J. Stuart, 168
Tombazis, Alexandros, 21
Tominaga, Yuzuru, 109
Tomorrowland (Disneyland), 123, *124*
TOTO Seminar House (Tsuna-gun; Ando), 108
Tournon, Paul, 22

Townes, Emilie, 25, 226
Trans World Airlines building, Idlewild (JFK)
    International Airport (New York; Saarinen),
    123, 229
transcendence
    aura of, experiencing, 53
    awareness of, as presupposition of human
        flourishing, 25
    descent of, into the visible, 59
    dynamism of, 59
    expressing, through the physical, 223
    loss of, 53–54
    sense of, arising from interplay of materiality
        and form, 18
Trautman, Catherine, 218
Tree of the Sephirot, 44
Trouin, Edouard, 14, 40
Turning Torso (Malmö; Calatrava), 53
Tzonis, Alexander, 53

U
Ultimate Mystery, answering the call of, 131
Umayyad Mosque (Damascus), 217
unheimlich (German: uninhabitable space), 140
Unitarianism, 38–40
Unité d'habitation (Marseilles; Le Corbusier),
    40–42
United States
    hope in, reduced to the "satisfied self," 62
    religiosity of, 54
    transplanting religious communities to, 119
United States Pavilion, 1967 World's Fair
    (Montreal; Fuller), 124n20
unity of mankind, 175
Unity Temple (Oak Park; Wright), 15, *17*, 38–40,
    149, 226, 229
University of Virginia, lawn of (Charlottesville;
    Jefferson), 228–29
unsayable, 207
Ur, ziggurat of, 30
urban fabric, 193
utopia, 53, 58

V
Valente et Pfister, 218
Venkateswara Temple (Pittsburgh), 118
Venturi, Robert, 43 , 160
vernacular architecture, 193
Verne, Jules, 121, 122–23
Vicariato di Roma (Church of Rome), 150
Vietnam Veterans Memorial (Washington, D.C.;
    Lin), 40, *63*
Villalpandus, 28

Villa Rotonda (Vicenza; Palladio), 37
violent destructiveness, associated with the
    sacred, 70
visionary architecture, 122, 123
visionary expression, 10–11
Vitruvian man (Leonardo da Vinci), 36
Vitruvius, 34
Volf, Miroslav, 25

W
Wagner, Otto, 16
war memorials, lacking religious connection, 40
Wasserstrom, Steven, 19–20
water, as one of two decorative elements in
    Lotus Temple, 178–79
Water Temple (Awaji Island; Ando), 105, *106*,
    107, 109, *111*, 119
Watsuji, Tetsuro, 106
way, the (Schwarz), *86*, 87–88, 90
way-form, 84, 87, 88, 89, 227
Western Wall piazzas (Jerusalem; Safdie),
    194–96
White, Roger, 180
Wilmotte, Jean-Marie, 218
window, architecture's function as, 62
wind towers, 178
Wittgenstein, Ludwig, 58
workers, Sahba's relationship with, 177
Works and Days (Heriod), 33
worship spaces, names of, 73–74, 78
Wren, Christopher, 230
Wright, Frank Lloyd, 15, 16, 38–40, 127, 149, 226

X
Xenakis, Iannis, 14

Y
Yad Vashem Children's Memorial (Jerusalem;
    Safdie), 196, *197*
Yad Vashem Holocaust Museum (Jerusalem;
    Safdie), *title page*, 198–205
Yale Art Gallery (New Haven; Kahn), 43
Yokogurayama National Forest Museum
    (Ando), 108

Z
Zwingli, Ulrich, 85–86

IMAGE CREDITS